The March to Zion

The Ma

ch to Zion

UNITED STATES POLICY AND
THE FOUNDING OF ISRAEL

By Kenneth Ray Bain

 TEXAS A&M UNIVERSITY PRESS
COLLEGE STATION AND LONDON

Library of Congress Cataloging in Publication Data

Bain, Kenneth Ray, 1942–
    The march to Zion.

    Bibliography: p.
    Includes index.
    1. United States—Foreign relations—Palestine.
2. Palestine—Foreign relations—United States.
3. United States—Foreign relations—1945–1953.
I. Title.
E183.8.17B34   327.73′05694   79-7413
ISBN 0-89096-076-3

To Marsha, Marshall, and Tonia

CONTENTS

Responses of Americans to the Palestine controversy of the late 1940's have attracted considerable attention from historians, but mostly from Zionist scholars. Convinced that a new Israel deserved support, these writers have measured U.S. policy against the needs of Jewish nationalism. In the process they have developed a widely accepted version of how and why the Truman administration came to the aid of Jewish statehood.[1]

The first outlines of that interpretation began to emerge in the 1949 work of Frank Manuel, *The Realities of American-Palestine Relations*. With the aid of a few memoirs, a handful of government documents, and some newspaper accounts, Manuel traced the development of Truman's policy. He had access to no archival materials, yet his study has had enormous impact on subsequent scholarship. Truman, according to Manuel's version, found himself in the happy circumstance of being able to serve his own desires, feather his political nest, and do the "right thing." The president had great sympathy for Jewish refugees and for a Zionist solution to their problems, Manuel argued. But Cold War considerations caused him to forego his own wishes temporarily and court Arab friendship. The president weaved his way through the conflicting claims of international poli-

---

[1] For indications of the impact of such interpretations, see, for example, Robert H. Ferrell, *George C. Marshall*, pp. 190–199; Robert Divine, *Foreign Policy and U.S. Presidential Elections, 1940–1948*, pp. 175–176; Jonathan Daniels, *The Man of Independence*, p. 317; Alonzo Hamby, *Beyond the New Deal: Harry S. Truman and American Liberalism*, p. 256; and Bert Cochran, *Harry Truman and the Crisis Presidency*, p. 196.

tics and his desires to emerge ultimately friendly to Jewish nationalism.[2]

While there were some disagreements in subsequent accounts, this scenario of a president working toward eventual devotion to Zion became standard in most of the studies that followed. With additional sources available in the 1960's, Zionist historians were able to provide only minor refinements to Manuel's version. Harry Truman emerges from these accounts as a leader struggling to maintain a commitment to humanitarian goals while the cold calculations of his diplomatic corps and military establishment constantly pressure him in the other direction.[3] The president's own memoirs, published in the mid-fifties, helped foster this image of a decent chief executive fighting for a downtrodden people despite the insensitive and even bigoted advice of the "striped-pants" boys in the State Department.

Zionist scholarship has offered only two significant variations on this theme. Both Joseph Schechtman's *The United States and the Jewish State Movement* and the 1973 work of Bernard Postal and Henry W. Levy argued that Truman did not begin his presidency as a Zionist. Schechtman noted that the chief executive initially called for the settlement of one hundred thousand Jews in Palestine while refusing to make any comment on the permanent political status of the Holy Land. Largely narrative rather than analytical, Schechtman's book traced a drama in which the administration finally saw the wisdom of Zionist approaches and committed itself in late 1947 to the creation of a Jewish state in part of Palestine. Postal and Levy

---

[2] Frank Edward Manuel, *The Realities of American-Palestine Relations*, pp. 319–333.

[3] For example, Herbert Feis, *The Birth of Israel: The Tousled Diplomatic Bed*, pp. 20–45; and Herbert Parzan, "President Truman and the Palestine Quandary: His Initial Experience, April–December, 1945," *Jewish Social Studies* 35 (January, 1973): 42–72. Parzan contended that Truman entered the White House "manifestly sympathetic" with Zionist goals in Palestine. State Department and military warnings about Arab threats plus conflicts with the British weakened the president's resolve to support Jewish nationalism. By December the president, according to Parzan, had abandoned his commitment to Zionism and had decided to limit his quest to the humanitarian goal of moving one hundred thousand refugees into the Holy Land.

also found the president eventually developing a keen appreciation for Jewish statehood.[4]

The other major variation came in the work of John Snetsinger in the early 1970's. Relying primarily on materials from the Truman Library, Snetsinger did much of his research in the late 1960's while completing a 1969 dissertation at Stanford University. With some minor revisions and additional trips to Independence, he published his conclusions in *Truman, the Jewish Vote, and the Creation of Israel* in 1974. Truman emerges from Snetsinger's pages slightly less humanitarian and considerably more political than he appears in earlier accounts. Reports on refugee conditions do invoke presidential sympathies, but domestic pressures from Zionists carry even more weight. With one eye on displaced persons camps and the other on the ballot box, Truman marches toward eventual support for a new Israel. On the way he rejects the 1946 Anglo-American plan because of Zionist lobbying and the supposed failure of the scheme to provide for adequate refugee relief. The president finally endorses the granting of Jewish control over major portions of Palestine after Arabs move troops to the borders of the Promised Land and Truman sees the United Nations partition plan as the only hope for peace.[5]

In the most recent version of the subject, Howard Sachar's *A History of Israel*, there is simply a new mixture of older interpretations. Sachar argues that it is an oversimplification to say that no more than political considerations motivated the president. Truman, according to Sachar, had a history of sympathy for the underdog and had been since early manhood a Zionist. The president was, however, primarily concerned with refugee resettlement. Sachar praises Truman for his decision to leave the political status of Palestine to the United Nations.[6]

[4] Joseph B. Schechtman, *The United States and the Jewish State Movement: The Crucial Decade, 1939–1949*, pp. 139, 241–249; Bernard Postal and Henry W. Levy, *And the Hills Shouted for Joy: The Day Israel Was Born*, pp. 86–87, 304–308.

[5] John Snetsinger, *Truman, the Jewish Vote, and the Creation of Israel*.

[6] Howard M. Sachar, *A History of Israel: From the Rise of Zionism to Our Time*, pp. 255–290.

Beyond this discussion of Truman's motivation and the timing of his alleged conversion to Jewish nationalism, Zionist scholars have developed some common assumptions about the course of policy development. According to their version, Truman reluctantly agreed to the establishment of the Anglo-American Committee of Inquiry in 1946. When that group filed its report in April, the president accepted its recommendations while the British refused.[7] In the summer another U.S. delegation headed by Henry Grady attempted to find a solution acceptable to London. The result, according to the standard account, was a surrender to the anti-Zionist (and therefore insensitive) British demands. After Truman recognized that the new scheme required Arab approval for any refugee resettlement in Palestine, he vetoed the plan because it meant there would be no relief for the uprooted. As Truman came closer to a Zionist perspective in the fall (or stayed there, depending on the version), he looked with favor on the newly adopted partition proposals of the Jewish Agency. In October, with some consideration to politics in New York, the president endorsed the division of Palestine between Arabs and Jews.

Throughout 1947, the standard version continues, the administration fought to execute its pro-Zionist policy despite the counteradvice of State and War Department spokesmen and the often obstructionist activities of the "bigots" in the diplomatic corps. While worry over oil concessions led the foreign-affairs planners to oppose partition, politics and humanity molded Truman's commitment to a new Israel. Finally, in October, the scenario concludes, the White House directed the U.S. delegation to the United Nations to vote for the General Assembly resolution favoring partition. When the State Department sought to redraw the borders of the proposed states and

---

[7] Zionist historians have had various ways to characterize Truman's "acceptance." Postal and Levy, *And the Hills Shouted*, p. 89, simply noted Truman's endorsement of the immigration provisions without any word on his approach to other parts of the report. Sachar, *History of Israel*, p. 263, wrote that "London had not envisaged official endorsement from the United States government" and that the president "concentrated" on the immigration provisions. Feis, *Birth of Israel*, p. 27, concluded that "these recommendations . . . were welcomed in Washington and rebuffed in London."

give the Negev to the Arab section, Truman intervened to kill the scheme.[8]

Zionist assessments of this record have seldom been more than mildly critical. Schechtman lambasted Truman for his attempt to divorce refugee solutions from Jewish nationalism, but even he ended his account with obvious approval for the president's final policy. Other writers have generally shared in this praise for anything which smacked of support for a new Israel. British policy, meanwhile, received most of the blame for its failure to find an acceptable solution to the Palestine struggle. While many of the Zionist writers offered little more than bitter denunciations of British moves, Christopher Sykes' 1965 *Crossroads to Israel* provided the most cogently and dispassionately reasoned critique of British policy. Sykes argued that Prime Minister Clement Attlee and his foreign minister, Ernest Bevin, blundered in their failure to follow Truman's lead and accept the proposal for admitting one hundred thousand Jewish displaced persons into Palestine. He contended that the British refusal ignored a workable compromise and encouraged extremist elements among the Zionists. In fact, Sykes theorized, if Attlee had permitted more downtrodden folk to enter Palestine, it might have been possible to prevent the creation of a Jewish state.[9]

While Zionist writers have been highly prolific in producing commentaries on U.S. policies toward Palestine, they have always had to share the topic with scholars who were unfriendly with Jewish nationalism. Yet beyond disagreements over the justice of Jewish claims in the Holy Land, the pro-Arab studies have had few arguments with the Zionist commentators. They have repeated much of the standard assessment of Truman's motives. The president was concerned about the plight of refugees and impressed with Zionist political pressure. Fred Khouri's 1968 book *The Arab-Israeli Dilemma* is

---

[8] Dan Kurzman, *Genesis 1948: The First Arab-Israel War*, p. 82; Sachar, *History of Israel*, pp. 255–290; and Ian J. Bickerton, "President Truman's Recognition of Israel," *American Jewish Historical Quarterly* 58 (December, 1968): 173–239.

[9] Christopher Sykes, *Crossroads to Israel, 1917–1948*, pp. 292–299.

typical. According to that work, Truman became convinced that a Zionist state could best solve the problems of refugees, satisfy domestic interests, and provide benefits to Moslem civilization. Thus, the chief executive eventually directed a U.S. vote for partition despite opposition from the Joint Chiefs of Staff and the State Department.[10]

All these earlier accounts, while often making impressive use of the sources available to them, nevertheless suffered from the limits of their own research. None of them were able to make a thorough examination of the presidential papers, State and Defense Department files, congressional manuscripts, and private archival collections as well as the more readily available published sources. In fact, many important records became available only within the last few years. Taking advantage of access to these materials, this study offers support for some of the earlier assertions but draws a number of important conclusions at odds with standard treatments. Most significant of these conclusions are the following:

1. Truman began his career with some sympathy for Jewish settlement in Palestine, both because of the Holocaust and because of a belief in Jewish cultural superiority over the Arabs. But neither sentiment was sufficient to push him into action. He advocated sending one hundred thousand refugees to Palestine in order to relieve economic difficulties in Europe, placate political elements at home, and keep the Zionist movement out of the hands of extremist elements. Truman was not an advocate of Jewish statehood and did not see his action as a step toward a new Israel. He was, instead, convinced that his move represented true compromise and could sufficiently appease Zionists while he kept the movement in check.

2. All previous accounts have grossly exaggerated the differences between White House and State Department policies. The diplomatic corps had no uniform opinion. It generally opposed the one-hundred-thousand program, but it operated from many of the same assumptions and goals that guided the president. Contrary

[10] Fred J. Khouri, *The Arab-Israeli Dilemma*, pp. 29–65.

to popular belief, the foreign-policy chiefs faithfully served the president's dictates and were not controlled by anti-Semitic prejudices.

3. Truman, not Clement Attlee, was largely responsible for rejecting and killing the Anglo-American plan of 1946. Britain was willing to act on the scheme, but only as long as the United States accepted the entire report. Domestic pressures convinced the president to endorse only selected provisions. Caught between political demands and strategic advice from the military, Truman eventually found it necessary to reject a solution he actually favored. That settlement, the Grady plan, offered the president the best hope for finding homes for the uprooted without major bloodshed.

4. Popular support for Jewish settlement in Palestine stemmed from much more than Zionist propaganda. It sprang from a deep cultural base that included both admiration for the achievements of Jewish settlers, bigoted opposition to Jewish immigration to the United States, and a widely accepted notion of Arab inferiority. Backing for Jewish admissions to the Holy Land did not, however, always include support for a new Israel.[11]

5. While many diplomatic chiefs did oppose Zionism because they wanted Arab oil, one faction in the State Department came to support the United Nations resolution on partition out of considerations of petroleum diplomacy. These men believed that the world organization might be able to impose a solution and that an early settlement, even if it included a truncated Jewish state, was less likely to alienate the Arabs than was continued uncertainty.

6. Truman played little direct role in the key U.S. decisions on the United Nations partition resolution. Even his celebrated intervention to save the Negev for Jewish control had limited impact. Secretary of State George Marshall and his colleagues formulated

---

[11] Scholars opposed to the creation of a Jewish state have generally tended to emphasize the power of Zionist propaganda in stimulating popular support for Jewish settlement in Palestine. See, for example, Kermit Roosevelt, "The Partition of Palestine: A Lesson in Pressure Politics," *Middle East Journal* 2 (January, 1948): 1–16; Evan Wilson, "The Palestine Papers, 1943–1947," *Journal of Palestine Studies* 2 (Summer, 1973): 33–54; and Khouri, *Arab-Israeli Dilemma*, pp. 29, 33.

basic strategy and tactics, including the Negev decision, while the Oval Office actually cautioned restraint in any U.S. commitment to the creation of a Jewish state.

7. Despite his own implications to the contrary, Truman was not willing to encourage United Nations responsibility for solving conflicts. Rather than striving for a world in which the new organization achieved sufficient prestige and power to settle disputes, the administration treated the world body like an unwanted stepchild. Foreign-policy chiefs were increasingly reluctant to allow the General Assembly any voice in even local trouble spots like Palestine. They eventually attempted to use the United Nations, not out of any dedication to its principles and prestige but for the sake of narrow national goals.

In addition, this study provides the first comprehensive examination of the Anglo-American Committee of Inquiry of 1946.

Most of the scholars writing about Truman's Palestine policy have treated the developments primarily as aspects of Israel's history. Yet they are also important episodes in the history of the United States. The whole affair reveals much not only about the diplomacy of two presidential administrations, but also about the prejudices, assumptions, values, ambitions, and habits that lay behind the policies. The Palestine controversy included patterns that repeated themselves frequently in the postwar age. On one side, aroused public groups, with their supporters in government, were trying to direct foreign policy. On the other, diplomatic officials and military strategists engaged in secret diplomacy and circumvention of the Congress, especially in pursuit of imperialistic interests. In the process there was no orderly procedure for formulating foreign policy. A beleaguered and accidental president, a product of a political system that required few other talents besides perseverance and loyalty, found it impossible to understand the complex situation and assume control over the direction of policy. Far from being the decisive president of popular mythology and campaign rhetoric, Truman was timid and frustrated, unable to make any of the hard decisions that lay beyond the one-hundred-thousand program.

The Palestine controversy reflects some disturbing aspects of the

American character. An assortment of prejudices helped shape the milieu from which policy emerged. Pity for Holocaust survivors and some sense of national benevolence played a role, but many people in the United States came to support Jewish aspirations in Palestine not only because of a sympathy for Jewish efforts, but also from a dislike for Arabs. Americans worshiped at the shrine of progress. They smiled with approval on Jewish successes and condemned the Arabs for their "failures." They developed a deprecating picture of the Moslems, an image that became far more significant than any sense of justice. Ethnocentrism, sometimes born of religious beliefs, must rank along with economic greed and politics as a major ingredient in the emerging national mind on the Holy Land controversy.

This study is not an attempt to weigh fully the long struggle between Arabs and Jews in Palestine. But in its assessment of U.S. policies it cannot escape some judgments on the merits of conflicting claims. It regards the outcome of national and international policy as a tragic failure, not because of any lack of commitment to a new Israel, but because of the inability of the world to find homes for Holocaust survivors without uprooting millions of Palestinians. It ultimately rejects the Zionist claim that only through the establishment of a Jewish state in the Promised Land could the seed of Abraham find peace and the proper consolation for centuries of Christian bigotry.

The staffs of many libraries aided this study, including those of the Harry S Truman Presidential Library, the Library of Congress Manuscript Division, several divisions of the National Archives, the Church Historical Society Archives, Georgetown University Library, Columbia University Library, the Herbert Lehman Collection at Columbia, Princeton University Library, Sterling Memorial Library at Yale University, Harvard University Library, Brandeis University Library, the University of Virginia Library, Clemson University Library, and the University of Texas Library. I also thank Marsha Marshall Bain and Ray Smith for research assistance and Suhail Hanna and Paul Travis for their willingness to read major portions of the manuscript and make excellent suggestions. Robert A. Divine provided immeasurable assistance from beginning to end. H. Wayne Morgan supplied valuable advice. I owe a special intellectual debt to Ralph Lynn.

Financial support for this study came from the International Studies Association, the Harry S Truman Institute, and the Graduate School and Department of History of the University of Texas at Austin.

My special thanks goes to Marsha Faye Marshall Bain, Tonia Larisa Bain, and Kenneth Marshall Bain for their patience.

The March to Zion

INTRODUCTION:
THE PALESTINE QUESTION

At the eastern end of the Mediterranean a small sliver of land called Palestine was home for seven hundred thousand Arabs in the early 1900's. Their ancestors had once commanded a domain stretching from Spain to Siam. Now they were subjects of the Ottoman Empire ruled by fellow-Moslem Turks. The domination from the north never completely pleased the residents of the Holy Land, but they generally reconciled themselves to a fate shared with other Arabs in much of Asia Minor.

Late in the nineteenth century these conquered people began to cultivate a sense of nationalism. Rumblings of rebellion often troubled the Turkish oppressors, but few opportunities for successful revolt emerged until 1914. That year the Ottomans went to war on the side of the Central Powers. Arabs eagerly seized the chance for which their ideology was well prepared and struck for independence. Turkey's enemies in the Great War, Great Britain and France, joined the Syrians, Palestinians, and others in a marriage of convenience to battle a common foe. An implied agreement guided the cooperation: when the conflict was over, the governments of the Allies would aid Arab nationalism.

Eight months after the Armistice, a national congress meeting in Damascus declared the existence of a constitutional monarchy to rule a Greater Syria, including Palestine. In late 1920, Iraqi leaders delivered a similar arrangement in Bagdad. But these twin triumphs of Arab nationalism soon fell victim to European ambitions. If the Moslems expected their former Christian comrades to honor the implied agreement, they were sorely disappointed. Great Britain and

France recarved the states and took control of them. Under the mandate system of the League of Nations, they pronounced the Arabs not yet ready to rule themselves. London would tutor Iraq and Palestine; Paris got Syria and Lebanon.

Bitterness and frustration rippled across Arabia in the wake of the cold betrayal. Insurrection tore Iraq. Blood flowed in Damascus when French troops occupied the city. But it did no good to resist. The Europeans had the weapons to impose their will. For a quarter of a century to come, they would possess their respective portions of the old Ottoman realm. The Arabs in Palestine would never realize any dreams of a national state.[1]

Two decades before the outbreak of the Great War, a Viennese journalist, Theodore Herzl (1860–1904), peered through the daily press coverage at the sickening spectacle of continuing mob violence against his fellow Jews throughout Europe. In Russia, Tsar Alexander III had stirred common bigotries and turned popular passions against the Jews because his father's assassin was Jewish. In Paris, anti-Semitic rabble vandalized synagogues because Dreyfus was Jewish. In eastern Europe some Junker lords found pogroms to be a convenient way to defeat liberalism. Herzl grew pessimistic about the chances that his coreligionists could ever win acceptance in Christendom. Cries of "Jesus-killer" resounded too loudly in his mind. In 1896, depressed by the news of discrimination in France, he wrote a pamphlet entitled *A Jewish State*. In it he argued that the classic problems of Jewry began when the Romans destroyed the Kingdom of Judea and turned its citizens into stateless and persecuted wanderers. Only through the revival of an Israel could the sojourning people find peace. It was not entirely a new idea, but Herzl sparked fresh interest in Jewish nationalism, called Zionism, and argued persuasively in behalf of a site for the proposed commonwealth: Palestine.[2]

[1] George Antonius, *The Arab Awakening: The Story of the Arab National Movement*; Zeine N. Zeine, *Arab-Turkish Relations and the Emergence of Arab Nationalism*.

[2] Walter Laqueur, *A History of Zionism*, pp. 84–135.

For centuries the Judean hills and the Holy City of Jerusalem had attracted special affections from the diaspora. They often longed to visit the site of ancient temples. Some made the journey. Others had themselves buried there. A few moved to Palestine. They talked about the end of time when the "Chosen People" would again occupy the "Promised Land." But until Herzl, they generally left to God any efforts to re-create a Jewish state in the Holy Land.

There were a few more than fifty thousand Jews living in Palestine in 1900. Many were descendants of families who had lived there for generations, with generally far less difficulty than their European cousins faced on the continent. Others came in the late nineteenth century, trying to escape the vicious pogroms that spread through much of eastern Europe. Few of them arrived with any plans to re-shape the political structure, but in the early part of the twentieth century many became converts to Zionism. The advent of Herzl's movement brought the Jewish population to eighty-five thousand in 1914, but it still remained barely more than 10 percent of the total population of the country. Regardless of the numbers, political Zionists sought to govern Palestine.[3]

It is not surprising that in the first two decades of this century Arab leaders seldom knew how to treat a Zionist community, isolated from them and demanding a separate state yet grafted onto them and sometimes making overtures of cooperation with Arab people. A few Islamic nationalists saw the immigrants as possible allies in fighting Ottoman, and then British, domination.[4] But it soon became clear that Zionist plans threatened Arab statehood no less than did imperialist aggression. The influx of pilgrims, coupled with the newcomers' general devotion to Herzl, meant that a growing Jewish population would eventually be able to gain control of governmental affairs in the country, excluding the Arabs from power. It took little

[3] For two different views on the rise of Zionism, see ibid. and Maxime Rodinson, *Israel and the Arabs.*

[4] See, for example, "The Feisal-Weizmann Agreement" and "Feisal-Frankfurter Letters," reprinted in Walter Laqueur, ed., *The Israel-Arab Reader,* pp. 18–22.

political acumen to realize that Zionism's call for a state run by Jews made no sense unless the children of Israel planned either to wrench political power from the Arab Palestinians or drive them from their homes. In 1920 the Arab natives of Jerusalem, embittered by the betrayals by Great Britain and France, struck at what they considered to be a territorial cancer supplied from the outside and eating away the chances for them to retain their fatherland and someday rule themselves. Violent conflicts between Zionists and Moslems became a permanent feature of the Holy Land.

The Jewish designs in Palestine touched more than the ambitions of those living in Judea. To Iraqis, Syrians, Lebanese, Jordanians, and others, the Zionist blueprint was part of a package of European aggression, less immediate than the mandate ploys of Britain and France but as dangerous to independence and unity. In every Arab country the rioters, strikers, and demonstrators protesting foreign domination after 1920 often directed part of their attack against Zionism, viewing colonialism and Herzl's program as two guises of the same villain. As long as the intended alien intrusion into an Arab territory had as its ultimate goal separation of that country from the rest of the Moslem world, it was, equally, an insult to Arab nationalism, Islamic civilization, and anti-imperialism.[5]

The British actually made their first foray into the scrap even before consummating the mandate arrangement. In November, 1917, Lord Balfour, the foreign minister, wrote the Zionist federation through Lord Rothchild to declare cabinet "sympathy" for the establishment in Palestine of a "national home for the Jewish people." The vague pledge, avoiding any specific statement on political structure, was partly an English bid for Jewish support during the war.[6] Five years later the Churchill Memorandum spelled out the nature of the British commitment to Zionism. London supported a "centre in which the Jewish people as a whole may take, on grounds of religion and race, an interest and pride." Great Britain did not endorse un-

---

[5] Antonius, *Arab Awakening*, pp. 350–421.

[6] U.S., Department of State, *Foreign Relations of the United States* [hereafter cited as *FR*], 1943, IV, 752, fn. 14, contains a copy of the letter written by Arthur James Balfour to Walter Rothschild on November 2, 1947.

limited immigration into Palestine or the "disappearance or the *sub-ordination* of the Arabic population, language or culture."[7] Despite the apparent exclusion of a Zionist state, future devotees of Jewish nationalism would bestow upon the British the right to dispense Arab land. They would invoke the Balfour Declaration as a just, legal, and irrevocable commitment to their complete ascendancy in Palestine.

During the twenties and thirties, the men in London straddled the controversy, torn between pro-Zionist sentiments at home and desires to protect imperialist interests by courting Arab friendships. A number of different commissions investigated the situation for the royal government, but policy usually flowed from events rather than from the reasoned conclusions of experts.[8]

The Jewish community, the Yishuv, continued to grow, especially after Hitler began his pogroms in the thirties. Between 1933 and 1939 a total of 215,000 Jews arrived in Palestine. While only a little more than 1,000 came from Germany in the previous decade, nearly 50,000 now streamed out of the Third Reich in the first seven years of Hitler's rule. In that time almost twice that number came from Poland, where anti-Semitism needed little encouragement from the Nazis. When World War II began in September, 1939, there were 400,000 Jews in the Holy Land out of a population of 1.5 million. They had developed some degree of local autonomy in areas where they were predominant and had a proto-parliament and an executive, the Jewish Agency. A world Zionist movement pushed for the fulfillment of Herzl's program. Immigrants from Europe brought with them the technology of the continent and some of its monetary capital, enabling them to make impressive progress in industrial development. The native opposition to Zionism in Palestine and the general Arab hatred for European domination did not abate. Violent resistance to Jewish growth and British duplicity spread through the Holy Land in both 1936 and 1938. The rise of the anti-British fascist

---

[7] "The Churchill White Paper—1922," reprinted in Laqueur, *Israel-Arab Reader*, pp. 46–47.

[8] Fred J. Khouri, *The Arab-Israeli Dilemma*, pp. 16–27; Laqueur, *History of Zionism*, pp. 516–528.

powers prompted some Arabs to consider them possible allies in the struggle against colonialism. But even some Nazis suggested shipping German Jews to Palestine.[9]

In 1939 the English government worried about the approaching war and the prospects that Hitler could exploit the Middle East situation. Accordingly, in May a British white paper tried to neutralize the issue. Under its terms, Great Britain would continue to rule Palestine but gradually grant independence after five years. Jewish immigration would slow down and then end in 1944 unless the majority of citizens agreed to admit more immigrants after that date. The plan allowed seventy-five thousand Jews to enter the country during the transition, but it limited their opportunity to buy land in regions of Arab predominance.[10] If the British enforced the document, there would be no Jewish state.

For nearly a decade the struggle over Palestine centered on the British White Paper of 1939. Zionist conventions denounced its provisions. Yishuv terrorists conducted guerrilla warfare against Mandate authorities and Palestinian residents. Jewish nationalists and their sympathizers on both sides of the Atlantic pressured the governments of the Allied Powers to alter the immigration limits. Some groups sponsored a flow of refugees to Palestine above the quota. But neither the Arabs nor the British initially bowed to the campaign. Until 1947, official British policy continued to endorse the White Paper of 1939 and thereby blocked the birth of a new Israel.

By the end of World War II the whole controversy was assuming elements that proved to be most decisive. In the spring of 1945 the ghastly extent of Nazi atrocities became visible as Allied armies liberated German concentration camps. The haunting scenes of human carcasses stacked in the dumps of Buchenwald, Auschwitz, and Bergen-Belsen morbidly confirmed earlier rumors of fascist brutality. When the Nuremberg trials began in November, the prosecutors of the Führer's deputies laid before the court and the world details of

[9] Rodinson, *Israel and the Arabs*, pp. 32–34; *Encyclopedia Judaica*, IX, 486, 527; Raphael Patai, ed., *Encyclopedia of Zionism and Israel*, I, 537, 538.
[10] Khouri, *Arab–Israeli Dilemma*, pp. 26–27; Laqueur, *History of Zionism*, pp. 528ff.

Third Reich crimes against humanity. Nazis slaughtered six million who wore the Star of David. Furthermore, they left behind several hundred thousand bitter, cynical, and homeless Jews who escaped the death chambers but languished in concentration camps at war's end. Allied deliverance initially meant little improvement for most of these displaced persons. Harried and uprooted, many existed for months after Hitler's death in barbed-wire-enclosed holes, unsanitary barracks, still wearing uniforms taken from dead German soldiers or, worse, Nazi-issued prison outfits. Death, depression, pessimism, stench, hunger, disease, suicide, insanity—like a festering sore the elements of life for surviving Jews marred the joys of victory.

A 1945 U.S. government report, later influential in shaping Washington's policy, enumerated the sins of occupation. "Beyond knowing that they are no longer in danger of gas chambers, torture and other forms of violent death," the survivors of fascist racism realized little change after liberation. "As matters now stand," the exposé somberly concluded, "we appear to be treating the Jews as the Nazis treated them, except that we do not exterminate them." [11]

Fall and winter news from Europe made it clear that many who escaped the Holocaust faced an unhappy future of more pogroms and discriminations. A new wave of uprooted, the belated victims of prejudice, inundated the already flooded streams of humanity pouring across the continent from Poland to France—tens, hundreds, thousands gushing into U.S. and British hands, drowning hopes that Nazi defeat would purify the Old World. Few responses seemed appropriate. Economic aid that might erase some battle scars from Christendom could not eliminate anti-Semitism. Multitudes of displaced persons, tired of mistreatment and impressed with Zionist promises, sought entrance to Palestine. To them it was the only possible salvation.

Actually, Jewish refugees had no direct connection with the squabble in the Holy Land any more than did millions of Gentiles who fell prey to Hitler's minions. There were really two separate

---

[11] "Report of Earl G. Harrison," *Department of State Bulletin* 13 (September 30, 1945): 456.

problems: (1) Who should control Judea? and (2) What should be done with the uprooted people in Europe? Yet the refugee question became inseparably intertwined with the Palestine debate. Jewish nationalists—well aware that adding to the non-Arab population would aid their cause and subvert the White Paper policy—dropped much of the direct appeal for political goals in favor of the more moving humanitarian expressions.

Their plan of redemption, however, meant trouble for Palestinians. Jewish migration to the Promised Land threatened far more than Arab nationalism; it also imperiled native economic well-being. Arab opposition came, in part, from the realization that the disputed country could not in 1945, nor in the foreseeable future, support a massive influx from Europe without displacing thousands of its own residents. That opposition also rose from the knowledge that Jewish nationalism equaled political control by a group that saw itself as separate and distinctly different from Arabs and that under such an arrangement, when shortages of food, jobs, and shelter developed, Arab subjects of the Jewish state would be the first to suffer.

Even before the beginning of any substantial migration, Jerusalem and every city in the region needed far more housing. A Middle East Supply Center investigation of September, 1944, concluded that the country had a deficiency of 126,000 rooms. In addition, it needed to replace another 33,000 slum quarters. The study reported that "it is common to find 5 to 7 people sleeping in one room." [12] While the largely Jewish-owned industries had relied on military sales during World War II, reconversion after the conflict threatened growing unemployment and economic dislocations that would hit especially hard at Arabs. The often endless debate over who caused Arab refugees to leave Palestine after 1948—Jews or Arab leaders hoping to stage a counteroffensive—ignores a central point. The country did not, and perhaps could not, absorb the arrivals from Europe without displacing its own inhabitants. Thousands eventually left, either flee-

---

[12] "Immigration in Palestine . . . ," August 29, 1945, 867N.01/8-3145, Record Group 59, National Archives, Washington, D.C. [hereafter cited as RG 59, NA].

ing the turmoil brewing from Zionist agitation or obeying Israeli banishment.[13]

Tragedy begets tragedy. Anti-Semitism aroused Herzl's ideology. Zionism matured on the bitterness of Nazi horror chambers. Struggles for a Jewish state turned Palestine into a battleground of hate, bombings, and murder. Many fugitives from Hitler's brutality assumed the methods of terror against their own enemies. Hundreds died in the process. By 1948, Zionists had a country, but a million Palestinians, living in the often squalid, "temporary" refugee camps of Jordan and Lebanon, had none. The birth of Israel spawned a legacy of blood, animosity, and nagging combat. In the wars of 1948, 1956, 1967, and 1973, thousands died either defending or attacking the Jewish state.[14]

Who was at fault? Was it possible to build a Jewish nation on the eastern banks of the Mediterranean without the ensuing tragedies? Were there other, less painful, ways of erasing from Europe the scars of bigotry and fascism? Are there justifications for Zionism that transcend the heartaches it wrought? Did the major powers have any obligations or opportunities to heal the wounds of the whole affair?

There was nothing inevitable about U.S. involvement in the controversy. Yet a succession of presidential administrations became entangled, beginning with Woodrow Wilson's expressed approval of the Balfour Declaration.[15] An Anglo-American treaty drafted in 1922 contained a British commitment to consult Washington before making any substantial changes in the status of the Mandate.[16] By the 1940's the issue entered national politics on a major scale. Zionism was popular and becoming increasingly so. Palestinian resisters won

---

[13] Khouri, *Arab-Israeli Dilemma*, pp. 123–181; "A Survey of the Arab Refugee Problem," *Department of State Bulletin* 30 (January 18, 1945): 101 ff.; U.S., Congress, Senate, *Hearing on the Palestine Refugee Problem before the Senate Subcommittee on the Near East and Africa of the Committee on Foreign Relations*, 82d Cong., 2d sess., 1953.

[14] Khouri, *Arab-Israeli Dilemma*, pp. 182–355; J. Bowyer Bell, *The Long War: Israel and the Arabs since 1946*.

[15] *FR*, 1917, Supp. 2, I, 317, 473, 483.

[16] Ibid., 1924, II, 203ff., 212–213.

only a few supporters. But there was one major obstacle blocking un-
diluted U.S. backing for Jewish nationalism. Arab countries along
the Persian Gulf sat atop the largest oil pool in the world. If Texaco,
Standard of California, and others hoped to tap those deposits,
Washington could not treat lightly Moslem complaints against
Herzl's movement.

But all that happened up to 1945 was merely a prelude to a decisive three-year political struggle after World War II. The tempo of
the conflict quickened as Zionists made their successful push for the
creation of Israel. The level of Yankee participation also increased as
President Harry Truman developed policies that both materially in-
fluenced the controversy and established deeply cut patterns for
future administrations. In the three years before Israel's birth in
1948, Americans were no longer subsidiary actors in the drama but
major players and directors, shaping much of what happened in Palestine and forming attitudes that often became permanent. It was a
critical time, both for the fate of Palestine and for U.S. approaches to
the problems of the Middle East. But the controversy was more; it
was a major test for the United Nations and for the Truman administration's willingness to work with the infant world organization.

For at least three years before the creation of Israel, U.S. conduct
in the Middle East emerged from a swirl of economic interests, popular sentiments, security planning, religious beliefs, Anglo-American
relations, United Nations maneuvering, economic problems in Europe, and Cold War fears and calculations as well as lust for Jewish
votes and money in domestic elections. Relations with Arabian countries deteriorated, while support for Israel grew. Yet Truman and his
advisers maintained the treasured oil leases while they befriended
the Zionists. It was a considerable feat, but it came at a high cost in
human tragedy, international conflict, and damage to the maturing
United Nations.

CHAPTER ONE

THE GREAT BITTER LAKE
CONVERSATION

When the president's plane landed near Great Bitter Lake
in the heart of the Suez Canal on February 12, 1945, Franklin Dela-
no Roosevelt was on his way home from the Yalta Conference, where
he had met with Winston Churchill and Josef Stalin. It had been a
tiring trip for the crippled chief executive. His frail body and with-
ered face made him appear much older than his sixty-three years. He
was stopping in Egypt to meet Abdul Aziz Ibn Saud, king of Saudi
Arabia. The squire of Hyde Park, dressed in a gray business suit
with a black cape draped across his back, greeted the fellow invalid
head of state aboard the U.S.S. *Quincy* anchored in the livid heat of
the Red Sea outlet. The aging Arab warrior was weakened and bent
from wounds suffered in youthful battles that had made him supreme lord over other chiefs of the desert. He was sixty-five years old
and had difficulty walking, his six-foot four-inch frame now requiring
the support of a cane. One of his eyes was missing. A checkered
hatta, a cloth head-wrap, framed his mustached, leathery face while
its long, warm-looking side panels flowed across his chest to the
waist. He wore a dark caftan robe.

His Royal Highness was a pious Moslem, a disciple of the strict,
fundamentalist Wahabi sect. A presidential aide cautioned the
heavy-smoking Roosevelt that his habit might offend the guest's religious sensitivities. Through the morning session the chief executive
heeded the warning. There was small talk about their common in-
firmities.

"I am your twin brother," Ibn Saud mused, "in years, in responsibility as Chief of State, and in physical disability."

"But you are fortunate," the American responded, "to still have the use of your legs to take you where ever you choose to go."

"It is you, Mr. President, who are fortunate. My legs grow feebler every year; with your more reliable wheel-chair you are assured that you will arrive."

"I have two of these chairs, which are also twins. Would you accept one as a personal gift from me?"

"Gratefully," the King nodded. "I shall use it daily and always recall affectionately the giver, my great and good friend." [1]

At one o'clock the two men stopped for lunch. The king rode the elevator to the wardroom, but Roosevelt stayed behind and took another lift. On the way down the president stopped the elevator between decks and smoked two cigarettes. In the afternoon the pair renewed their conversation. Ibn Saud offered his host some Arab coffee as the leaders amiably discussed the fate of ancient lands. An aura of good will—indispensable to all that happened there—filled the meeting.[2] Each man indelibly impressed the other. Roosevelt died two months later, but during his last days he spoke with admiration of his Saudi Arabian friend. Ibn Saud said on more than one occasion, "I have never met the equal of the President in character, wisdom and gentility."[3]

The White House report of the meeting paid more attention to the colorful ceremonies than to the substance of the discussion. "The President, seated on the forward gun deck of his ship, received the royal visitors as the crew manned the rails, bugle calls sounded and shrill notes of the boatswain's pipe kept all hands standing rigidly at attention." The purpose of the conference was to fulfill Roosevelt's desire that "heads of Government should get together whenever possible to talk as friends."[4]

But the conversation was far less casual than the sparse official account implied. The chief executive of the United States met the king of Saudi Arabia because of two major, interconnected problems

[1] *FR*, 1945, VIII, 7–9.

[2] Cyrus Leo Sulzberger, *A Long Row of Candles: Memoirs and Diaries, 1934–1954*, pp. 296, 326; Robert E. Sherwood, *Roosevelt and Hopkins*, pp. 871–872.

[3] *FR*, 1945, VIII, 8.

[4] *Time*, March 5, 1945, pp. 21–23.

to which both countries attached considerable significance. First, the Near Eastern kingdom had assets that vitally affected U.S. welfare. Its oil deposits, largely untapped, were bigger than any other known fields on Earth. The Arabian peninsula was strategically located; military and commercial airlines needed permission for air space and landing fields there for trans-world flights. But second, these material concerns conflicted with another U.S. interest. Ibn Saud strongly objected to U.S. support for the creation of a Jewish state in Palestine. Roosevelt was in Egypt to try to diminish the conflict.

The meeting at Great Bitter Lake was the pivotal event in a drama of policy making that stretched from the early years of the war to the last days of Franklin Roosevelt's life. In that time the president explored the issues of a troubled Middle East, searching for a response best suited to U.S. interests. It was no easy task, despite the self-assurance of a good many would-be advisers who thought they had the answer. In the beginning Roosevelt had considerable affinity for the cultural, political, and economic goals of Zionism. But in time he began to count the cost of building a Jewish commonwealth, and increasingly he doubted that a new Israel could be worth the inevitable bloodshed between Arabs and Jews. The world could find other, less painful, solutions to the refugee problem. Then, too, the fulfillment of Herzl's dream, with its large number of U.S. patrons, might antagonize Moslem rulers at the expense of the United States. For months before the meeting in Egypt, the president had been inching toward some major decisions on Palestine. A kaleidoscope of events and advice had tugged at his mind, slowly molding attitudes and opinions, bringing him to the verge of positions that ultimately surfaced in the talks with Ibn Saud.

Long before Franklin Roosevelt arrived at Great Bitter Lake, he had heard all the basic arguments on the Palestine question. There had always been plenty of associates, including old friend Felix Frankfurter, to tell him of the glories of the march to Zion.[5] In 1944 alone, seventy-seven senators, 318 representatives, scores of gover-

---

[5] Franklin Roosevelt, *Franklin Roosevelt and Frankfurter: Their Correspondence, 1928–1945*, annotated by Max Freedman, pp. 451, 463, 466, 661, 662, 678.

nors, state legislators, and city councils, and droves of other would-be coaches had urged him to push for Jewish nationalism. The Star of David had soaked up too much blood, they contended. Recompense for the Holocaust required the creation of a Jewish commonwealth.[6]

He had watched as the debate over the Holy Land emerged in Congress and became a burning obsession with Emanuel Celler, Robert Wagner, Robert Taft, and others. On several occasions the House and Senate had come quite close to passing a resolution petitioning the executive branch to oppose immigration restrictions in Palestine and support the creation of a Jewish commonwealth there.[7] During the 1944 election, both his Democrats and the opposition Republicans had included pro-Zionist planks in their national platforms.[8] On each side of the aisle in Congress a majority of members strongly believed that the cause embodied simple goodness and harmed no one. "If the spirit of fair play prevails," said Senator Wagner of New York in behalf of many of his colleagues, "there need be no enmity between the great Arab lands and the small country reserved by the nations of the world for the righting of an age-old historic injustice."[9]

But not all that Roosevelt heard favored Jewish nationalists. The State Department had consistently raised serious questions about the justice of Zionist demands in the Promised Land. Secretary of State Cordell Hull and his confederates had pondered the claims of Herzl's disciples, had wrestled with them, and had often found them wanting. More than one diplomat told the president that the advocates of a commonwealth held no clear title to the ground they coveted. Most outspoken was the minister to Iraq, Loy Henderson, who vigorously opposed displacing Palestinians. He had preached the virtues of anti-

---

[6] U.S., Congress, House, *Report No. 1997*, 78th Cong., 2d sess., 1944; Reuben Fink, ed., *America and Palestine: The Attitude of Official America and of the American People Toward the Rebuilding of Palestine as a Free and Democratic Jewish Commonwealth.*

[7] Kenneth R. Bain, "American Foreign Policy and the Palestine Resolution: 1944," *Paisano: The Historian of the University of Texas* 9–10 (1970–1972): 63–76.

[8] House, *Report No. 1997*, 78th Cong., 2d sess., 1944, p. 4.

[9] *New York Times*, March 2, 1944, p. 4.

Zionism with subtle explanations of Arab nationalism and discourses on the emotional and symbolic nature of the dispute. He had constantly prodded Washington with warnings about the dire consequences of alienating Arabs.[10]

Support for the Zionist program would cost the United States dearly, State Department leaders told their president. Force was necessary to install and maintain a Jewish state in the Middle East, they reasoned. An angry Moslem world had the potential for great mischief. Embittered Arabs could cut oil supplies, deny access to vital air space, befriend the Axis powers, or delay construction of a proposed Persian Gulf–Mediterranean Sea pipeline.[11] They might even cast favors on apparent postwar rivals of the United States. Both London and Moscow could enhance their own positions with the Middle East capitals if Washington flirted with Jewish nationalism. "If now the Soviet Government comes out opposing all Zionist ambitions," wrote one State Department division head, "it . . . will place us in a greatly inferior position to the British and the Russians in that area. When we think of our stake in Saudi Arabia alone, this situation should cause us to do some very serious thinking."[12]

Roosevelt's own position on Palestine during World War II appeared to be hopelessly inconsistent. In 1944 the president let the State Department and the military brass persuade Congress to shelve a pro-Zionist resolution.[13] But four days later he told two rabbis that his government had never blessed British limits on Jewish immigration into the Holy Land and that "when future decisions are reached, full justice will be done to those who seek a Jewish national home."[14] After Arab governments poured a torrent of protests on Washington, the White House employed State Department sophistry to cool the crisis. Under orders from home, U.S. ministers in the Middle East assured their hosts that while the United States had never endorsed

[10] *FR*, 1944, V, 565–569, 604–605, 617–620, 631–633; Cordell Hull, *The Memoirs of Cordell Hull*, II, 1528–1537.
[11] Hull, *Memoirs*, II, 1508, 1522, 1531; *FR*, 1944, V, 576, 585, 618, 622, 625, 632, 633, 649, 656, 766.
[12] *FR*, 1944, V, 622–623.
[13] Ibid., pp. 569, 645 fn. 68.
[14] Ibid., pp. 588–599; Hull, *Memoirs*, II, 1536.

the British immigration restrictions, it had not opposed them, either. The president promised a Jewish homeland, the diplomats pointed out, not a new Israel.[15] On one day in March, 1944, Roosevelt led Zionist leaders to believe he supported their cause, then congratulated House Speaker Sam Rayburn for blocking a resolution friendly to the movement.[16] Realistically, Roosevelt had two policies: pro-Zionist promises to satisfy domestic appetites, but discouragement of Jewish nationalism to answer Moslem complaints.

Beneath these contradictions lay more than hypocrisy. Roosevelt never appreciated the depth of convictions surrounding the Palestine question. To him, squabbles over the "Promised Land" were petty affairs that paled into triviality in comparison to the tasks of defeating the fascist powers, maintaining access to Arab oil, and keeping U.S. Jewry loyal to the Democratic party. Locked in a deadly struggle with the Axis nations, he had to prevent a political explosion in the Holy Land that could ignite the whole region, cut vital supply lines, and damage Allied military posture. Political wisdom made the president acutely aware of Jewish nationalism's popularity, but the realities of petroleum diplomacy left him with a sense of caution. He had to pacify both Arabs and Jews. Roosevelt was never sure which side he really supported in the contest. Zionists' arguments were politically and emotionally attractive, yet their logic often puzzled him. The Arabs will fight to keep Palestine, he once reminded his wife, and fifteen to twenty million of them live in and around that country.[17]

So Doctor Win-the-War chose to avoid any lasting commitments to either side. He responded to each crisis individually, shifted positions to meet immediate goals, and concentrated attention on the main arenas of military strategy and wartime diplomacy. Nothing in the war situation demanded that he devise a permanent policy. To the contrary, the fighting gave him both reason and opportunity to

---

[15] *FR*, 1944, V, 591, 596–597; Hull, *Memoirs*, II, 1536.
[16] Roosevelt to Rayburn, March 9, 1944, Official File 700 (Palestine), Franklin D. Roosevelt Papers, Franklin D. Roosevelt Presidential Library, Hyde Park, N.Y.; *FR*, 1944, V, 588.
[17] *FR*, 1945, VIII, 690–691.

delay a final decision. He deliberately avoided a consistent response and made occasional promises to Zionists and Arabs, not to develop binding arrangements, but rather to postpone crises and pacify current passions. After the war he could weigh the advice that daily came his way and formulate a permanent policy. But while Hitler and Tojo survived, it was better to have an uneasy peace in the Holy Land than to attempt a settlement that might ignite smoldering tensions.[18]

Part of Roosevelt's indecision and inconsistency stemmed from a conflict between his desires and his perceived options. At first the chief executive exhibited far more sympathy for Zionist aspirations than he did for Arab complaints. On more than one occasion he expressed admiration for the economic advances of Jewish communities in Palestine. The dream of building a civilization out of a wilderness, "making the desert bloom," seemed to excite the president in much the same way that this vision captured public imagination. In a meeting in early 1940 with future Israeli President Chaim Weizmann, Roosevelt talked enthusiastically about conclusions reached in the U.S. Department of Agriculture relating to Palestine's economic potential. "It was a wonderful report," he told the British Zionist, "The Jews had done very well."[19]

Roosevelt probably never completely lost his cultural predispositions toward Zionism. But the hard realities of Middle Eastern politics slowly tamed his enthusiasm and eventually pushed him into an appreciation for the competing tensions of Arab nationalism. Even in his conversation with Jewish leaders in 1940 he recognized that no one could completely ignore Moslem complaints, but at that time he thought "a little backsheesh"—a bribe—might neutralize such opposition.[20] As the war progressed, State Department advisers were largely responsible for convincing the chief executive that Arab protests were legitimate and would not easily fade away.[21]

[18] Ibid., 1944, V, 640, 645 fn. 68; Hull, *Memoirs*, II, 1536.
[19] Samuel Halperin and Irvin Oder, "The United States in Search of a Policy: Franklin D. Roosevelt and Palestine," *Review of Politics* 24 (July, 1962): 321.
[20] Halperin and Oder, "United States in Search of a Policy," p. 321.
[21] The president received advice from a good many different sources, in-

Highly influential in this regard was a 1943 report from Lieutenant Colonel Harold B. Hoskins, who had gone to Saudi Arabia at the behest of the White House to talk with Ibn Saud. Hoskins was supposed to test the king's reaction to a proposal to pay Arabs for relinquishing Palestine to Jewish settlers from abroad. The plan, first discussed in the late 1930s in some international circles, was to remove all Arabs from their homes in Palestine, resettle them elsewhere at the expense of Zionists, leave the Holy Land to Jewish immigrants, and give Ibn Saud twenty million pounds sterling for his cooperation.[22] When the Arabian monarch talked with Hoskins, the old warrior was incensed at what appeared to him to be an attempted bribe in return for betrayal of his own people. He blamed Zionist leader Chaim Weizmann for initiating the move and rejected Hoskins's suggestion that he meet with the English Jew.[23]

After Hoskins returned to Washington, he reported to Roosevelt that there was no peaceful way to create a Jewish state in Arab territory. It was hopeless to expect Ibn Saud's acceptance. During a White House meeting between the president and Hoskins, the chief executive received the news stoically. He quickly abandoned any discussion of Palestine as a future Zionist state and lapsed into talk about making the disputed country an international "Holy Land" for Jews, Christians, and Moslems. He also suggested that there were other solutions to the Jewish refugee problem besides settlement in the Promised Land.[24]

Until his death Roosevelt occasionally voiced encouragement for Zionist aspirations, but he never again exhibited much faith in the movement's prospects for success. Rather, he grew increasingly pessimistic. While thousands of Jews wanted passage to Jerusalem, he

---

cluding Brigadier General Patrick J. Hurley, who traveled the Middle East in early 1943 as a personal representative of the president. *FR*, 1943, IV, 776–780. For State Department advice to Roosevelt, see *FR*, 1944, V, 586–587, 606–607.

[22] H. St. John B. Philby, *Arabian Jubilee*, pp. 210–212; Chaim Weizmann, *Trial and Error: The Autobiography of Chaim Weizmann*, pp. 426–433; *FR*, 1942, IV, 550–551; 1943, IV, 795, 812; Selig Adler, "Franklin D. Roosevelt and Zionism—The Wartime Record," *Judaism* 21 (Summer, 1972): 267.

[23] *FR*, 1943, IV, 809.

[24] Ibid., 1943, IV, 807–810, 811–814.

reminded Senator Wagner, several million Arabs were ready "to cut their throats the day they land."[25] From such vain expectations he began slowly to nurture an appreciation for Arab complaints and for State Department arguments that strategic U.S. interests required friendship with the Middle East majority. Increasingly he followed the lead of State Department advisers, except when political pressures made it uncomfortable to associate with their mainly pro-Arab views. It was Congress that constantly pushed to get more Jews into Palestine and to reorganize the government. When Arab capitals complained about such pushes, Roosevelt played the role of disinterested peacemaker, setting his diplomats into action to assure Moslem leaders that rumblings from Capitol Hill meant nothing to U.S. policy.[26]

But even if Roosevelt was pessimistic about Zionism's prospects, he could not escape the necessity of pleasing the right elements at the right time. When he faced a relection bid in 1944, he responded to the immediate political pressures. Early in the year, friends of Zionism introduced twin resolutions in the House and Senate. The measures threatened to put Congress on record as opposing British White Paper restrictions on Jewish immigration and favoring creation of a new Israel.[27] The matter presented a prickly dilemma for the administration. Passage meant alienating Middle Eastern countries, and Roosevelt knew it. Defeat might offend Jewish votes and money, important ingredients in the Democratic coalition and in Roosevelt's quest for a fourth term. Zionism had broad support, even among Gentiles. Republicans were eager and ready to capitalize on any signs that the White House was less than enthusiastic about the birth of a Jewish state.[28]

---

[25] Roosevelt to Wagner, December 3, 1944, Box 23, Robert F. Wagner Papers, Georgetown University Library, Washington, D.C.

[26] *FR*, 1944, V, 589–590, 591, 596–597, 615, 625, 629, 633, 656.

[27] U.S., Congress, *Congressional Record*, 78th Cong., 2d sess., 1944, 90, pt. 1, p. 856; *FR*, 1944, V, 560–561, 563; *New York Times*, January 28, 1944, p. 10.

[28] House, *Report No. 1997*, 78th Cong., 2d sess., 1944, pp. 2–3; *New York Times*, June 28, 1944, p. 6; June 29, 1944, p. 21; October 11, 1944, p. 30; October 13, 1944, p. 15; October 28, 1944, p. 11.

To surmount this problem, Roosevelt divided chores with his diplomats and military leaders. While they comforted worried Arabs
and persuaded Congress to shelve its resolution, he courted Jewish
votes. First, U.S. ministers in the Middle East excused and belittled
the actions of Congress, telling their host governments that the pro-
Zionist statements of politicians back home had little to do with the
foreign commitments of the United States. The executive branch,
they insisted, was solely responsible for the development of the nation's international policy. Then, with the approval of the president,
the State and War departments trotted out their biggest guns to sink
the Palestine measure on Capitol Hill. Cordell Hull joined Secretary
of War Henry Stimson and Generals George Marshall and Thomas
Handy in appeals to the lawmakers. All four warned that alienating
Arabs might hurt the war effort. Meanwhile, Roosevelt campaigned
as a champion of Jewish nationalism. His party platform contained
a Zionist plank, an extension of a Republican statement.[29] And in the
closing hours of October he affirmed his own dedication to the proposition in an open letter to Senator Wagner commending the Palestine section of the Democratic program.[30]

In December, with his reelection bid a success, Roosevelt once
again turned his back on a pro-Zionist measure. He sent his new secretary of state, Edward Stettinius, to testify in secrecy before the
Senate Foreign Relations Committee. The administration, or at least
the State Department, now agreed to take public responsibility in
return for defeat of the Palestine resolution. On December 10 the
committee agreed to the bargain.

There was within Roosevelt's policy some apparent hope that time
might close divisions between Zionists and Arabs and reward an administration that patiently allowed the crisis to run its course. Thus,

[29] Secretary of State Hull wrote Roosevelt in late July, 1944: "I believe
that it would be advisable for leaders of both parties to refrain from making
statements on Palestine during the campaign that might tend to arouse the
Arabs or upset the precarious balance of forces in Palestine itself" (*FR*, 1944,
V, 606). For information on campaign statements, see U.S., Congress, Senate,
Report No. 179, 79th Cong., 1st sess., 1945, p. 2; House, *Report No. 1997*, 78th
Cong., 2d sess., 1944, p. 2–4.
[30] *FR*, 1944, V, 615–616.

he did what the immediate situation required and avoided any elaborate settlements. His *ad hoc* approach might produce enormous inconsistency, but it would buy time. Time for the president to ponder the tragedy, survey the scene, and reach his own conclusions. Time for the squire of Hyde Park to travel east, talk with the leaders of Arabia, use his powers of personal diplomacy, and cultivate a compromise solution. Time for the chief executive to cut through conflicting ideologies, satisfy the majority, and find a workable answer—to do what he had always done in New Deal politics when confronted with competing philosophies or factions. Time for Roosevelt to charm Ibn Saud and convince the old monarch to moderate his own position—not because the American leader was devoted to a Jewish state, but because he saw a token victory for Jewish nationalism as a simple way to quiet Zionist agitation in domestic politics.

In late December, 1944, Franklin Roosevelt prepared for his February trip to Yalta. He told his secretary of state that he hoped for a respite from Palestine's controversy. But the nagging question would not go away, and Roosevelt knew it.[31] Even though he no longer had much enthusiasm for Zionist plans, he could not forget them without some mental anguish. It was more than political consideration. The election was behind him. In part, the promises made to Zionist leaders like Rabbi Stephen Wise, an old friend since the days when Roosevelt was governor of New York, may have bothered him.[32] Equally important, he could not resist the temptation to tread where diplomats feared to go. The president had enormous confidence in his own abilities in personal diplomacy. In January he began planning for his post-Yalta journey to Great Bitter Lake and a personal confrontation with Ibn Saud.[33]

If the president did have any hope of reaching a compromise

[31] Ibid., p. 655.

[32] Roosevelt certainly supported efforts in late 1944 to keep Congress from adopting a pro-Zionist resolution (*FR*, 1944, V, 637). Yet the president continued to toy with possible ways to realize part of the Zionist dream. In his letter to Senator Wagner in early December he said, "Everybody knows what American hopes are. If we talk about them too much we will hurt fulfillment" (Roosevelt to Wagner, December 3, 1944, Box 23, Wagner Papers).

[33] *FR*, 1945, VIII, 1.

solution over Palestine, however, his first step toward the Egyptian conference must have been a disappointing one. He asked the U.S. director of economic operations in the Middle East, James M. Landis, for advice on how he might achieve a rapprochement with the Arabian king on the Palestine problem. Landis had sobering thoughts on the subject. "You must be warned," he wrote the president, ". . . Ibn Saud both personally and as a political matter feels very intensely about this subject." The Moslem leader is the "spearhead of a true pan-Islam movement . . . that is unwilling to have any dealings with Infidels," including Jews. "Indeed of recent years Ibn Saud has had to defend against increasing hostility his actions in being friendly with Christians and admitting them into the country," Landis observed. It may be best to avoid the subject entirely, he counselled. But if the matter must come up, Roosevelt should abandon any hope that Ibn Saud would accept the creation of a Jewish commonwealth. In fact, Landis concluded, "the political objective implicit in the Jewish State idea . . . is not consistent with the Principles of the Atlantic Charter." If Palestinian policy became an international responsibility, Zionists might, at most, achieve the establishment of a Jewish homeland where "the extent of immigration can be related to the economic absorptive capacity of Palestine rather than to the political issues of a Jewish minority or majority."[34]

While Landis was making his assessment, the State Department and diplomats abroad sent their own views to the White House. Colonel William A. Eddy, U.S. minister in Saudi Arabia, reported in early January that King Ibn Saud said he "would be honored to die on [the] battlefield himself, a champion of Palestine Arabs." Secretary of State Edward Stettinius later forwarded the warning to the president, while much the same sort of appraisal came from other Near Eastern envoys.[35]

When February arrived and Roosevelt left Yalta to fly south toward Egypt, he still harbored some hopeful expectation of winning

[34] Ibid., pp. 680–682.
[35] Ibid., p. 679; 1944, V, 649, 652, 638–640.

concessions for Zionism. Yet even the view from his airplane window carried bad omens. Halfway between the Crimea and Great Bitter Lake the president flew over the disputed territory. To Roosevelt the land appeared rocky and barren, except for the coastal plain. Could it support an influx of thousands of Jews? Not without dislocations and bloodshed, he reasoned.[36]

If there was any chance of influencing Ibn Saud, every detail of protocol on board the U.S.S. *Quincy* had to be right. There could be no women allowed aboard the ship—not even the president's daughter, who left for a Cairo shopping spree. Ibn Saud arrived with his retinue of royal attendants "like something transported by magic from the middle ages," observed Chief of Staff William D. Leahy. For lunch in his honor the desert king got rice, lamb stew, and grapefruit. But no amount of rose water could sway the ruler from his opposition to Zionism.[37]

Roosevelt's plan was to offer Arab states massive technological assistance from the West in return for acceptance of a Jewish state. He may also have had in mind a scheme to mold a semiautonomous Jewish commonwealth with a regional federation that included neighboring Arab countries, but the evidence is inconclusive.[38] At any rate, Ibn Saud rejected every overture. He knew all the arguments—the pleas to save European refugees, the demands for Holocaust compensation, the historical claims to promised land—and was ready with clear and consistent answers. There was no need to tie the refugee problem to a Middle East solution, he argued. Displaced persons should find homes on the continent. If there was any indemnification, it should come from those responsible for fascist atrocities. In fact, he pointed out, so much death and destruction in the old Third Reich undoubtedly left depopulated areas where resettlement

---

[36] Later reported by FDR to Harold Hoskins in ibid., 1945, VIII, 690–691.
[37] William D. Leahy, *I was There: The Personal Story of the Chief of Staff to Presidents Roosevelt and Truman, Based on His Notes and Diaries Made at the Time*, p. 326; *FR*, 1945, VIII, 2–3.
[38] Adler, "Roosevelt and Zionism," p. 271.

would present few problems. Palestine must not bear the cross of European sins.[39]

Franklin Roosevelt came to his meeting hoping to moderate the Moslem ruler's position on the Holy Land debate. But in the end it was the U.S. president who shifted ground. He made a promise to his guest that went further than any previous commitment. He pledged that the United States would not aid Jewish nationalists in their fight against Arabs. The guarantee was the most direct statement to that date on U.S. intentions in Palestine. It was all that Ibn Saud and Arab leaders wanted for the time being, for without U.S. assistance to Zionism, they thought, there was little threat that the movement for a Jewish state in the Middle East would succeed.[40]

For Roosevelt's part, the whole conference was a lesson with grave implications. On the way home from Yalta he shared his feelings with Edward Stettinius. The meeting had convinced him that he must confer with congressional leaders to "examine our entire policy in Palestine." There is real danger, he told the secretary of state, that "if nature [takes] its course there [will] be bloodshed" in the Holy Land. "Some formula, not yet discovered, [will] have to prevent this warfare."[41]

Roosevelt was truly puzzled. There seemed to be no satisfactory solution. It was in these moments of doubt and frustration that he gained some renewed appreciation for State Department advice. Foreign-policy experts had generated elaborate plans—most of which the White House never saw—for a Palestine settlement.[42] Roosevelt was not yet ready to embrace any detailed formula but was now sure he could not ignore Arab wishes. In an early March appearance before Congress he told his audience, "I learned more about the whole problem of Arabia—the Moslems—the Jewish problem—by talking to Ibn Saud for five minutes than I could have learned in the exchange of two or three dozen letters."[43] In the weeks

---

[39] *FR*, 1945, VIII, 2–3.
[40] Ibid.
[41] Edward R. Stettinius, *Roosevelt and the Russians*, pp. 289–290.
[42] See, for example, *FR*, 1944, V, 655–657.
[43] *Time*, March 12, 1945, p. 18.

to come he sent a series of messages to Arab leaders reassuring them on an old pledge: he would consult them before making any decision on Palestine's destiny.[44]

For a time the president appeared to be making major shifts in U.S. policy and preparing public and Congress to accept the hard realities he had discovered. Then suddenly he reversed himself again. His remark to Congress about learning so much from Ibn Saud stirred the wrath of U.S. Zionists. Rabbi Stephen Wise called on the president in mid-March and asked if the comment meant Roosevelt would not support the aims of Jewish nationalism. On the contrary, the chief executive replied. The Jewish leader emerged from his White House parley reassured. He told reporters his host had authorized him to say, "I made my position on Zionism clear in October. That position I have not changed, and shall continue to seek to bring about its earliest realization."[45] Even if Roosevelt was preparing major reevaluations of national policy, he still could not escape the old patterns of soothing Zionist friends. The task of shattering their illusions would be difficult and painful. Roosevelt was not yet ready to undertake that burden. One month later he died with unfinished business.

Roosevelt's conduct toward the Palestine question produced a curious pattern of public responses. Most of the reactions came from people with unmistakable sympathies for Zionism. The president got high marks for any assistance to Jewish nationalism, but hints of indifference, opposition, or misgivings toward a New Israel inspired either open ridicule or a thinly veiled hostility. Promises to Arab leaders were seen as disgraceful betrayals of decency, appeasements of sinister petroleum potentates, deadly cuts at the legitimate interests of thousands of Jewish refugees—all for the sake of liquid riches from Arabia.[46]

On one level, considering the Holocaust and its aftermath, it was

[44] *FR*, 1945, VIII, 697, 698, 704.

[45] Ibid., p. 693 fn. 42.

[46] Historians have offered many of the same criticisms of Roosevelt. See, for example, Herbert Parzan, "The Roosevelt Palestine Policy, 1943–1945," *American Jewish Archives* 26 (April, 1974): 31–65.

not difficult to appreciate why people might condemn failures to promote the movement of Jewish refugees out of Europe and into new
homes in Palestine. Yet the criticisms using Zionist criteria were justified only with the assumption that the creation of a new Israel was
the best solution—or even the only answer—to the problem of the
uprooted Jews. Any fair assessment of Roosevelt had to recognize
that there were other possible solutions—alternatives to Jewish nationalism that might have served Holocaust surivivors best. Reason
also demanded some appreciation for Roosevelt's view of the problems of creating a Jewish state in Palestine. As the past quarter-
century of Arab-Israeli conflict, bitterness, hate, and terror has indicated, Roosevelt's vision of a "throat-cutting" greeting was all too
accurate.[47]

It made more sense to fault Roosevelt for not finding other havens
for Jewish refugees. He flirted with Zionist proposals much too long,
continuing to see them as acceptable solutions long after much evidence told him that the plans for a Jewish state meant great trouble.
On several occasions he toyed with various rescue schemes, including
a "world budget" under which the refugee problem would receive international solution.[48] But he never stuck with any plan long enough
to see its realization. There was no major effort to increase U.S. immigration quotas, no dedication to any workable scheme, nothing
except the recurring flirtation with Zionism. In his inability and lack
of courage to put aside Zionist proposals and seek alternatives, Roosevelt left plans for rescuing Hitler's victims in a constant state of

---

[47] Selig Adler's 1972 article in *Judaism* is perhaps the best statement of
the Zionist review of Roosevelt's policies. While ending his survey with a friendly attempt to explain why the president faced a "peculiarly difficult" problem,
Adler's main thrust is that FDR committed a series of "blunders," and "misrep-
resentations" on his way to a "sorry record." For Adler, executive conduct was
reprehensible because Palestine was such an easy and "logical solution" to Jewish woes in Europe. Uprooted people, fleeing Hitler's gas chambers, "would receive a cheering welcome" in the Holy Land—"an immediate asylum." In
retrospect, Roosevelt's prediction of a "throat-cutting" greeting seems far more
accurate than historian Adler's depiction of a "cheering welcome" (Adler, "Roosevelt and Zionism," pp. 270, 272).

[48] *FR*, 1943, IV, 792–794, 807–810, 811–814.

flux. While he wallowed in indecision, precious time passed with tragic consequences. Thus, it was his inability to abandon Zionism completely that caused more trouble than did his lack of dedication to Herzl's cause.

Palestine may have had some responsibility to accept part of the world Jewish refugee burden, and Roosevelt may have had a duty to command fulfillment of that responsibility. Yet justice should not have expected the disputed country, with its meager economic base, to absorb all of the displaced Jews, or even any major portion of them, while the rest of the world took practically none of them. Even offers to help Palestine enlarge its economy were small comfort to Arabs. If the territory eventually became a Jewish state, they would not be around to enjoy the financial rewards. In order to win welcome for Holocaust survivors, Roosevelt needed to persuade the Arabs that increased immigration did not represent a step toward Jewish statehood. Such persuasion would have been difficult in light of the Zionists' agitations brewing among the Arabs since the 1920's. But the only hope of persuading the skeptical Arabs rested not in continued overtures in behalf of Jewish nationalism or even in the promise of nonintervention, but in a presidential assurance that the United States would prevent the creation of a Zionist state in return for Arab acceptance of part of the refugee burden.

Ironically, Roosevelt did recognize the problems of depending on Palestine to absorb most of the uprooted Jews. He realized early that Zionism meant trouble and bloodshed, yet he failed to act effectively on that knowledge. Instead, he clung tenaciously to the hope of winning concessions for Jewish nationalism, allowing a cultural affinity and political considerations to modify his otherwise rational conclusions. His failure to act decisively on his own observations in 1945 made his policy vulnerable.

It is equally regrettable that Roosevelt's conduct was riddled with deception. His policy came to depend heavily on his ability to sell false impressions. FDR arrogantly tossed honesty and candor aside. His flaws were the defects of a regime too long in power, too accustomed to making matters work out in the long term, too familiar with the opportunity to correct yesterday's lies, and too little impressed with what might happen when a new man sat in the oval office. The parade of fictions, half-truths, self-contradictions, and secrets left his successor an inconsistent legacy of advice that did more to confuse than to enlighten.

CHAPTER TWO

MARCHING TO ZION

I n February, 1947, the *Atlantic Monthly* carried an article by Princeton University philosopher W. T. Stace. It argued that any attempt to force Palestine to accept massive immigration was an act of aggression against the Arab people and contrary to the "self-determination" doctrine of the Atlantic Charter. Suffering in the Holocaust gave Jews a claim against "England, America, Russia, France, and Palestine too. . . , but not more against Palestine than any other country." Yet, he concluded, "The inhabitants of the United States, of Canada, of Australia, of Great Britain, of the rest of the countries concerned do not want . . . to take our fair share of the burden. We have found a small country, Palestine, and a remote and defenseless people, the Arabs, on whom we can unjustly shove the burden of our duties." Neither the Jewish desire for Palestine, Stace argued, nor the American wish to fulfill that desire justified Zionist claims.[1]

"Let us suppose," Kermit Roosevelt, grandson of Theodore Roosevelt, theorized in *Harper's* in late 1946, "that the United States, having undertaken to assist the Filipinos to self-government, had then turned to another people suffering under Japanese oppression who had lived in the Philippines many centuries ago but were now wholly foreign to the islands. Suppose that the United States had promised them these islands to form a commonwealth of their own. Even if . . . the Filipinos agreed that victims of Japanese oppression should be given every possible aid and comfort, they would not

[1] W. T. Stace, "The Zionist Illusion," *Atlantic Monthly* 179 (February, 1947): 82–86.

admit the right of the United States to make such a promise. They would resist all efforts to fulfill it. American public opinion would surely support them." So it was with any promises from the British to give Palestine to the Jews. Great Britain did not have the right, the young Roosevelt argued, to give away Arab land.[2]

For anti-Zionist Jews there were even additional reasons to oppose the creation of a new Israel. Lessing J. Rosenwald, president of the American Council of Judaism, constantly insisted that Judaism was a religion, not a nationality, and that it had universal significance, not narrow tribal meaning. Zionism, with its contention to the contrary, had accepted anti-Semitism's argument that Jews did not belong in Gentile society. It had capitulated to the forces of bigotry and had given ammunition to the enemies of enlightenment. Israel, could become only "another self-imposed ghetto." Palestine was not a sanctuary from the troubles of the world. "War-weary Jewish refugees may find," he warned, "they have jumped from a Central European frying pan into a Palestine fire."[3]

Yet for all their efforts at persuasion, neither Stace, Kermit Roosevelt, Rosenwald, nor any of the other anti-Zionists had much impact on public opinion. Actually, when the Second World War ended in Europe, most Americans knew little about the political status of Palestine. One public opinion poll in late 1945 discovered that half of the people had never heard of the dispute over the Holy Land; another poll, a year earlier, found that only one-third realized that Great Britain held a mandate over the territory.[4] Yet such ignorance about details did not hinder the quick development of opinions. Jews of the United States, generally better informed on the issue than were their Gentile countrymen, had for several previous decades steadily increased their collective support for both political Zionism and the proposals to send more of their coreligionists to the Jordan

---

[2] Kermit Roosevelt, "The Arabs Live There Too," *Harper's* 193 (October, 1946): 289–294.

[3] Lessing J. Rosenwald, "The Fallacies of Palestine," *Collier's* 121 (March 13, 1948): 30, 32.

[4] *The Gallup Poll: Public Opinion, 1935–1971*, I, 584; *Opinion News*, October 16, 1945, p. 4.

Valley.[5] In the wake of Hitler's defeat, larger immigration quotas for the Promised Land soon gained overwhelming national popularity.

The plight of Jewish refugees seeking admission to the Holy Land became a cause célèbre for hundreds of leading American citizens, including scores of prominent Gentiles. Catholic priests and Protestant clergymen joined their rabbi brethren to champion the needs of displaced persons. Congressmen, senators, state legislators, and governors urged bigger flows of humanity to the Promised Land. Liberals were often in the forefront of the movement, but powerful conservatives like Robert Taft also joined the crusade. A poll in late 1945 found that 80 percent of the citizens favored increased immigration to Palestine.[6]

Such attitudes, however, did not necessarily imply support for the creation of a Zionist state. At most, only a sizeable minority sought the founding of a Jewish commonwealth. Even a large body of Jewish leaders strongly denounced the drive for a nation based on their religion. Other friends of increased immigration either knew little and cared less about the political status or offered various degrees of opposition to a new Israel. Finding a place for thousands of displaced persons in Europe became the dominant issue, to the virtual exclusion of practically all other considerations. Even many mild opponents of political Zionism were willing to tolerate a Jewish commonwealth as long as it provided a sanctuary for the Holocaust survivors.[7]

Sympathy for Hitler's victims helped crystallize public opinion. But it would be a mistake to think that wartime passions accounted for all of the American good will toward Jewish ambitions in Palestine. Long before Nazi concentration camps shocked the world, Jew-

[5] *Gallup Poll*, I, 554.
[6] Ibid. In this poll actually only 55 percent of the respondents had "followed the discussion about permitting Jews to settle in Palestine." In that informed group, 76 percent favored the immigration and another 4 percent liked the idea "if the Jews do."
[7] See, for example, "Interim Policy for Palestine," *New Republic* 113 (November 26, 1945): 692–693, and the discussion in Irwin Oder, "The United States and the Palestine Mandate, 1920–1948: A Study of the Impact of Interest Groups on Foreign Policy" (Ph.D. diss., Columbia University, 1956).

ish immigration to the Promised Land attracted considerable support from Americans. Two different, but related, trains of thought had generated admiration for the efforts of the Yishuv. To a large segment of the population, pioneering in the Holy Land deserved approval because it was part of a great historical process, a new and peculiar form of manifest destiny. Jews were doing their own version of the Great American Drama, so the argument ran, playing the role of pilgrim settlers, battling against "savages," and trying to carve a civilization out of a wilderness. A Jewish community in Palestine— whether it be a "homeland" or a commonwealth—promised an outpost of Americanism in the Middle East, a comforting outlook in an age drifting toward Cold War paranoia. To another segment, one justification for Jewish ascendency in Palestine outweighed all others —it was God's will. The return of the "chosen people" to the Holy Land was a fulfillment of a biblical prophecy that commanded respect and appreciation.

Pity for Holocaust survivors still played a large role in shaping American responses. It became the capstone in the growth of public attitudes. Tribulations had, so the argument ran, earned for the Jews a place in Palestine. Through a peculiar kind of reasoning some observers even viewed dispossessing Arabs as a way to punish Axis criminals— a logic made easier to digest by the alleged fraternization of the mufti of Jerusalem with the Führer. But the Holocaust generated more than pity and vengeance. Jewish suffering in Europe created a potentially embarrassing situation. If the uprooted did not find homes in Palestine, they might pressure for admission to the United States. Rhetoric and emotions from the war demanded attention to the "first enemies of Nazism," but little support existed for bringing any sizeable number of Jews to this side of the Atlantic. Compassion conflicted with xenophobia and ethnocentrism. Even those observers who exhibited no personal anti-Semitism had to face the realities of popular biases and bow to the wishes of the majority. The forces of prejudice, plus a surrender by the benevolent to the weight of that bigotry, produced an almost automatic assumption that Palestine was the proper destination for Holocaust survivors.

In an important sense, admiration for Jewish settlement in Palestine was merely an extension of an old pattern of national attitudes. In professional journals, in church magazines, in newspapers for school children, and throughout the mass media, writers pictured Zionist efforts in the disputed territory as a repetition of U.S. history. According to the analogy, all of the major elements were present. Immigrants from Europe were pilgrims arriving at the Jewish substitute for Plymouth Rock, fleeing the tyranny and degradation of the Old World and hoping to carve a civilization out of a wilderness. The pioneers were encountering enormous difficulties, including the opposition of backward natives and reactionary imperial authorities. Arabs were playing the part of Indians, while the British re-created their own role from the eighteenth century.

But the comparisons did not stop there. Articulate observers constantly used the language of nineteenth- and twentieth-century expansionists to glorify Jewish ascendancy in the disputed territory. There was even considerable discussion of bringing elements of the New Deal to the Holy Land. A proposal to create a Jordan Valley Authority, modeled after the Tennessee Valley Authority, sparked an enthusiastic response. The entire analogy was comforting, not only because it reminded readers of their own national past, but also because it promised them friends and an expansion of influence in an increasingly hostile world. Jewish history became U.S. history. Zionist struggles were "like the fight the American colonies carried on in 1776," Henry Wallace wrote. "Just as British stirred up the Iroquois to fight the colonist, so today they are stirring up the Arabs."[8] Zionist acts of terror and sabotage were comparable to Boston Tea Party tactics, a New England newspaper editor concluded.[9]

There were striking similarities between the way commentators described Jewish settlement in Palestine and the way earlier generations of Americans discussed their own colonization of North Amer-

[8] Henry Wallace, "The Problem of Palestine," *New Republic* 116 (April 21, 1947): 12.
[9] As quoted in Joseph Schechtman, *The United States and the Jewish State Movement: The Crucial Decade, 1939–1949,* pp. 150–151.

35

ican territory. From the early years of the century, many writers began to marvel at the technological achievements of the Zionists. The pilgrims made the desert bloom, according to the prevailing account. They created a virtual paradise on once arid and barren land. A touch of their hand had transformed ancient Judea into a cornucopia of milk and honey. Tractors, hydroelectric plants, lush vineyards, fields of grain, and collective farms with lavish assortments of vegetables symbolized the Jewish presence.[10] The proper use of the soil, so the argument ran, had won for the Zionists the right to claim the land from its more recent, but less progressive, owners. The reasoning was reminiscent of Jacksonians defending Indian removal or dispossession of Mexicans. It was the language of settlers moving West with the conviction that they could stick a Christian plow into the ground and make Kansas bloom.[11]

Americans had long thought of themselves as special people, endowed by their Creator with enormous powers to transform a wilderness and a high responsibility to use that potential. Advocates of nineteenth-century expansion had often used biblical symbols, borrowed from ancient Hebrew experiences, to express their Manifest Destiny. Anglo-Saxons were "chosen people" and recipients of a promised land. It was easy for twentieth-century observers to transfer images and idioms back to the earlier "children of God."

An important part of the argument was that the potential for growth was always in the land but that the Arabs had failed to tap its power. Jews were better suited to make full use of the resources because of their special status with the Almighty and their unique relationship to the soil. "Israel," a Baptist minister argued, "belongs

[10] See, for example, Andree Choveaux, "The New Palestine," *Geographical Review* 17 (January, 1927): 75–88; Milton Steinberg, "The Creed of an American Zionist," *Atlantic Monthly* 175 (February, 1945): 101–106; and William H. Stringer, "A Peace for Palestine," *New Republic* 113 (November 12, 1945): 633–635.

[11] For a brilliant discussion of this theme, see Paul D. Travis, "Charlatans, Sharpers, and Climatology: The Symbolism and Mythology of Late Nineteenth Century Expansionism in Kansas" (Ph.D. diss., University of Oklahoma, 1975); and Albert K. Weinberg, *Manifest Destiny: A Study of Nationalist Expansionism in American History.*

to the 'land' and the 'land' belongs to her. Like spirit and body, neither can function without the other."[12]

Commentators were fond of making comparisons between Arab "failures" and Zionist "successes." The literature on Palestine was full of descriptions that contrasted the old and the new. "Jewish pioneers . . . have built modern cities on what used to be sand dunes," *Senior Scholastic* writers told school children in late 1945.[13] "It is, of course, the modern objection against the Arabs," one reporter concluded, "that they developed Palestine less in 1300 years than present day Jews [did] in 30 years."[14] Another account was more graphic. It displayed pairs of photographs with telling dissimilarities: Bedouins living in grass huts versus the modern homes of Jewish settlers. "Here are camels, the ancient burden bearers, carrying from the field the harvest of the Arabs" contrasted with the "modern machinery now largely being used in reaping the fields of grain" on Jewish farms.[15]

Some of the more benevolent suggested that, far from routing the Arabs from their homes, Jewish settlement in Palestine could actually benefit the natives. Zionist communities could become models for Arab efforts. They could function as beacons to light the way to progress for the undeveloped. Innumerable blessings could flow from the kind of example and guidance that Jewish civilization was ready to provide for its neighbors. The rising Israel could become a showcase of westernization, displaying for all its neighbors the wisdom of adopting Americanization.[16]

Implicit in this whole approach was the conviction that the Arabs

---

[12] W. A. Jamlett, "The Palestine Question," *Florida Baptist Witness*, May 27, 1948, p. 3. For a Zionist expression of this idea, see Eliahu Ben-Horin, "The Future of the Middle East," *Harper's* 190 (December, 1944): 82–90.

[13] "Palestine . . . Much Promised Land," *Scholastic* 47 (December 3, 1945): 7.

[14] Eugene S. Geissler, "Jewish Farming in Palestine," *America* 14 (January 19, 1946): 428.

[15] George T. B. Davis, *Rebuilding Palestine According to Prophecy*, p. 83.

[16] See, for example, I. F. Stone, "The Palestine Report," *The Nation* 162 (May 11, 1946): 562–564; and "The Atlantic Report on the World Today: Palestine," *Atlantic Monthly* 173 (September, 1946): 17–22.

were inferior beings, incapable of leading any struggle for moderni-
zation. With great slashes of ethnocentric and racist thinking, Americans reasoned that technological advancement had unquestioned
value and that any people who lagged behind in material achievements was obviously deficient. Like the natives of North America,
the Moslems had forfeited their title to the land when they failed to
make "proper" use of the soil. "Who legally owns Palestine?" Charles
Alexander of Dallas asked in the *Baptist Standard*. "Do the Arabs?
No! . . . When some races become so low down as to become a pes-
tilence to others about them, then justice demands that they be
wiped off the earth." [17]

The image of Arabs as hostile, "lesser" breeds who "deserved"
displacement appeared in a vast array of media, but nowhere was
it better reflected than in motion picture versions of the Middle East
people. For a generation the film world had both reflected and en-
trenched popular attitudes. In many minds, Arabs were all barbarian
bedouins, roaming the desert, occasionally stealing unsuspecting
white maidens, and often fighting British or French foreign legions.
They were an inferior species—highly superstitious, savage, and
lecherous. They were nearly always the enemy. They were the crea-
tures who attacked Ronald Coleman in *Beau Geste*, raided Gary
Cooper and his party in *Beau Sabreur*, and ambushed a John Ford–
directed cast in *The Lost Patrol*. In the hazy impressions that
emerged from celluloid images, Arabs were often brutish and crude,
consumed by sexual desires, and constantly preoccupied with danc-
ing girls, marriage fairs, and the trading of wives. "When an Arab
sees a woman he wants," Rudolph Valentino said in *The Sheik*, "he
takes her." [18] It was a collective national experience that helped generate a legacy of animosity toward the Moslem people.

[17] Charles T. Alexander, "Who Owns Palestine?" *Baptist Standard*, September 16, 1948, p. 3. The Reverend Wendell Phillips of Christ's Episcopal
Church, Rye, New York, told a meeting of the American Christian Palestine
Committee in late 1945: "There is no Arab problem. They wouldn't fight if it
were too warm, or too rainy. I know the Arabs; I taught them. They came to
classes without prepared lessons, but they gave such charming excuses. . . . The
Arabs like working under the Jews" ("Palestine," *Churchman*, November 1,
1945, p. 16).
[18] *The Sheik*, Jesse L. Lasky Pictures, 1921, Motion Picture Division, Li-

Most Americans knew relatively little about Arabs and had few opportunities to learn much. In 1940 only a handful of colleges and universities offered graduate work in Islamic studies. A small group of Arabiaphils maintained meager cultural contacts with the Near East. There were three American-sponsored colleges in Lebanon and Syria. Several Protestant denominations maintained small missionary endeavors in Asia Minor and North Africa. *Muslim World* had led scholarly interests in Arab matters since its founding in 1911, but its circulation touched no more than a few centers of learning.[19]

The whole thrust of popular attitudes drew a clear line between Arabs and "civilized" whites. In reflection of the deep sense of racial categories so prevalent in American thought, Arabs joined Indians, blacks, Chinese, and other people in the public notion of inferior breeds. American thought had plenty of precedents for assigning people to untouchable status. To do the same for one more group was merely an extension of an old pattern.[20]

Much of this whole approach came into clear focus in the proposals for the creation of a Jordan Valley Authority. Dr. Walter Lowdermilk of the Soil Conservation Service of the Department of Agriculture outlined his ideas for development of the river in a 1944 book

---

brary of Congress. Other films that reflected the Arab stereotype or featured Arabs in attacks on westerners included *The Silent Lover* (1926), *She's a Sheik* (1927), *The Desert Bride* (1928), *The Desert Sheik* (1927), *The Son of the Sheik* (1925), *A Son of the Desert* (1928), *A Son of the Sahara* (1929), *The Desert Song* (1929 and 1943), *One Stolen Night* (1923) and the two-million-dollar classic rendition of *The Thief of Bagdad* (1925). Most of these films are deposited in the Motion Picture Division, Library of Congress.

[19] Robert L. Daniel, *American Philanthropy in the Near East, 1820–1960*; Joseph L. Grabill, *Protestant Diplomacy and the Near East: Missionary Influence on American Policy, 1810–1927*; and George Dimitri Selim, *American Doctoral Dissertations on the Arab World, 1883–1968*.

[20] The movies of the era also often stereotyped Jews, but apparently with kinder images. One reviewer argued that the portrayal of Jews in films was done with "great sympathy, . . . an aura of religiosity and gentleness." Jews in films were rarely realistic and sometimes "a bit of a buffoon" but ultimately "Americanized." In the 1930's and early 1940's Jews rarely appeared as Jews except to blurt out "one-liners" with the proper "Jewish accent" (Gary Carey, "The Long Long Road to Brenda Patimkin," *National Jewish Monthly*, October, 1971, reprinted in Richard A. Maynard, ed., *The Black Man on Film: Racial Stereotyping*, pp. 113–124).

entitled *Palestine, Land of Promise*. The book generated considerable enthusiasm in a good many observers. New Dealers found much to favor in the idea of extending the application of Tennessee Valley Authority concepts. Lowdermilk, openly Zionist in his politics, had a long career in forestry, engineering, hydrology, geophysics, and soil conservation. He had spent five years as research professor of forestry at the University of Nanking and was the assistant chief of the Soil Conservation Service at the time he wrote the book. In 1938 and 1939 the Department of Agriculture had sent him to Europe and the Near East to study denudation and conservation of soil. His book was the product of his observations from that journey.

Lowdermilk's plan called for the building of hydroelectric dams to take advantage of the Jordan's proximity to the Mediterranean and the river's descent to a thirteen-hundred-foot depth below sea level at the Dead Sea. Saltwater, diverted from the ocean along canals to the edge of the river valley, could create enormous energy as it fell to the level of the Jordan. Dams could store floodwaters during wet periods and later release them for irrigation. Lowdermilk argued that such development could significantly increase the capacity of Palestine to absorb more immigrants—he estimated a potential four million—and benefit the Arab population at the same time.

Lowdermilk contended that Palestine, after generations of prosperity, had been in a man-made economic decline since the seventh century. Human devastation and neglect of the land and its potential stemmed from the cultural, political, and economic habits of the Turks and Arabs. Nomadic traditions of the Bedouins had played a major role in the decline. Lowdermilk celebrated the twentieth-century achievements of Zionist settlers in western Palestine as the first significant improvements in a thousand years. In his mind the technological advances of Jewish pilgrims promised a great future for Judea. Already, he claimed, Arab prosperity had increased as a result of Zionist immigration. More arrivals from Europe could only mean greater benefits for everyone.

It was an appealing analysis even if it did ethnocentrically assume the superiority of technical advances and the degeneracy of nomadic existence. It contained so much that reminded Americans of their own past. Surely Arabs, like the Indians before them, so the argument ran, could benefit from the standards of Western civilization. A few might complain about alien intrusions, but there could be no legitimate, sustained opposition because of the enormous advantages for the natives. "How could there be . . . a clash," asked a reviewer from the *New York Times* when discussing Lowdermilk's book, "when Arab prosperity and population have increased in the neighborhood of all Jewish settlements and when in the space of fourteen years (1927–1940) the Arab death rate has dropped by one-third?" Just as European leadership had helped "civilize" Cherokees and other American Indian tribes, Jewish guidance could lead backward bedouins into the blessings of modern life. "The Arab shows his ability," the *New York Times* writer boasted, "to improve himself when a good example is set before him. The good example in Palestine happens to be Jewish."[21] It was not a matter of racial superiority. It was a matter of having the "proper" culture.

Yet for most observers the significance of Lowdermilk's dream went far beyond the prospects for improving the lot of Arabs and Jews. *Palestine, Land of Promise* offered what many people considered to be a completely dispassionate and scientific solution to a difficult political squabble. Most reviewers remained skeptical about the prospects for the plan's realization and often critical of Lowdermilk for doing his thinking in a political vacuum. Yet it was the seemingly nonpolitical character of the scheme that had the most appeal. The book was rational and devoid of value judgments, so the argument ran. "It tries to inject sober economic deliberations into heated political arguments," Werner J. Cahman wrote in the *American Journal of Sociology*. "Unlike so many recent books on Palestine," *Foreign Affairs* noted, "this one is not concerned with politics." *Booklist* recognized some discussion of "racial and political questions," but concluded, "the author's viewpoint is chiefly economic and agricultural." Historian Louis Adamic called the work a "hard-headed statement of facts and means, possibilities and results."[22]

[21] R. L. Duffus, "Practical View of Palestine," *New York Times Book Review*, May 21, 1944, p. 20.
[22] Werner J. Cahman, "Review: *Palestine, Land of Promise*," *American*

Palestine simply needed the application of modern technology. Millions of Jews and Arabs could benefit. Dr. Lowdermilk's good engineering techniques could improve the economic capacity of the country, thereby allowing more immigrants to enter the territory without harming local Moslems. The Promised Land could become a showcase of progress to light the way for neighboring Moslem countries, a model to guide a whole region into the twentieth century. "There . . . is a wonderful opportunity for such development," wrote a *Nation* book reviewer, if politics allowed the proper use of advanced engineering. "What has been done in southern California, which in many respects is a land like Palestine," concluded the *New York Times* reviewer, "could be done along the eastern shores of the Mediterranean." [23]

Strangely missing from this whole approach was any discussion of the difficult problems that lay beyond decisions on immigration policy and economic development. It was as if all matters would peacefully take care of themselves once the Jordan Valley Authority became a reality. There was little recognition that Zionism meant something more than the immigration of large numbers of Jews into Palestine. Neither Lowdermilk nor his reviewers offered any hints about the political status of a postdevelopment Holy Land. They failed to confront questions about who would rule, whether there would be a Jewish state, or what such a political entity would mean for non-Jews in the area. They offered few comments on the possibility that increased Jewish immigration might give extreme Zionists the political muscle with which to displace Arabs from Palestine or at least to dominate them. They reflected little sensitivity to the Arab fears that even if major technological advances took place, the rise of a Jewish commonwealth might mean few Arabs would be in a position to enjoy the rewards. There was little discussion of the time it

---

Journal of Sociology 50 (September, 1944): 155–156; *Foreign Affairs* 22 (July, 1944): 666; *Booklist* 40 (April 1, 1944): 262; quotation in an advertisement for the book in *New York Times Book Review*, October 1, 1944, p. 26.

[23] W. F. Albright, "Palestine Transformed," *The Nation* 158 (June 3, 1944): 656; Duffus, "Practical View of Palestine," p. 20.

would take to develop Lowdermilk's plans or what to do about immigration in the meantime.

The whole approach, typical of a large body of American opinion, was willing to risk the possibility that increased immigration into Palestine might very well mean dispossession for Arabs. The promises of a rational use of the soil justified the risks. "Dr. Lowdermilk's outline of a JVA project," wrote Louis Adamic, "much like our TVA, holds forth a tremendous promise for Palestine's future."[24] It was this promise which outweighed Arab objections.

Lowdermilk's book attracted considerable attention and went through several printings in the first few years after its initial publication. Included in its champions were a good many prominent voices, but none more distinguished than Vice-President Henry Wallace and Senator George W. Norris, father of the TVA. "My own interest in Zionism," Wallace recalled when he became editor of the *New Republic* in 1947, "began when, as Secretary of Agriculture, I sent Walter Lowdermilk . . . abroad to study the soils of the Near East."[25] It was the good doctor's report on the potentials of Palestine that attracted Wallace's attention and enthusiasm.

With coaching from old friend and ardent Zionist Louis Brandeis, who shared his excitement, Wallace was able to see the Jewish settlement and Lowdermilk's proposals in typically American terms. Brandeis and Wallace talked about developments in Palestine in language that was Jeffersonian, reminiscent of Progressive Era struggles for the New Freedom. Wallace said of Brandeis, with obvious agreement, "His faith in Zionism was associated with his belief in the virtue of doing things with your own hands in a small way." He wanted, Wallace wrote with continuing approval, "to give an opportunity to every human being to earn his livelihood on a small farm or a small business."[26] A Jordan Valley Authority was exciting because it promised to promote the ideal society.

[24] Quoted in an advertisement for the book in *New York Times Book Review*, October 1, 1944, p. 26.
[25] Wallace, "Problem of Palestine," pp. 12–13.
[26] Ibid.

George W. Norris was equally enthusiastic about the plans. The Nebraska senator had struggled for much of his congressional career to help achieve what he considered to be unprecedented development along the Tennesse River. When Lowdermilk proposed to accomplish the same task on the ancient waterway of the Holy Land, Norris responded with the pride and approval of a doting father. "From the very beginning," he wrote ". . . the [TVA] project excited the curiosity and admiration of engineers and scientists the world over." But it was not just Lowdermilk's dream for advancement of Palestine that thrilled the Nebraskan. It was the possibility that the Jordan Valley Authority could become, in Lowdermilk's phrase, "the leaven that will transform other lands in the Near East." After Norris read *Palestine, Land of Promise*, he knew few bounds for his thinking on the subject. "If the TVA could be developed here without regard to state lines, why could not Europe, the Near East, or any other region develop a TVA without regard to national boundaries?" he asked. "Who knows what the effect would be on the future peace of the world?"[27]

Both Wallace and Norris favored the Jewish settlement in Palestine because it promised to create a civilization much like their own. It was a cheap way to spread the "American dream." Both men relished the thought of having an outpost of Americanism on the banks of the Jordan River. The Jews deserved support because they were doing what progressives had done in the New World. They were carving a civilization out of a wilderness, providing guidance for "backward" natives, and reclaiming the land to its proper and productive use. There could be no question about the wisdom of admitting more of these advanced people to the Promised Land. If there was some risk that Arabs might suffer dispossession in the process of Zionist colonization, such was the small price of progress.[28]

This whole devotion to an American brand of progress was, how-

---

[27] George W. Norris, "TVA on the Jordan," *The Nation* 158 (May 20, 1944): 589–590.

[28] Lowdermilk's proposals attracted widespread comments. See, for example, "The Atlantic Report on the World Today: Palestine," *Atlantic Monthly* 178 (September, 1946): 17–22.

ever, more than a commitment to aphoristic principles. It was also a pursuit of concrete advantages. In the context of growing Cold War tensions, advocates of Zionist colonization could fault Arabs for more than a failure to till the soil properly. They could also easily dismiss them as unlikely allies because of their "ancient" ways. Few people expected the anachronistic Moslems to side with Washington in future confrontations of the United States with the Soviet Union.

In contrast, the Jewish settlements appeared to be friendly islands in an increasingly hostile world. They could provide outlets for the expansion of influence and culture. To Howard LeSourd, co-director of the American Christian Palestine Committee, the Zionist community in the Holy Land "constituted" an "arsenal of democracy." For George T. Renner, professor of geography at Columbia, "guarantee of future security [in the Middle East] . . . would be a strong Jewish state in Palestine." It could, he concluded, "serve as an outpost of democracy."[29]

Dreams of a partisan compound in the Middle East stimulated much of the support for Jewish colonization of Palestine. Yet such visions were not the only thoughts to encourage sympathy for Holy Land settlement. For millions of fundamentalist Christians the return of "chosen people" to the Promised Land had unquestioned value simply because in their view God predestined and prophesied the creation of Israel. Beginning in the nineteenth century, a growing chorus of eschatological believers focused much of their attention on Jewish progress in Palestine. In the two decades before Zionists achieved their goal, a flood of literature celebrated the fulfilling of divine predictions and reminded the faithful that migration to the Holy Land was part of a celestial plan. Large numbers of Protestants saw the flow to Judea as a sign that human history was coming to an

[29] Howard M. Lesourd, "A Sacred Promise—Still Valid," *Churchman*, November 1, 1945, p. 7; George T. Renner, "America's Outpost for Peace," *American* 139 (May, 1945): 116. Much of the same sentiment often came from Zionist leaders. See, for example, David McClure to Harry Selden, March 13, 1947, Series I, Box 2, Palestine Statehood Papers, Sterling Memorial Library, Yale University, New Haven, Conn.; and Emanuel Celler to James V. Forrestal, December 10, 1947, Box 23, Emanuel Celler Papers, Manuscript Division, Library of Congress, Washington, D.C.

end. For these people it made little difference whether they aided the Jews or not. God's chosen people were going to prevail.

Details of the belief varied considerably, but the basic approach centered on the notion that the return of Jews to power in the Promised Land was a sign from God that time was coming to an end. Jesus Christ would return to the world to establish a thousand-year rule of peace. Such millennialist views, which frequently arise in cultures during times of social stress, enjoyed a considerable revival beginning in the nineteenth century. Converts were usually bothered by the growth of liberal theologies, frustrated with the strains of modern living, and disturbed about changing social mores. They often came from economically downtrodden groups but just as often included people who had achieved some measure of material success yet were disappointed and bitter over their inability to obtain all they had expected from life. In some sense millennialism was a reaction to the harsh realities of modern life in the western world. Wars and rumors of wars, social turmoil and violence, corruption and growing materialism all combined to convince many that the dire predictions from the Revelation were true.[30]

Emphasis on an imminent Second Coming appeared in Dispensationalism and the Bible conference movement after the Civil War and in Holiness and Pentecostal crusades near the turn of the century. It cut across traditional denominational lines and found a home in a number of Protestant sects, including the Baptists, Presbyterians, and Episcopalians. Even though it eventually declined in the last two groups, it helped spark the development of several new clans of believers, including the Church of the Nazarene and the Assembly of God, From religious publishing houses in Michigan, Missouri, and elsewhere, and from Bible schools like the famous Moody Bible Institute in Chicago, interdenominational writers proclaimed their belief in so-called Premillennialist notions (the contention that Jesus would

---

[30] Yonina Talmon, "Millenarism," in David L. Sills, ed., *International Encyclopedia of the Social Sciences*, X, 349–360; Ernest R. Sandeen, *The Roots of Fundamentalism: British and American Millenarianism, 1800–1930*, pp. 81–102, 208–232; Shirley Jackson Case, *The Millennial Hope, A Phase of War-Time Thinking*, pp. 6–35.

return before the beginning of the period of peace). Some other spokesmen denied many of the specifics of the Premillennialist catechism yet still insisted that the return of the Jews to Palestine was part of God's plans.[31]

Premillennialists in the nineteenth century searched the scriptures for clues about the timing of the Second Coming. They watched with fascination as the Zionist movement gained momentum in the 1890's. But even long before any major influx of Jews to the Holy Land, they were convinced that the migration would eventually take place. The belief in a new Israel had become so widespread among evangelical groups by 1865 that several traditional Christian spokesmen felt it necessary to denounce the movement. A decade and one-half later a rash of prophecy and Bible conferences predicted the end of the Dispersion. Some of the statements, like the 1878 Niagara Creed, an extremely influential expression of the Fundamentalists' position, implied that Israel's rebirth would come after the return of Christ. Herzl's efforts near the turn of the century convinced most millennialists, however, that the "chosen people" would find their way to Jerusalem before the Second Coming. "The climacteric sign," Baptist leader Isaac M. Haldeman wrote in 1914, "is the organized movement known as—Zionism." God has declared, the evangelist concluded, "that the Jews shall go back to their own land —that Israel shall be restored to Palestine."[32] At an international prophetic conference in Philadelphia in May, 1918, the participants celebrated the British capture of Jerusalem as a significant step toward eschatological goals. One speaker told the gathered multitude that "even before Great Britain took possession of Egypt, there were keen-sighted seers who foresaw the day when God would use the Anglo-Saxon peoples to restore Jerusalem."[33]

In the 1920's and 1930's there was far less emphasis on millennial-

---

[31] Sandeen, *Roots of Fundamentalism*, pp. 132–187; Sydney E. Ahlstrom, *A Religious History of the American People*, pp. 807–824.
[32] I. M. Haldeman, *The Signs of the Times*, p. 450.
[33] *Light on Prophecy: A Coordinated Constructive Teaching: The Proceedings and Addresses at the Philadelphia Prophetic Conference*, May 28–30, 1918, p. 17.

ism but an increased concentration on Jewish successes in Palestine as proof that the Bible was correct in its prophecies. In a widely distributed book called *Seeing the Future*, published in 1929, Christabel Pankhurst celebrated the Zionist successes in Palestine as the greatest sign of a Second Coming, predicted less Arab opposition in the future, and called the Holy Land a domain of milk and honey, capable of supporting massive Jewish immigration. Some of the literature took on a tone almost reminiscent of the Crusades, evoking both the images of Premillennialism with its emphasis on a celestial plan and the older symbols of a struggle against the infidel Moslem. As late as 1933 Fundamentalist writers were rejoicing over British General Allenby's capture of Jerusalem during World War I. The English triumph was, Ross Wood concluded in *The Present in the Light of Prophecy*, "a great surprise that sent a thrill of joy to the hearts of Jews and Christians—the end of Mohammedan oppression in the Holy City—the end of Turkish tyranny in the Holy Land." [34]

Much as the first Great War had done, World War II sparked a fresh interest in Premillennialism. Large crowds gathered in the Calvary Baptist Church in New York City in November, 1942, for the New York Congress on Prophecy. A line of speakers proclaimed their belief in the return of Christ and cited Jewish successes in Palestine as supporting evidence for that conviction. They blended the emotions of the war with their religious doctrines. "We will win [the war] chiefly because the governments of America, Britain, and our allies have deep sympathy for the Jews," one delegate proclaimed. It was a sentiment with important implications for the Palestine dispute. Anyone who opposed the "chosen people" was an enemy of God. The British White Paper policy limiting immigration to the Promised Land was "Satan's effort to hinder God's plan from being carried out." [35]

M. R. DeHaan, a widely broadcast radio evangelist, took up the cry with rhetoric that sang praises to Zionism and celebrated its es-

---

[34] Ross Wood, *The Present in the Light of Prophecy*, pp. 87–116.

[35] L. Sale-Harrison, "The Right of the Jews to Palestine," in *The Sure Word of Prophecy*, ed. John W. Bradbury, p. 247; John Wilkinson, *God's Plan for the Jews*, p. 47.

chatological meaning. God is, "as it were, shouting that the day—that glorious day—is near at hand when the Lord shall redeem His people Israel, plant them again in their own land . . . so that none shall make them afraid. May God hasten the glad day!"[36]

A major part of Fundamentalist prophecies had always been the prediction that the forces of good and the armies of evil would meet in the Battle of Armageddon. In the first year after World War II, several evangelical writers became convinced they had unraveled the details of that forthcoming struggle. Zionists would reestablish Israel in Palestine. Russia would represent Satan. The United States would fight for God. And the great battle described in the book of Revelation would take place in the Middle East. Some literalists even contended that both the Soviet Union and its U.S. adversaries were preparing to use major detachments of mounted cavalry to fulfill the specific descriptions of the Bible. In evangelical declarations of the Cold War, the Fundamentalists clearly labeled Russia an enemy and sought to align the United States with God's "chosen people." For these observers the disputes over the Near East were far more important than the disagreements over Eastern Europe.[37]

Several generations of emphasis on the Second Coming and the restoration of Israel had left their mark on the American mind. In the period from 1945 to 1948 when the struggle over Palestine reached decisive levels, several conservative Protestant sects were ready with unqualified support for Zionist causes. Evangelical theologians still debated the details of eschatological theories, and some even maintained that there would be no literal creation of a Jewish state. But for the overwhelming majority of spokesmen in several denominations there was no question that Israel would rise from the ashes of Middle East struggles.

In the 1940's the pages of *The Pentecostal Evangel*, the denominational publication of the Assembly of God, were filled with cele-

---

[36] M. R. DeHaan, *The Second Coming of Jesus*, p. 12.

[37] See, for example, Harry Rimmer, *The Shadow of Coming Events*, pp. 69–132; and Mark Kagan, "God and the World Crisis," *Pentecostal Evangel*, April 24, 1948, pp. 7–8. For other works by pro-Zionist fundamental Christians, see appropriate titles in the bibliography.

brations of Zionist successes. The editors kept a close eye on events surrounding the Palestine issue and reported the developments in great detail. Nearly every reference to the Near East dispute reflected an abiding sympathy for Jewish ascendancy in the Holy Land. The paper became a voice for pro-Zionist rhetoric, using its space to answer complaints against the migration of God's "chosen people" to the "Promised Land." It covered the problem of the displaced persons in Europe and told its readers that most of the Jewish refugees had nowhere to go except Palestine. It reported on industrial development in the Holy Land, reviewed the proposals to expand the absorptive capacity of the country, and concluded that the disputed territory could support thousands of additional residents. In November, 1945, the journal called for the creation of Israel as a reward to Jewish scientists who had worked on the atomic bomb.[38]

Church leaders saw most of the developments in the Holy Land as a fulfillment of biblical prophecy. Even the Holocaust appeared to be the enactment of God's threat that "Ye shall be left few in number . . . : because thou wouldest not obey the voice of the Lord thy God." When stories circulated among the Allies that the Nazis were tattooing numbers on prisoners, the editors concluded that the book of Revelation had forecast the practice. As the Holy Land dispute developed into a major international issue, the paper pronounced that "Palestine will yet be the bone of contention over which the wild beasts (as the nations are pictured in the Bible) will wage their fiercest war." Reports that the Iraq Petroleum Company planned to build an oil pipeline through Palestine prompted denominational writers to view the situation as a fulfillment of prophecy that the Hebrew tribe of Asher "shall 'dip his foot in oil.'" The whole Jewish desire to migrate to Palestine stemmed, *The Pentecostal Evangel* concluded, from divinely planted desires.[39]

Southern Baptists were much more divided in opinion than were the members of the Assembly of God. Denominational leaders often

[38] *Pentecostal Evangel*, February 10, 1945, p. 8; March 11, 1945, p. 16; March 24, 1945, p. 8; November 24, 1945, p. 11; January 26, 1946, p. 16.

[39] Ibid., March 31, 1945, p. 16; December 15, 1945, p. 10; July 31, 1948, p. 7; September 25, 1948, pp. 3, 10.

strongly disagreed with each other about the prospects for Zionism's success or whether the movement was a fulfillment of scriptural predictions. Yet beneath the doctrinal debates Baptists exhibited considerable sympathy for Jewish ascendancy in Palestine. Arabs could count on little more than occasional pockets of indifference. Most church leaders followed events in the Middle East, sometimes puzzled over their meaning, but usually equated the enemies of Zionism with the forces of evil and darkness. Ministers frequently spoke in the language of prophecy, eschatology, and fatalistic resignation to the "inevitable." [40]

For a denomination that traditionally made few forays into political questions, there were a surprising number of Baptist spokesmen who took an active interest in the foreign-policy implications of the Middle East dispute. Several pastors wrote the State Department and the White House urging favorable treatment for Zionist requests. In 1948 they exhibited their greatest concern. Within days after Israel's declaration of independence, Southern Baptist representatives met in Memphis for their annual convention. Amidst readoption of old statements endorsing complete separation of church and state, two prominent leaders introduced separate resolutions applauding Truman's quick recognition of the new Tel Aviv government. [41] "It is prophecy not politics," wrote E. D. Solomon, one of the resolution sponsors. Good Christians should cast their lot with God's "chosen people." But it made little difference to the outcome. Good would triumph. "Israel will succeed," Solomon pronounced. "It is God's will." [42]

Both the notions of a Jewish Manifest Destiny and the belief in a divinely inspired restoration of Israel deeply affected U.S. attitudes. Yet neither concept could generate the sensational feelings that

[40] For examples of Baptist eschatology, see *Florida Baptist Witness*, May 13, 1948, p. 4; June 17, 1948, p. 4; *Baptist Standard*, July 29, 1948, p. 3; *Alabama Baptist*, February 26, 1948, p. 3.

[41] *Annual of the Southern Baptist Convention, 1948: Ninety-First Session*, pp. 34, 48, 52, 53. See also J. Frank Norris to Harry S Truman, October 2, 1947, Official File 204, Harry S Truman Papers, Harry S Truman Presidential Library, Independence, Mo.

[42] E. D. Solomon, "Editorial," *Florida Baptist Witness*, June 17, 1948, p. 4.

eventually sprang from war-related issues. The world conflict and the Holocaust finally produced the critical situation conducive to Jewish colonization's great popularity. Hitler's madness sparked fresh and broader interest in the old movements for settlement in Palestine, giving the efforts a sense of urgency and providing important additional reasons for U.S. support for settlement of the Holy Land. However, Americans' awareness of Nazi persecutions and of the Holocaust was actually slow to develop. In May, 1933, a U.S. church journal published a letter from the German-born priest of the American Episcopal Church in Munich. Father Frederick Wissenback reported that international rumors of Third Reich anti-Semitic atrocities were simply not true. In fact, he contended, the Nazis were a restraining factor against mob bigotry. "If it had not been for Reichskanzler Adolph Hitler," he wrote, "many thousands of Jews would be corpses."[43]

For the next decade Americans heard conflicting accounts, charges, and countercharges about massive brutality under the Führer. Nearly ten years after Father Wissenback's naïve denial, the U.S. government finally leveled specific charges against enemy Deutschland: fascist tyrants were systematically murdering massive numbers of civilians and captured soldiers.[44] But even beyond such official recognition of a Holocaust, large segments of the American people continued to doubt. Perhaps such skepticism stemmed from a pseudosophistication born of the knowledge that atrocity stories from other wars were often exaggerated. Whatever the cause, as late as November, 1944, nearly one-fourth of a Gallup opinion poll sample either did not believe accounts of genocide or had no opinion. Only a tiny percentage suspected the magnitude of the killing.[45]

Spring offensives rolling across Europe in 1945 finally dispelled most of the uncertainty. Allied armies liberated prison compounds

[43] Frederick Wissenbach, "The Jewish Situation in Germany," *The Living Church*, May 6, 1933, p. 11.

[44] U.S., Department of State, *Department of State Bulletin* 7 (December 19, 1942): 1009.

[45] Hadley Cantril and Mildred Strunk, eds., *Public Opinion, 1935–1946*, p. 1070.

to discover a nightmare of slaughter far beyond the expectations of most observers. Ghastly proof of concentration camp atrocities appeared in the daily press; in *Life, Time,* and *Newsweek*; in a variety of other popular journals; and at local movie theaters in weekly newsreels. As *Life* concluded in its May 7 issue: "Last week Americans would no longer doubt stories of Nazi cruelty. For the first time there was irrefutable evidence as the advancing Allied armies captured camps filled with political and slave laborers, living and dead." With pictures that seared the minds of a whole generation, the magazine offered graphic examples of that "irrefutable evidence." Page after page of photography displayed a monotonous parade of human carcasses and skeletal figures. Could anyone doubt now? The day after *Life* published its coverage, Gallup found only a sprinkling of disbelievers.[46]

From this initial encounter with Nazi madness there slowly emerged the special problems of European Jewry. With the opening of the Nuremberg war trials in December, chief U.S. prosecutor Robert Jackson delineated for the jury and the world the extent of Hitler's brutality. Among other atrocities, the Führer and his minions had attempted to eradicate all of the house of Israel. In the United States attention suddenly focused on the horrors. John Dos Passos, the celebrated American author, covered the testimony in Nuremberg for *Life*. A *Time* reporter sat nearby and watched the judges view a film of German concentration camps. "It was," he recorded in a cover story for that weekly, "an endless stream of corpses—single corpses and small mountains of them, corpses lying still and corpses being carted away by bulldozers, corpses shrunk by starvation and corpses battered by boots or clubs, staring corpses and corpses which,

---

[46] Ibid., p. 1071; *Time,* January 15, 1945, p. 18; April 23, 1945, p. 38; April 30, 1945, pp. 38–44; May 7, 1945, pp. 32–35; May 14, 1945, pp. 43, 60; May 21, 1945, p. 24; *Life,* May 7, 1945, pp. 32–37; May 14, 1945, pp. 38, 103–104, 107–108, 110; *Paramount News,* Paramount Pictures, April 28, 1945; May 2, 1945; May 23, 1945, Motion Picture Division, National Archives, Washington, D.C. Some early war feature films attempted to depict concentration camp life, but Hollywood's imagination could not match Hitler's realities. See, for example, *Night Train,* Twentieth Century Fox, 1940, Motion Picture Division, National Archives.

miraculously, had still some life in them and feebly moved about before the camera." In movie houses audiences caught glimpses of the evidence excerpted for inclusion in the weekly newsreels. It was a news story not easily forgotten.[47]

But already, months before the full extent of the Holocaust became clear in the Nuremberg testimony, Americans were learning something of the problems of those who survived the threat of gas chambers. A remnant of European Jewry escaped execution but faced a future of continuing anti-Semitism on the continent. Thousands remained in concentration camps weeks after Hitler's death, many unable to return home because of threats of renewed persecutions. New waves of malevolence swept across Europe, creating a fresh class of refugees. In U.S. newspapers, weekly magazines, and movie newsreels, the plight of displaced Jews became a pitiful reminder of the war's legacy.[48]

It was revelations of the Holocaust and of continuing discrimination in Europe that first focused major attention on Jewish refugees and helped shape public opinion. Articulate observers began to concentrate on the immigration policy in the Holy Land to the virtual exclusion of all other matters. In the eyes of many commentators the United States could, and should, respond to the problems of uprooted Europeans without affecting the political status of Palestine. There was no need for any decision on whether the disputed country would become a Zionist commonwealth, an Arab nation, or a binational state. There was an immediate need to aid downtrodden people. Within this viewpoint there was even occasional criticism of Jewish nationalism, but always the insistence that the Allies could, somehow, send one hundred thousand immigrants to Palestine and still

---

[47] *Time*, December 10, 1945, pp. 25–28; John Dos Passos, "Report from Nurnburg," *Life*, December 10, 1945, pp. 28–31; *Paramount News*, Paramount Pictures, October 12, 1946, Motion Picture Division, National Archives.

[48] *Time*, July 23, 1945, p. 37; Earl G. Harrison, "The Last Hundred Thousand," *Survey Graphic* 34 (December, 1945): 73–77; Paul W. Massing and Maxwell Miller, "Should Jews Return to Germany?" *Atlantic Monthly* 176 (July, 1945): 87–90; *The Year 1945*, United News, Motion Picture Division, National Archives.

maintain complete neutrality in the political struggle between Zionists and Arabs.

The *New Republic*, an old and respected champion of underdogs, became a frequent pulpit for this approach to the problem. The liberal journal first confronted the issue in August, 1943, with a twenty-one-page special section entitled "The Jews of Europe: How to Help Them." After discussing the Nazi persecutions in terms known at that time, the editors reviewed ways to relieve the misery. One article concentrated on Great Britain and the United States as places of asylum. Another emphasized that only Palestine offered an extensive solution. The question of a Jewish state could wait, the writer concluded, but there must be open immigration to Palestine immediately.[49]

Two years later the *New Republic* writers knew far more about the magnitude of the genocide. In October, 1945, they could ponder the findings of former U.S. Immigration Commissioner Earl Harrison, who went to Europe in mid-summer to investigate refugee camps. Harrison spent several weeks touring the continent, and he came back with bleak news about conditions in war-torn areas. "The ugliest of all the ugly stories now coming out of 'liberated' Europe," on October editorial concluded, "is that of the continued plight of European Jewry." The situation demanded immediate attention. "Whether or not Palestine and the creation of a Jewish state, as demanded by the Zionist movement, is *the* solution of the so-called Jewish 'question,' Palestine today offers Europe's Jewry its only chance to survive 'liberation.' . . . They are haunted by the ghosts of spiritual and physical starvation or death. Their moral, legal, and political claims to be permitted to go to Palestine may be debatable. But their practical need cannot be a matter for protracted discussion."[50] The situation was so desperate that its difficulty thrust aside

[49] "The Jews of Europe: How to Help Them," *New Republic* 109 (August 30, 1943): 295–316.
[50] "Nowhere to Lay Their Heads," *New Republic* 113 (October 29, 1945): 556–557.

all consideration, save one: the problems that daily faced surviving Jews.

Any inconveniences to Arabs, so the popular view held, were minor in comparison to the immense problems of European Jewry. "Certainly it is preferable," William H. Stringer wrote in November, "to bruise slightly the sensibilities of Arabs . . . than to risk bruising heavily both the bodies and spirits of those refugees by leaving them in Europe."[51] Palestine must be the answer, John Lewis, editor of *PM* concluded, "There isn't any other place for them to go. . . . It's not a question of whether the Arabs like it or not. It's a matter of simple humanity."[52] Few admitted that sending thousands of European Jews to Palestine might virtually insure the establishment of a Zionist state. World society could, and should, resolve the refugee matter in a near vacuum, completely separated from debates over the future political status of the area.

Even many strong opponents of Zionism felt moved to advocate some increases in Jewish admissions to Palestine. The anti-Zionist American Council of Judaism endorsed the sending of one hundred thousand Jews to Palestine as a measure of refugee relief. Kermit Roosevelt suggested that the Holy Land could become a "sanctuary" for one hundred thousand refugees only after the immigrants and their leaders renounced the idea that the disputed land would never become a Jewish state.[53]

A homestead in Palestine was a token offering to atone for both the Allies' failure to recognize the enormity of Hitler's executions and their inability to do anything about them. Promised land could partially compensate European Jewry for Nazi sins. Yet for all the words of remorse over the Holocaust and refugee conditions, pity alone could not account for the American reaction. In retrospect it was legitimate to ask why so many people were eager to give away

---

[51] William H. Stringer, "A Peace for Palestine," *New Republic* 113 (November 12, 1945): 633–635.

[52] John P. Lewis, "For Human Decency," *Churchman*, November 1, 1945, p. 10.

[53] Lessing J. Rosenwald, "The Fallacies of Palestine," *Collier's*, March 13, 1948, pp. 30–32; Kermit Roosevelt, "The Arabs Live There Too," *Harper's* 193 (October, 1946): 289–298.

Arab land and to encourage the creation of a state based on a single religion. If sympathy alone had driven popular responses, attention might have focused on more U.S. assistance to the downtrodden.

But little Yankee help was freely given. While support for Palestinian settlement grew, approval for refugee admissions to the United States did not. Any complete explanation of national attitudes looked beyond the simple expressions of compassion. Many commentators simply came to see a large flow of humanity to Palestine as a way not only to aid downtrodden people, but also to exact punishment for the Holocaust and to avoid unwelcomed immigration to the United States. This vengeance and bigotry made it so easy to place heavy emphasis on using Judea to relocate the uprooted rather than on providing more U.S. assistance.

In a bizarre twist of spite, Arab people living in Palestine became "legitimate" targets for anti-Nazi revenge because of the alleged friendship between Adolph Hitler and Haj Amin el-Husseini, mufti of Jerusalem. The most extreme version of this thinking centered on the charge that the mufti actually designed the extermination policy of the Third Reich. Less unwieldy accusations pointed to Husseini's fascist tendencies and his contact with Nazis since the early thirties. Some critics lumped most Arab leaders into fascist categories and complained that Middle East masses were also susceptible to persuasion from "the brutal slogans of Nazi philosophy."

Zionist writers were particularly fond of calling the policy of the British White Paper of 1939 a "Middle Eastern Munich," an appeasement of Arab "fascists," clearly implying that while it was too late to undo the damage of Neville Chamberlain's deals on Czechoslovakia, it was not too late to correct the mistakes of British immigration bans in Palestine. It was all a strange case of guilt by association. Palestinian Arabs had the wrong leaders during the war, so they were partly responsible for the Holocaust, and the Allies were completely justified in thrusting, as an act of vengeance against war criminals, large flows of humanity on the small, disputed country.[54]

[54] Henry A. Atkinson, "Betrayal from the Left," *Churchman*, November 1, 1945, pp. 7–8; Eliahu Epstein, "Middle Eastern Munich," *The Nation* 162

But even beyond vengeance, there was still another major pressure pushing for a Holy Land answer to refugee needs. Most Americans simply did not want the displaced persons in the United States. In January, 1939, one group of pollsters asked interviewees if the government should permit ten thousand refugee children from Germany—most of them Jewish—to enter the United States. Sixty-one percent said no. When Fortune Poll later that year asked people their attitudes on raising immigration quotas to accommodate more refugees, over 84 percent of Protestant and Catholic respondents were opposed. Opposition to refugee admissions flourished throughout the war, and peace brought few changes. In 1946 one national poll found that only 43 percent of the people favored allowing "Polish people, Jews, and other displaced persons" to enter the United States.[55]

Additional evidence of anti-immigration sentiment comes from signs of continuing prejudice against Jews who already lived in the United States. In fact, Jews constantly evoked more resentment, fear, and animosity than did any other ethnic group except blacks. In November, 1942, for example, *Fortune* asked a national cross-section of factory workers which group they would least like to see move into their neighborhood. Negroes and Jews far outdistanced all other targets of resentment. The *New York Herald Tribune* found exactly the same results when polling a national cross-section of high school students about prospective college roommates. The Fair Employment Practices Commission, meanwhile, discovered that in "one of

---

(March 9, 1946): 287–288; I. F. Stone, "The Case of the Mufti," *The Nation* 162 (May 4, 1946): 526–527; Edgar Ansel Mowrer, "Call the Mufti!" *Forum* 109 (March, 1946): 611–612. In 1947 the American Christian Palestine Committee of New York issued a forty-eight-page brochure entitled *The Arab War Effort* which "exposed the pro-Nazi antecedents of the present leaders of the Arab League and of Arab States." See also American Zionist Emergency Council's use of correspondence between the Mufti and Hitler, *New York Times*, September 25, 1945, p. 13.

[55] Cantril and Strunk, *Public Opinion*, pp. 477, 1081, 1089; *Opinion News*, February 15, 1948, p. 15; March 1, 1948, p. 7; *Time*, August 6, 1945, p. 27.

the largest commercial" agencies in Chicago, "60% of the executive jobs, 50% of the sales executive jobs, and 41% of the male clerical openings were closed to Jews."[56]

Even most of the unprejudiced apparently found it easier to confront Arab opposition than to oppose American bigotry. Ernest Bevin's celebrated charge that Americans wanted Jews in Palestine "because they did not want too many of them in New York" found disturbing verification in samples of public opinion.[57]

By 1945, U.S. support for Jewish efforts in Palestine was extensive, yet qualified. Opinion polls consistently reflected large majorities favoring an end to immigration bans in the Holy Land. Backing for a new Israel never enjoyed as much affirmation, but when in 1947 the United Nations finally proposed a division of the country into Arab and Jewish nations, most Americans favored the idea. There was, in fact, always more agreement with any Jewish position than with any Arab counterpoint. When fighting erupted between Zionists and Palestinians, a heavy plurality sympathized with the Jewish nationalists.[58]

Yet few people were willing to assume any major burdens in pushing for Jewish settlement in the Holy Land. Palestine became a way to shed responsibilities, not to assume more of them. Only a tiny percentage favored the use of U.S. troops, or even the sale of ammunition to either belligerent. To most citizens the dispute was apparently a task for the United Nations, where the United States might play a carefully proportioned role without assuming any national responsibilities.[59]

The general tenor of public opinion meant there would be a large, well-organized, and active lobby of Jews and Gentiles ready to sup-

[56] Cantril and Strunk, *Public Opinion*, pp. 477, 1081, 1089; *Opinion News*, February 15, 1948, p. 15; March 1, 1948, p. 7.
[57] Bevin quoted in Freda Kirchwey, "Palestine and Bevin," *The Nation* 162 (June 22, 1946): 737–739.
[58] *Opinion News*, February 15, 1948, p. 15; March 15, 1948, p. 16; July 1, 1948, pp. 11–14, 16; *Gallup Poll*, I, 554, 584, 686.
[59] *Gallup Poll*, I, 554, 584, 686; *Opinion News*, February 1, 1948, p. 15; March 15, 1948, p. 16; July 1, 1948, pp. 11–14.

port Jewish settlement in Palestine. It meant also that as long as the Promised Land could be redeemed at no cost in American lives, there was little threat of much opposition to Zionism and considerable promise of extensive support.

CHAPTER THREE

TRUMAN AND THE
PALESTINE PROBLEM

Harry Truman came to the presidency with little knowledge of what his predecessor had been doing in the Middle East. He also came lacking any strong convictions about the Palestine question. As a U.S. senator and then vice-president he had paid routine tribute to Jewish aspirations in the Holy Land largely in deference to the pleas of constituents. But his support was far from unqualified and less than enthusiastic. Like most Americans he sympathized with Hitler's victims and easily translated that sympathy into a vague appreciation for a Jewish homeland. At least the Missouri Democrat endorsed the creation of a refuge where Jews might escape from Gentile persecutions. But he specifically opposed foundation of a Zionist state that might exclude Arabs from political power. He never attached much significance to the matter. To the new president the debate over the Holy Land was initially a low-priority item, one of those often pesky minor questions that political considerations could settle best.

In the few months after his sudden elevation, Truman quickly realized the intensity of feelings surrounding the Middle East squabble. Congressmen, rabbis, diplomats, and a bevy of other petitioners sought to educate the president on the matter. Zionists and most politicians urged him to aid Jewish nationalism. Most State Department memoranda carried the opposite advice, warning him about the ploys of politicians and Zionists. Into the summer of 1945 Harry Truman remained largely silent on the question. Then in late July he made his first major commitment to either side. He wrote Prime Minister Winston Churchill, while both men were at Potsdam, and asked him to end White Paper restrictions on Jewish immigration to Palestine. Six weeks later he sent a note to Churchill's successor, Clement Attlee, in London and requested admission to the Holy Land for one hundred thousand displaced persons.

Zionists had scored important points. They were centering their initial postwar efforts largely on lifting the immigration restrictions, increasing the Jewish population in Palestine, and letting statehood evolve from the force of a Jewish majority. Truman's appeals contained much of what they wanted. Yet the president still had little interest in promoting a new Israel. His position stemmed almost entirely from domestic political pressures, from a desire to discourage extremism in the Jewish statehood movement, and from a concern for the problems surrounding Jewish refugees in Europe—both the suffering of displaced persons and the burden they created for the continent. Truman pitied the uprooted, but he also worried that thousands of refugees might aggravate food and fuel shortages and create severe economic and strategic consequences for Europe. At the same time, he wanted to solve Old World problems without imposing heavy financial responsibilities on U.S. taxpayers. If Truman had any concerns about Palestine, it was to cool Zionist aspirations, not to encourage them.

In 1945 he believed he could send the Holocaust survivors to Palestine, relieve Europe's pains, and still not affect the political structure of the Holy Land. With naïve disregard for the emotional and symbolic elements of the Middle East dispute (a disregard spawned in part by expediency), and almost complete insensitivity to Arab nationalism, the chief executive assumed that the Palestinians would welcome an influx of what he regarded as culturally advanced immigrants. He continued to oppose the creation of a Jewish commonwealth and believed that a "homeland" was not automatically a step toward statehood. The president adopted a solution that was politically easy and popular, oblivious to the problems it would encounter and the implications it would have for the Middle East debate.

On the day after Franklin Roosevelt died in Warm Springs, Georgia, a deputy office director from the State Department had little time to mourn the passing of the old leader. He was busy preparing to deal with the successor to power and setting into motion a campaign to mold Harry Truman's attitudes on the Palestine question. In that same hour of grief, Zionist leaders in New York, in Washington, and throughout the world and a wide variety of other interested parties were planning their own efforts to educate the new president. In the weeks to come the White House lived through a crossfire of advice that presented Truman with a classic contest between an elite corp of experts advisers and a substantial and vocal segment of public opinion. State Department officers were eager to have Truman see that he could aid displaced persons and still maintain immigration limits in the Holy Land. Advocates of Jewish nationalism joined with champions of refugee causes to tell the chief executive that compassion and justice should compel British authorities to allow uprooted Jews in Europe to enter Palestine.[1]

For the battle of influence the State Department had developed a sophisticated machine for gathering information, weighing the raw data of diplomatic communications, and formulating advice for the Oval Office. Through its network of representatives in the Middle East it kept a close watch on Arab reactions to U.S. policy. The whole organization was well suited to care for what its members saw as national interests. Its directors understood the importance of maintaining friendships with Ibn Saud and other possessors of oil and strategic real estate. In the last year of the war they had become increasingly concerned about their ability to compete with Soviet influence in Asia Minor if the United States supported Zionist efforts in Palestine. But it was more than the calculations of potential petroleum resources that made State Department people responsive to Moslem complaints. Several men who had served in Middle East capitals had developed a keen appreciation for Arab nationalism

---

[1] Paul Alling to Edward Stettinius, April 13, 1945, 867N.01/4-1345; Loy Henderson to Joseph Grew, May 25, 1945, 867N.01/5-2545; RG59, NA; *FR*, 1945, VIII, 704ff.; Andrew F. Schoeppel to Truman, June 4, 1945, Official File 204 (Misc.), Harry S Truman Papers, Harry S Truman Presidential Library, Independence, Mo.; Wagner to C. Venn Pilcher, May 17, 1945, Folder 8, Robert F. Wagner Papers, Georgetown University Library, Washington, D.C.; Harry Truman, *Memoirs: Years of Decisions*, pp. 83–89.

and enjoyed the happy coincidence of being able to promote national interests without sacrificing any convictions on the justice of con-flicting claims over the Holy Land.[2]

Development of policy on the Palestine controversy centered on the desk of Loy Henderson, director of the Office of Near Eastern and African Affairs, who had wrestled with the question since his ear-lier service as minister to Iraq. Like a good many of his colleagues who had served in Moslem capitals, he was acutely aware of Arab resentment of Zionism. His task, both as overseas envoy to Bagdad and as head of a department office, was to safeguard U.S. interests. His duties made him sensitive to protests from Cairo, Damascus, Jidda, or elsewhere in the region and helped cultivate an admiration for Arab nationalism. But Henderson was not alone in his sympa-thies for anti-Zionist complaints. Other men in the diplomatic ser-vice, including Paul H. Alling, Henderson's deputy director; Gordon P. Merriam, chief of the Division of Near Eastern Affairs; Wallace Murray, Henderson's immediate predecessor in the Near Eastern and African Affairs Office and later ambassador to Iran; Dean Acheson, assistant secretary of state; and Joseph Grew, under secretary, had developed similar attitudes. In addition, most of the members of U.S. delegations to the Middle East sided with Arab protests.[3]

These State Department planners realized that their courtship of Moslem states could easily fail if Truman's reaction to the Palestine controversy displeased Middle East leaders. In an effort to find an acceptable solution, the collective mind of the planners of foreign policy had produced a variety of approaches. But increasingly in 1945 much of the thinking centered on a scheme to create a United Nations trusteeship for the disputed territory. That scheme was mostly the product of William Yale, a Harvard historian who had

[2] *FR*, 1944, V, 615, 618, 622, 629, 641, 656; 1945, VIII, 10–18; Cordell Hull, *The Memoirs of Cordell Hull*, II, 1528–1537.

[3] For information on Henderson's career, see George F. Kennan, *Memoirs, 1925–1950*, pp. 61, 87, 132; *New York Times*, June 25, 1943, p. 9; September 20, 1945, p. 2; Dean Acheson, *Present at the Creation: My Years in the State Department*, p. 231; *FR*, 1944, V, 598–599, 619–620; 1945, VIII, 10–18.

for thirty years served as an occasional State Department adviser on the Middle East. The plan, making the Holy Land a special international province sacred to Moslems, Jews, and Christians, received so much attention in intradepartmental channels that it was obviously more than a passing fancy with foreign-policy planners. The design called for Great Britain to remain as trustee and dominate a supreme government with direct responsibility for four principal cities and undeveloped regions of Judea and the Negev. Elsewhere, an Arab communal government would control regions with an Arab majority, and a Jewish counterpart would govern Jewish areas. A central government, with its British-appointed chief administrator, would control immigration. Quotas for admissions would depend on the economic absorptive capacity of the country, and local Jewish and Arab authorities would separately provide the statistics to determine that capacity. The plan sought to prohibit any discrimination on the basis of race, religion, or nationality in admitting refugees. Local governments (Jewish and Arab) had the power to control land transfers in their own regions, while the central trustee authority regulated such matters where it had direct control.[4]

The Near Eastern branch may have harbored a solid consensus against the establishment of a Jewish state. But Henderson and his colleagues were not callously disregarding the plight of Jewish refugees. Their anti-Zionism was not tantamount to anti-Semitism. They simply thought there was no compelling reason to tie the problem of the displaced persons to a solution based exclusively on the Holy Land. They also believed that in order to win Arab acceptance of more immigrants to Palestine, there had to be a settlement of the political questions first. Arabs must know that they would not become subjects of a Jewish-dominated state. A proposal from adviser Yale even suggested a formula for admitting more immigrants to Palestine in the interim before a political settlement became a reality.

[4] "Proposed Trusteeship Agreement for Palestine," July 28, 1945, 867N.01/7-2845, RG59, NA; Yale to Merriam, July 30, 1945, Palestine Folder, William Yale Papers, Harvard University Library, Cambridge, Mass.

Yale was unalterably opposed to state Zionism. He regarded any massive and unlimited migration of Jews to the Holy Land as a step toward a Jewish commonwealth and a provocation of Arab protests. Yet he suggested that the Truman administration support limited and restricted admission of refugees to Palestine as long as the flow was "not . . . of such dimensions as seriously to disturb the political situation."[5]

While the State Department people prepared their messages to the president, the task of convincing the chief executive passed quickly from the hands of a fourth-level bureaucrat to the big names of foreign policy, including Secretary of State Edward Stettinius and Under Secretary Joseph Grew. Initial scrimmages in the struggle for influence used only the light artillery of persuasion. The chiefs of diplomacy tried to impress their commander with the complexities of the question. It was more involved, they told him, than merely deciding the fate of Holocaust survivors. Hasty and blind decisions could inflame the "continual tenseness" in the Near East and threaten vital U.S. interests in that area.[6]

By May they were peppering the president with their best arguments and invoking the name of Truman's dead predecessor. They wondered whether the former senator in the White House appreciated all the delicacies of Roosevelt's approach. If the Missourian knew only of the public commitments to Zionism, he might think consistency meant simply more blessings for Jewish nationalism. The president must understand the promises to Arab leaders. He must comprehend what might happen to U.S. interests in the Middle East if the United States played midwife to the birth of Israel. Franklin Roosevelt may have openly appeared sympathetic "to certain Zionist aims," a State Department memorandum advised, but he had also assured Moslem leaders that he would consult them before making any decision "altering the basic situation in Palestine." Joseph Grew sent Truman a transcription of the Great Bitter Lake conversation.

---

[5] "Proposed Trusteeship Agreement for Palestine," July 28, 1945, 867N .01/7-2845, RG 59, NA.
[6] *FR*, 1945, VIII, 704–705.

Roosevelt had, Grew noted, promised Ibn Saud that he would make no move hostile to the Arab people and would not "assist the Jews as against Arabs." [7]

No one in the State Department could be sure what kind of impact their efforts were making on the president. After the first series of memorandums and conferences, Henderson, Grew, and others could only hope for the best. "We did not feel particularly alarmed at the result of this opening round," Gordon P. Merriam wrote Wallace Murray in mid-June. "The President . . . is a very sensible and reasonable man, and we now feel that he is well grounded in the essentials of the Palestine question and will go pretty slow in the future." It is "my personal impression," Merriam confided, ". . . that President Truman is a straight shooter and that, now that he knows the difficulties and dangers, we will hear much less on the subject of Palestine in the future." [8]

But Merriam in his satisfaction could not know all the elements in the inventory of persuasion. During the same period that advice flowed freely from the diplomatic experts, Truman faced a similar barrage of petitions from other quarters. Within days of Roosevelt's death, a deluge of visitors, resolutions, and letters began arriving at the White House. Nearly all of them urged the new president to support more immigration of Jews into Palestine. Appeals came from every direction. A week and one-half after Truman took office Stephen Wise of the American Zionist Emergency Committee (AZEC) came to the White House to plead for assistance to Jewish refugees in Europe. Mass rallies in New York and elsewhere—including one that drew sixty thousand people to Madison Square Garden—dramatized the issue. In May the National Zionist Organization (NZO) released a public statement from twelve U.S. senators urging creation of a Jewish state in Palestine. [9]

Through the spring both the State Department and the White

---

[7] Ibid., pp. 705–706.

[8] Merriam to Murray, June 15, 1945, 867N.01/6-1545, RG 59, NA.

[9] Robert F. Wagner to Truman, July 3, 1945, Official File 204 (Misc.), Truman Papers; Harry Truman, *Memoirs: Year of Decisions*, pp. 83–84; *New York Times*, June 11, 1945; July 5, 1945, p. 14.

House received a steady stream of letters on the Holy Land debate. Senators, governors, state legislatures, mayors, and city councils joined the procession of appeals. The American Christian Palestine Committee staged a national radio broadcast in early July, featuring an impressive list of prominent entertainers. That same week Senator Robert Wagner carried to the White House a letter from fifty-four colleagues in the Senate and 251 representatives in the House, a majority in both cases. The letter urged the chief executive to implore the British to "open forthwith the doors of Palestine to unrestricted Jewish immigration and colonization."[10]

One theme permeated nearly all of these petitions: Jewish refugees in Europe required immediate abrogation of the White Paper policy on immigration to Palestine. While State Department advisers saw the Holy Land as a place for emergency, limited, and even temporary relocation of displaced persons, most of the would-be counselors wanted the area to become the principal absorber for several hundred thousand survivors of the Holocaust. When it came to the eventual political status of Palestine, however, there was less argument. Many appeals to Truman never mentioned questions of government. Others neatly fluctuated from advocacy of a Jewish homeland to proposals for a Zionist commonwealth. The American League for a Free Palestine initially insisted that the disputed territory simply become an independent state with equal citizenship for both Arabs and Jews. One major group, the American Council for Judaism, supported proposals to send refugees to Palestine while it opposed creation of a Jewish commonwealth there.[11]

The NZO was never united in its efforts or opinions, but much of the movement's postwar campaign centered on opposition to the

[10] Fifty-four senators and 251 representatives to Truman, July 2, 1945, Folder 8, Wagner Papers. See numerous resolutions in State Department files 867N.01/4-145 to 867N.01/5-3045, RG59, NA; an in Official File 204 (Misc.), Truman Papers.

[11] *FR*, 1945, VIII, 710–712; memorandum of conversation with Guy M. Gillette, April 23, 1945, Conversations, Volume 7, Folder 3, Joseph Clark Grew Papers, Harvard University Library, Cambridge, Mass.; John W. McCormack to Baruch Korff, May 5, 1945, Series I, Folder 18, Palestine Statehood Papers, Sterling Memorial Library, Yale University, New Haven, Conn.

White Paper and the hope that a Jewish state would emerge from the force of a Jewish majority. It continued to advocate political goals but emphasized humanitarian concerns in an attempt to obscure any differences they might otherwise have with other spokesmen for refugee causes. Actually, the potential differences were considerable. Zionists in the NZO and the AZEC often saw refugee settlement as a means to a Jewish commonwealth, while the American Jewish Congress and others were willing to forsake statehood in order to win aid for uprooted people. Many Zionists never let the immediate needs of displaced persons interrupt their quest for a new Israel. They wanted refugee settlement in Palestine, but not under any terms that might compromise long-range ideological targets. Yet Zionists and non-Zionists worked together on behalf of free and unlimited immigration of Jews to Palestine, both convinced that the Holy Land offered the only hope for early relief to the downtrodden.[12]

But even without the pulls and pushes from Congress, statehouses, and lobbyists, Truman faced a commanding array of pro-immigration advice from within the White House. Two presidential advisers, David Niles and Samuel I. Rosenman (both carryovers from Roosevelt's staff), were strong advocates of sending Holocaust survivors to Palestine. Niles, an ardent Zionist, was constantly alert to any arguments that might sway the president, even if it took slight distortions to achieve the desired result. He once told Truman that the chief executive need not fear much opposition from Moslems because a "good part" of the Islamic world "follows Ghandi and his philosophy of non-resistance." Arab protests were easy to overcome, he assured the president. "You know," he confided, "that President Roosevelt said to some of us privately he could do anything that needed to be done with Ibn Saud with a few million dollars."[13]

Rosenman, initially much closer to the inner circle of the White House, was a more careful adviser, often expressing his views with confessed reluctance but always favoring higher immigration quotas

---

[12] *FR*, 1945, VIII, 713–715; Charles Schwager to William D. Hassett, July 3, 1945, Official File 204 (Misc.) Truman Papers.
[13] Niles to Truman, May 27, 1946, Official File 204 (Misc.), Truman Papers.

and ridiculing any suggestions that such a policy might create trouble. He kept Truman constantly advised on the political implications of the president's policies in the Middle East, frequently reminding the chief executive that moves hostile to Jewish demands might cost the party dearly in New York elections.[14]

While the State Department had its sophisticated machinery for gathering information, advocates of the abrogation of White Paper policy had their own organization for collecting intelligence and directing influence. In the months to come, top-level documents often appeared in private hands before they arrived at the president's desk. Advanced information on major policy decisions leaked prematurely to Zionist organizations. In the summer of 1946 the British reported that they found U.S. government documents in the confiscated files of a suspected Jewish terrorist organization in Jerusalem. Earlier, a White House secretary reported that "very trustful and confidential . . . information is regularly being relayed from Judge Rosenman to Justice Frankfurter and in the absence of Judge Rosenman Mr. Niles imports these secrets to the Justice."[15] But for all of the leaks, Zionists still did not know what decisions Truman might make.

Ultimately, it was Harry Truman who had to weigh the advice and pressures directed his way. When he became president, the former county judge from Missouri was not a Zionist, although long hours of discussion with a former business partner and friend, Eddie Jacobson, may have acquainted him with the movement. As a U.S. senator he had even demonstrated some hostility toward Jewish nationalism. He had allowed his name to be used as a member of the American Christian Palestine Committee but had opposed the creation of a religious state that excluded Arabs from political power.

14 Rosenman to Truman, October 23, 1945; October 17, 1945; September 7, 1945, Box 2, Samuel I. Rosenman Papers, Harry S Truman Presidential Library, Independence, Mo.
15 Betty Weatherspoon to Mr. Hannegan, n.d., Folder 596(2), James F. Byrnes Papers, Clemson University Library, Clemson, S.C.; Earl Harrison to Peter H. Bergson, September 10, 1945, Series I, Box 1, Palestine Statehood Papers; Acheson to U.S. Consul, Jerusalem, July 31, 1946, 867N.01/7-2346, RG59, NA.

When Senators Wagner and Taft introduced their Palestine resolution in 1944 calling for the immediate creation of a Jewish national home, Truman initially advocated that Congress postpone any decision on the matter until after the war. On more than one occasion the Missouri senator received communications from Zionist leaders in his state who were trying to affect his attitudes on the question. The tone of those letters clearly indicated that they certainly did not regard Truman as an automatic supporter of their cause. He required constant guidance lest he go astray on a binge of anti-Zionism. By the end of the war the proddings were having some effect. Truman no longer voiced any resistance to Zionist demands. He spoke in generalities, said he hoped to carry on with Roosevelt's policy (whatever that meant), and vowed to leave long-range political settlements to the United Nations.[16]

When Truman entered office, he did not even have an unrestrained commitment to rescue Jewish refugees from European misery. At least he was cautious about several cabinet suggestions, unwilling to move boldly on all fronts and initially refusing to offer his own approaches, if indeed he had any. Throughout the war he had paid routine tribute to beleaguered Jewish victims of Nazism. His name appeared in support of appeals for help. But few members of Congress left themselves out of such lists. Once Truman was in a position of power, however, the implied promises of his earlier appeals turned into delays and indecision. Secretary of the Treasury Henry J. Morgenthau, Jr., for example, suggested in May that the president appoint a cabinet committee to deal specifically with "non-repatriable" refugees—which meant Jews in most cases. Truman toyed with the idea for a week, scribbled at the bottom of Morgenthau's memorandum that he did not see "what good . . . such a board would accom-

16 Truman to Stephen Wise, June 1, 1943, Folder 8, Wagner Papers; David Berenstein to William Boyle, February 23, 1944, Official File 502; Wise to Truman, January 28, 1943; Truman to A. H. Silver, December 31, 1941; Senatorial and Vice-Presidential File (Jews); Emanuel Neumann to Truman, December 15, 1941, Senatorial and Vice-Presidential File (Zionist Organizations), Truman Papers.

plish," and then in early June rejected the proposal. In the meantime he had no substitutes to offer. At least in the last weeks of spring his approach to refugee problems was clearly negative.[17]

Yet some of his attitudes did make fertile ground for the advocates of increased immigration into Palestine. Like so many of his fellow countrymen, Truman believed that Jewish pioneers to the Promised Land were generally more talented than were their Arab neighbors. According to his view, derived from years of dabbling in ancient history, the "fertile crescent" was formerly the center of magnificent achievements. "I knew," he confessed in his memoirs, "that it had once been the seat of great world powers. . . . the empires of Nebuchadnezzar and Darius the Great . . . had made full use of the riches of the area." But Asia Minor had fallen on bad times in the last two thousand years. "There had been divisions and internal warfare and general decline," Truman wrote. Yet the region still had great potential. The Arabs simply lacked the ability to use the resources wisely, he concluded: "Except for a short period [they] . . . had never brought the area back to the position of influence and power it had once had." Now it was time for representatives of western technology to move into the motherland of civilization and redeem the land. He thought of the Jewish pilgrims into Judea as superior missionaries of progress who could aid the "backward" Arabs: "I felt that . . . a great industrial system could be set up under the Jews, and the productive potential of this region could be used to the mutual benefit of the Jews and Arabs."[18]

But much like Roosevelt before him, the Missouri Democrat still viewed Palestine as a sideshow to the major American concerns in

[17] Edward D. McKim to Truman, May 28, 1945; Morgenthau to Truman, May 23, 1945; Truman to Morgenthau, June 2, 1945, Official File 127, Truman Papers. It was Morgenthau, not Truman, who suggested sending Earl Harrison on his famous study of refugee problems. Morgenthau to McKim, May 30, 1945, Official File 127; Joseph Grew to Truman, June 21, 1945, Official File 127A, Truman Papers. Truman was apparently very reluctant even to meet with James G. McDonald, chairman of the President's Advisory Committee on Political Refugees. M. C. Latta to Joseph Grew, June 29, 1945, 840.48Refugees/6-2945, RG59, NA.
[18] Harry Truman, *Memoirs: Years of Trial and Hope, 1946–1952*, pp. 132–133, 140, 156.

foreign policy. In the wake of Hitler's defeat, and with Tojo's doom impending, the president was preoccupied with the larger issues of international relations: expanding U.S. influence, dealing with the Soviet Union, and avoiding situations conducive to Soviet advances. Struggles over the Promised Land, even the rescue of Holocaust survivors, always came second to the demands of protecting the American empire. Staying in office always outranked Arab objections to Zionist ambitions. Except for a vague belief in Jewish abilities to transform the desert, he showed little concern about the issues that excited Stephen Wise, A. H. Silver, and other U.S. Zionists. His attention was on Europe and the broader Middle East. To the degree that he worried about Palestine, per se, it was either for the sake of satisfying elements at home or of avoiding a bloody crisis.

In the spring of 1945 Truman appeared most sensitive to Arab anxieties over Palestine. In April and May he echoed an earlier commitment from his predecessor: there would be no "basic change in the situation" without consultation with both Arabs and Jews. Leaders in Cairo and other Middle East capitals could believe with satisfaction that the president was eschewing a United States–imposed Jewish state. Yet such statements did little to foreshadow the future course of Truman's policy in the Holy Land debate. State Department advisers had drafted the promises and had sent them to the White House for the president's signature before mailing them to Arab governments. Truman had signed them in almost routine fashion, apparently reluctant to resist any quest for continuity with Roosevelt's program.[19]

By July, however, the president was seemingly less reticent to move on his own. A series of considerations propelled him into action. No doubt he was growing more accustomed to his position, urged on by pro-Zionist White House advisers. But there were also more substantive inducements. Troubles in Europe ranked high on the list.

Within days of Truman's taking office, signs of continental difficulties began to accumulate in the president's mind. Experts from several departments showered him with extensive evidence that the

[19] *FR*, 1945, VIII, 706–709.

Nazis had bequeathed staggering devastation to the Old World. Every vital commodity from food to fuel was in short supply. Department of Agriculture experts, measuring the depths of the hunger crisis, uncovered a deficiency in Europe of twelve million tons of food. They reported that massive starvation was a strong possibility. Closer analysis found two residues of war—a large uprooted population, and legions of mines and explosives dotting farmers' fields—that dimmed any hopes of quickly remedying the situation.[20]

But statistics on bushels of wheat and tons of coal did not tell the whole story for Truman. In late June, Acting Secretary of State Joseph Grew sent the president a top secret memorandum outlining the implications of European troubles. The document, a product of "long study" and "intensive research," reflected a growing concern that victims of postwar misery might choose an unacceptable solution to their own problems. "There is so much poverty and destitution . . . [that] Europe affords now a perfect background for spontaneous class hatred to be channeled by a skillful agitator." Grew warned that to save the downtrodden folk from themselves and the appeals of "extreme leftist activities," Truman must act quickly. Clearly, in State Department eyes, communism, not hunger, was the true enemy.[21]

If cold memorandums were not enough to convince the chief executive that the situation was desperate, he received a first-hand education during his journey to Potsdam in July. He landed in Europe at Antwerp, Belgium, aboard the U.S.S. *Augusta* and drove to Brussels on Sunday morning, July 15. As the presidential motorcade sped along the road, Adolph Hitler's legacy rolled past the window in a panorama of destruction and horror. Bombed-out homes and factories, a Nazi concentration camp at Breendock, and seemingly endless lines of refugees punctuated the drab panorama. In Brussels the president boarded his plane for the flight to the heart of the defeated

[20] Herbert Hoover to Henry L. Stimson, May 31, 1945, Henry L. Stimson Papers, Sterling Memorial Library, Yale University, New Haven, Conn.; Truman, *Year of Decisions*, p. 344; *FR, Potsdam*, I, 614–621, 781; Henry Stimson to Truman, July 22, 1945, File 628, Byrnes Papers.

[21] *FR, Potsdam*, I, 267–280.

Third Reich. From an altitude of several thousand feet the scenes of rubble appeared everywhere. Over the cities of Kassel and Magdeburg, a military aide later wrote, "we could not see a single house that was left standing."[22]

Late that afternoon Truman arrived at his destination in Babelsberg, a suburb of Berlin, not far from Potsdam. On Monday morning the U.S. chief executive went sightseeing. James F. Byrnes and William Leahy rode with the president to Berlin. In a two-hour drive they caught a glimpse of what defeat meant in Germany. The destruction in Belgium was minor in comparison to the scenes of wreckage passing before their eyes. "Every building we saw was either badly damaged or completely destroyed," the military aide reported. "Much more distressing," Leahy told his diary, ". . . was a long procession of old men, women, children, marching in great numbers along the country roads." They were "carrying, pushing or pulling what was left of their belongings," Truman related. "I saw evidence of a great world tragedy, and I was thankful that the United States had been spared the unbelievable devastation of this war." It was "a beginning," Leahy added, "of the disintegration of a highly cultured, proud people who are racial kinsmen of the English and the Americans."[23]

In Germany the president could weigh the advice of Grew and others, contemplate the destruction around him, and measure his response against some requirements of his own. Truman was convinced that it had been a mistake after the First World War for the United States to become economically overextended in Europe. He hoped this time to avoid any substantial U.S. financial burden for reconstructing the continent. Yet he had no inclination to leave the Old World to its own misery. Neither compassion nor the considerations of national security would allow him to deny all responsibility. He

---

[22] "Log of the President's Trip to the Berlin Conference (July 6, 1945, to August 7, 1945), written and compiled by Lieutenant William M. Rigdon" (manuscript on file at Harry S Truman Presidential Library).

[23] Ibid.; diaries of William D. Leahy, July 16, 1945, p. 108, William D. Leahy Papers, Library of Congress, Washington, D.C.; Truman, *Year of Decisions*, p. 378.

was thus attuned to any approaches that could minimize U.S. expenses. The notion of using Palestine to relieve part of the refugee burden undoubtedly became more attractive as the problems of Europe unfolded.[24]

A few weeks after he returned home, Truman received even more counsel and information on European troubles. This time the advice linked answers directly to the Holy Land. In June, Earl G. Harrison, U.S. member of the Intergovernmental Committee on Refugees, had gone to Europe as a special envoy to investigate refugee matters. Through the summer months the former dean of the University of Pennsylvania Law School toured camps of uprooted people, talking with the survivors of the Holocaust. In August he returned from his study mission while the president came home from Potsdam. Late in the month they met in Truman's office. Harrison spent thirty minutes enumerating the sins of occupation and left the chief executive a pointed summary of conditions and recommendations.[25]

He argued that while Allied authorities should repatriate as many refugees as possible, most uprooted Jews had "special needs." The severity of Nazi anti-Semitic persecutions permanently separated Jews from "their nationality categories" and placed them in a unique position, unable and unwilling to return to their former homes. Continuing prejudice and discrimination against Jews after the war left them in "crude, over-crowded camps," the worst conditions of any displaced group. Harrison contended that "humanitarian" considerations demanded that these people have permission to settle wherever they might choose. Some wanted passage to the United States or Great Britain, but most of them sought admission to Palestine. "The civilized world owes it to this handful of survivors to provide them

[24] Robert D. Murphy, *Diplomat Among Warriors*, p. 270; Truman, *Year of Decisions*, pp. 343, 454. Also in 1945 Truman told a Jewish congressman that he was trying to improve conditions in Europe in order to eliminate the necessity for Jews to emigrate to Palestine (Schechtman, *United States and the Jewish State Movement*, p. 124).

[25] Truman, *Year of Decision*, p. 346; Livingston T. Merchant, "The Rosenman Mission," *Department of State Bulletin* 13 (July 8, 1945): 55–57; "Report of Earl G. Harrison," *Department of State Bulletin* 13 (September 30, 1945): 456–463.

with a home where they can again settle down and begin to live as human beings."[26]

Truman did have a direct interest in the refugee problem in Germany, but that concern stemmed from more than pity for the downtrodden. He was alarmed about the shortages, the economic pinch, and, most of all, the threat of communist expansion with its corresponding decline of U.S. influence. It really made little difference whether charity or power politics carried more weight; Jewish settlement in Palestine appeared more attractive after a thorough view of continental destitution.

Political realities certainly made it easy for Truman to favor large-scale Jewish immigration to the Promised Land as a way to end the European nightmare. Few people opposed such a move. But in the summer there were, for a while, other aspects of the Zionist movement which affected the president more than did its popularity. Truman wanted to keep the Palestine situation from boiling over into a major conflict. He cared little about who won control of the disputed territory as long as the struggle did not hinder broader U.S. interests. He had no desire to see the Zionist movement fall into the hands of diehards who might precipitate a holy war with the Arabs. He preferred moderate elements willing to accept compromises on political questions. He wanted to maintain peace in the Middle East.

He was, accordingly, much disturbed when, in June, the Office of Strategic Services (OSS) reported to the State Department that "the more extreme elements among the Zionists in this country are gaining ground" over "moderate leaders" like Rabbi Stephen Wise and Dr. Nahum Goldmann. A "mood of impatience and desperation" was sweeping Jewish communities. People were disillusioned with the failure of the United States and Great Britain to relieve refugee burdens in Europe. Tragic consequences were in the making. A failure to grant some token concessions in Palestine, the document warned, might either drive "Jewish youth 'into the arms of Moscow,'" spawn serious violence in Judea, or both.[27]

---

[26] "Report of Earl G. Harrison," pp. 456–463.
[27] *FR*, 1945, VIII, 712.

Secretary of State Byrnes was enough concerned about the report to ask the U.S. consul general in Jerusalem, Lowell C. Pinkerton, to assess the situation there. Pinkerton responded with gloomy conclusions. Terrorism from Zionist groups in the Holy Land was virtually inevitable. Fighting between Arabs and Jews was already a regular occurrence. But a general Jewish uprising over unfavorable British immigration policy was unlikely. Pinkerton did admit that continued enforcement of White Paper limits on immigration did endanger the "present [Jewish] agency leadership."[28]

If Pinkerton's reply was even slightly reassuring, communications from London were not. Soon after Truman and his party left the United States for Potsdam, the ambassador to Great Britain, John G. Winant, sent Byrnes a telegram which seemed to confirm the OSS report. Winant's message, relayed to Byrnes aboard the U.S.S. *Augusta* at sea, warned of ominous possibilities. "There is a problem that gives me considerable concern," the ambassador noted. If there were no concessions to Jews seeking admission to Palestine, Dr. Chaim Weizmann, president of the World Zionist Organization, might resign his position. "The man is tired and ill and completely discouraged because of the tragedies that have befallen his people, but he is also aware that a more militant policy would undoubtedly follow his retirement." Winant wrote with a sense of grave impending crisis. It was clear he viewed Weizmann's possible departure with misgivings. "It might lead," he concluded, "to serious trouble in the Middle East with inevitable outside repercussions."[29]

While still in Germany, Truman sent Winston Churchill a note on his thoughts. He asked the British prime minister to end restrictions on Jewish immigration into Palestine. It was the first time either he or Roosevelt had made such an appeal to the mandate power. But the appeal had no immediate results. When Clement Attlee became prime minister, he responded with a terse note that said little more

---

[28] Ibid., p. 715; *FR, Potsdam*, 1945, I, 978.

[29] A copy of Winant's telegram was attached to the copy of Truman's July 24 telegram to Churchill found in the Truman Papers. *FR, Potsdam*, 1945, II, 1402; I, 977.

than "we will give early and careful consideration to your memorandum." No reaction came from either Zionists or Arabs, because the message remained secret for several weeks.[30]

In a press conference on August 16 the president finally revealed his activities. He told reporters that he had requested that Palestine admit as many Jews as possible. Yet, he added, he wanted to settle the matter diplomatically with the British and the Arabs. He had no desire to send half a million U.S. soldiers to keep the peace in the Holy Land. When someone asked him if he had also talked with Josef Stalin about the Middle East squabble, Truman said he had not. Furthermore, he had little intention of consulting with the Soviets. It was none of their business.[31]

His pronouncements produced no more British response than did his earlier letter to Churchill. With the public statement of policy, however, he could at least expect some reaction from Arab capitals. But when it came, it was surprisingly mild. Most of them expressed concern over the endorsement of substantial increases in Jewish immigration, and several were a little disturbed over the exclusion of the Soviet Union from any voice in a Middle East settlement. But promises to consult with Arab states won high praise, as did the desire to avoid U.S. military intervention in the matter. Truman's position "indicates sagacity and deep wisdom," the Syrian prime minister told a Damascus newspaper. "When he states that the United States will not send soldiers to Palestine, he means that both parties will be satisfied." [32]

Thus far the president had managed policy with some success. Without stirring any violent Arab reactions, he had kept open the possibility of using Palestine as a partial answer to refugee problems. Furthermore, he had done so without the assistance of the vast State Department machinery. He did consult with Secretary of State Byrnes and Admiral William Leahy, both of whom were present at Postdam. But he did not even notify the senior diplomatic people in

---

[30] *FR*, 1945, VIII, 716, 719.

[31] Ibid., p. 722; *New York Times*, August 17, 1945, p. 8; Henderson to Byrnes, August 18, 1945, 867N.01/8-1845, RG59, NA.

[32] *FR*, 1945, VIII, 727.

the department about his plans, let alone ask them for any technical information or cooperation in executing his chosen policy. Either through direct design or inadvertent good luck he had managed to drive a small wedge between the question of resettling displaced persons and the issue of a future government in Palestine.

But if his initial pronouncements moderated any Arab minds, his second major statement did not. In the wake of Earl Harrison's exposé of refugee conditions in Europe, the president wrote Clement Attlee on the last day of August and asked the British leader to push for the admission of one hundred thousand Jews into Judea.[33] Even beyond the proportions of the request, Truman's subsequent handling of the matter convinced Arab leaders that the United States had decided to violate its earlier pledges and unilaterally dictate Palestine's future.

The first sign of a drastic shift in U.S. policy came from former Senator Guy Gillette and Senators Brewster and Magnuson, who visited the White House on September 10 at the president's request. Truman showed them a copy of his letter to Attlee and told them the State Department was "fully alert to the situation."[34] One day later, news of the meeting and its content appeared in the *Washington Post*, where Gordon Merriam, Loy Henderson, and their colleagues in the Near Eastern Office first learned of the matter. Despite Truman's reassurances, cooperation between the State Department and the White House was grinding to a halt. Henderson could do little more than complain to Acheson: "We will undoubtedly receive inquiries from our missions in the Near East and quite possibly protests from the Arab States. We feel that we should be in a position to tell our representatives what the facts are."[35]

Henderson was correct on at least one matter: Arab states did

[33] Ibid., pp. 737–740.

[34] Gordon Merriam to H. Reams, September 13, 1945, 867N.01/9-1345, RG59, NA.

[35] Henderson to Acheson, September 14, 1945, 867N.01/9-1445. A number of people knew about Truman's plan before the State Department did. See, for example, Earl Harrison to Peter Bergson, September 10, 1945, Series I, Box 1, Palestine Statehood Papers; Henderson to Acheson, September 21, 1945, 867N.01/9-2145, RG59, NA.

flood Washington with complaints once they realized what was taking place. On September 25 the Iraqi prime minister handed the U.S. chargé d'affaires a note explaining much of what Arabs feared. The note stated: "[We] sympathize with the destitute of Europe—victims of Nazism. . . . It has been proved to [us] . . . beyond all doubt, that the Zionists intend to invade other Arab countries after they have overrun Palestine." No doubt the "strength and military power of the US is more than sufficient to compel the Arabs to acquiesce in any policy which the US may impose on the nations." But if force is intended, "why all these charters and pledges, to which America has bound itself, for safeguarding human rights and liberties?" Press reaction in Bagdad was even stronger. One editorial condemned Truman's "frank hostility" to Arabs and called the U.S. intervention "aggression" against the rights of Palestine. To Iraqis, protection of the Four Freedoms appeared to be inconsistent with support for "imperialistic Zionism." Similar reports came from Syria, Transjordan, and Saudi Arabia. In early October, ministers from Egypt, Iraq, Syria, and Lebanon called at the State Department in Washington to express their disapproval.[36]

Truman simply ignored the chorus of protests. Even when confronted with accusations that his policy violated U.S. pledges to foreign governments, he initially refused to make any concessions to the complaints. Iraqi, Syrian, Lebanese, and other delegations insisted that the endorsement of one hundred thousand additional Jewish settlers violated pledges from two U.S. presidents. But Truman seemed to worry little about previous commitments or the stream of complaints coming from the Middle East.

On September 26 he told the press that a search of White House files had revealed no commitments from his predecessor that might exclude unilateral U.S. pronouncements on Palestine.[37] He was wrong, and he knew it. Truman had viewed a copy of the Great Bitter Lake conversation within weeks after taking office. In late August and early September his White House staff had carried on a busy

---

[36] *FR*, 1945, VIII, 744–745, 749, 750, 756–758.
[37] *New York Times*, September 27, 1945, p. 14.

exchange of memorandums about the talks between Roosevelt and Ibn Saud. Rosenman and Leahy had each sent directly to the president notes discussing the February meeting between the previous chief executive and the king. Truman had read Roosevelt's letter of April 5 in which FDR reiterated his commitment that he "would take no action . . . which might prove hostile to the Arab people." Within a month of Roosevelt's death, Truman had sent several Arab governments his own commitments "that no decision should be taken respecting the basic situation . . . without full consultation with both Arabs and Jews."[38]

It is doubtful that the president forgot so quickly. More likely his denial of previous pledges stemmed from the impact of several key advisers in the White House. Working from both domestic political considerations and an affinity for Jewish ascendancy in Palestine, Rosenman and Leahy lead Truman through a series of denials of promises to consult with Arab leaders.[39]

Middle East governments did, however, have one trump card which eventually caused the president some concern. They had their own copies of all the commitments from both Roosevelt and Truman. If the president could not find his files on the matter, Saudi Arabia was graciously willing to supply the world with a duplicate of the Great Bitter Lake conversation. When Ibn Saud's government proposed publication of that transcript and the April 5 letter from FDR, the administration quickly sprang to attention. In the wake of Truman's confident denials that any such pledges existed, public exposure of the documents could prove embarrassing.[40]

Saudi Arabia's publication threat did at least offer the State Department its first opportunity in weeks to have any meaningful impact on the execution of policy. Henderson and his colleagues had quietly pursued their tasks, developing a wide variety of possible

[38] *FR*, 1945, VIII, 705–708; George Elsey to George Vardaman, August 25, 1945; Rosenman to Truman, September 7, 1945, Box 2, Rosenman Papers.
[39] Leahy to Truman, n.d.; Rosenman to Truman, September 7, 1945, Box 2, Rosenman Papers, *FR*; 1945, VIII, 753–755; diaries of William D. Leahy, October 2, 1945, p. 165, Leahy Papers.
[40] *FR*, 1945, VIII, 755–756.

plans for settlement of the whole controversy. They had gathered technical information on military requirements for executing the president's wishes. But they had also viewed with some alarm the drift in Truman's policy. In late September, Paul H. Alling and Gordon Merriam had contemplated recent developments and considered possible action.[41]

"It seems apparent to me," Alling wrote Loy Henderson, "that the President (and perhaps Mr. Byrnes as well) have decided to have a go at Palestine negotiations without bringing [the Near Eastern Office] into the picture for the time being. The question we must answer is: Should we nevertheless inject ourselves actively into the negotiations with further recommendations at this state, or should we wait to be called?" In the end Alling decided it was best to be patient. "We have already given Mr. Byrnes our fully considered recommendations on Palestine," he concluded. "I see nothing further we can appropriately do for the moment," he added, "except carry on our current work, answering letters and telegrams, receiving callers, etc., as best we can, pending the time (which will come soon) when the whole thing will be dumped in our laps."[42]

Merriam was less willing to lose the initiative. "Recent developments . . . have . . . rendered it all the more essential that the Department should do everything possible to bring about a more unified and positive Government policy on Palestine," he wrote in late September. "Such a policy should . . . be made public and be adhered to by all branches of the Government in the future handling of the Palestine question." Merriam wanted the administration to emphasize efforts to improve the situation for refugees in Europe. "Every effort should be made," he advised, ". . . to get the Jews out of the camps as soon as possible." He proposed a program of resettlement in Europe coupled with, for the "hard core of the stateless and non-repatriable persons," increased immigration to both the United States and Palestine.[43]

[41] Ibid., pp. 717–719, 724–743.
[42] Ibid., pp. 734–736, 742–746; Henderson to Byrnes, August 21, 1945, 867N.01/8-2145.
[43] *FR*, 1945, VIII, 745–748.

Merriam's suggestions came to naught, but Alling's patient predictions proved at least temporarily correct. Faced with threats of embarrassing disclosures from Saudi Arabia, the White House relied on the State Department to handle the dilemma. When Dean Acheson received the telegram proposing publication of the Great Bitter Lake conversation, he immediately tried to buy time. While he sent Truman a memorandum advising him of the situation and continued to communicate with the president over the next week, he sent word to the Saudi government that Truman's absence from Washington prevented him from responding immediately. But it was certainly apparent that Acheson could not delay the inevitable. Henderson suggested that the president might extract himself from embarrassment through another press conference announcement. Truman could tell some future gathering of reporters that there had been no change in the policy of the U.S. government to consult with both Jewish and Arab leaders before any decision on the basic situation in Palestine. He also advised that the administration agree to publication of Roosevelt's April 5 letter while opposing release of the Great Bitter Lake conversation.[44]

Administration advisers, with State Department participation, contemplated possible action. By mid-October, Byrnes began pushing for Truman to agree to disclosure of Roosevelt's letter. He also wanted the president to state publicly that U.S. promises to consult with Arab leaders remained unchanged. Rosenman strongly disagreed. He flooded Truman with a host of objections. Since the current administration had never made any personal endorsements of Roosevelt's pledges (an incorrect assumption on Rosenman's part), Truman could refuse to support them. It is even proper, the White House counselor wrote, "for you to take the position that the admission of 100,000 Jews into Palestine is not a 'change in the basic situation.'" Besides, "consultation" could easily become a meaningless commitment. "You or the Secretary of State . . . [should] call the Jewish and Arab leaders into conference at an early date, and 'consult' with them so that

[44] Ibid., pp. 751–753, 756, 763–764; Acheson to Truman, October 5, 1945, 867N.01/10-545, RG59, NA.

the Arab consultation will be fulfilled—and then you can take whatever action you wish." [45]

But Truman had already decided to follow the advice of the State Department and Byrnes. On October 13 he sent Ibn Saud a telegram agreeing to publication of FDR's letter. He also told the king that he was contemplating a public statement for October 18 "that . . . the policy of the Govt. of the US is unchanged." When October 18 came, it was Secretary of State Byrnes who spoke for the administration. "Should any proposals emerge which in our opinion would change the basic situation in Palestine, it would be the policy of the Government not to reach final conclusions without full consultation with Jews and Arabs." [46]

State Department intervention had saved Truman considerable embarrassment, but the department's permanent influence was minor. It became increasingly clear that Truman was primarily attuned to the kind of advice coming from men who worried about the political impact of plans for the Holy Land and who had advised action that would serve election needs. White House files became full of warnings to the president. John Stanley Grauel, executive director of the American Christian Palestine Committee, spoke of political considerations, as did the Democratic state chairman of Iowa, who wrote Matt Connelly, secretary to the president, warning that Jews in his state were concerned over the drift of policy. From within the White House, Rosenman bemoaned the political impact of the publication of Roosevelt's April 5 letter: "Repercussions over it in New York are terrific, as Bob Hannegan can tell you." [47]

Harry Truman had entered the White House relatively inexperienced and unprepared to handle the massive problems besetting the country. German and Japanese surrenders had brought no respite to

[45] Rosenman to Truman, October 17, 1945; October 23, 1945, Box 2, Rosenman Papers; *Time*, October 15, 1945, p. 29.

[46] *FR*, 1945, VIII, 769–771. Truman took the position that he had said merely that there was "no record of any such commitment" (*Time*, October 29, 1945, p. 32).

[47] Rosenman to Truman, October 23, 1945, Box 2, Rosenman Papers; Jake More to Connelly, October 1, 1945; Grauel to Truman, October 1, 1945; Official File 204 (Misc.), Truman Papers.

the weary executive. Economic questions, Democratic party fortunes, and relations with the Allies and with the defeated powers demanded careful consideration. Palestine could not occupy much of the president's attention. In the face of so many other pressing matters, it seemed excusable, no doubt, to let politics dictate Holy Land policy. Public opinion polls reflected a wide sympathy for Jewish settlement in the Promised Land. One Gallup survey late in the year indicated 80 percent support for Jewish colonization of the disputed country. Truman had neither the time nor the commitment to develop any appreciation for Arab fears. Increasingly his administration simply reacted to the demands of domestic forces.[48]

Nowhere was this reaction more apparent than in dealings with the British and with Congress. There was some evidence that when Truman talked with Churchill and Attlee at Potsdam about the Palestine situation, he rejected their suggestion that any Yankee contributions to policy should also include more U.S. responsibility for the consequences of policy. Accordingly, when Attlee received Truman's call for the admission of one hundred thousand refugees to Palestine, the prime minister made a noncommittal reply and then proposed the creation of an Anglo-American committee to investigate the whole refugee-Palestine question and make recommendations. It was the British attempt to force Washington into a position of responsibility.[49]

Truman's response was cool. In late October meetings between Byrnes and Lord Halifax, the British ambassador in Washington, one consideration appeared constantly on the secretary's lips. "Quite frankly, I am thinking of the New York City election," he told the British envoy. Every detail of policy, from the wording of public announcements to the timing of their release, had to hinge on such matters. "When this is submitted to the President he has to think about that," Byrnes explained. Even if the chief executive's thoughts did not instantly revert to party victories, Rosenman was there to remind him. The White House adviser never wanted the establishment

---

[48] *The Gallup Poll: Public Opinion, 1935–1971,* I, 584.
[49] *FR,* 1945, VIII, 719, 739, 740–741; *FR, Potsdam,* I, 972–979; II, 1402–1407.

of an Anglo-American committee, but even more, he opposed announcing its creation before the New York election.[50]

Through October and November, Byrnes and Lord Halifax haggled over the terms of reference for the Anglo-American inquiry. The British hoped the investigation would concentrate on refugee problems, with Palestine being merely one of many possible schemes for resettlement. For domestic political reasons the Truman administration sought to confine considerations to the Holy Land. "We are interested," the secretary told Halifax, "in Jews going to Palestine and not to be scattered all over the earth."[51]

Central to the dispute was the relative placement of two terms. Washington demanded that the first item in a statement of committee responsibilities stress that the investigation sought ways to get more people into the Promised Land. London feared that such an emphasis might suggest to Arabs that the inquiry really favored Zionism, not humanitarianism. Lord Halifax and the British constantly urged a less provocative wording which could keep open the option of allowing Jewish refugees to settle in Palestine but which would convey to Moslem capitals that Americans and British wanted comfort for uprooted people, not Jewish nationalism, and that the burden of relief would be shared with Europe and the United States. Truman might have been able to accept the British position except that any detraction from Palestine had unwanted political consequences. In late October, Byrnes even abruptly terminated all discussion on the matter for fear that news might leak to the press before the November 6 election in New York. When talks resumed in early November, the two governments finally reached agreement on the terms of reference. But the final version bore almost no British imprint.[52]

Truman's policy could at least make him appear to be moving boldly in defense of uprooted folks. His whole public posture suggested that he had taken every possible step to secure homes for the

---

[50] Rosenman to Truman, October 23, 1945, Box 2, Rosenman Papers; memorandum of conversation, October 19, 1945, 867N.01/10-1945, RG59, NA.
[51] Memorandum of conversation, October 29, 1945, 867N.01/10-2945, RG59, NA.
[52] *FR*, 1945, VIII, 779–790, 800, 812–823.

Holocaust survivors. But he made no major moves in behalf of refugee settlement in the United States, where the political rewards were meager and the liabilities extensive. He did issue an executive order to the effect that unused portions of the immigration quotas should go to displaced persons. But that effort proved to be pitifully inadequate. Over the next six months fewer than four thousand people actually won admission under the program. Truman failed, however, to push Congress to expand the quotas for refugees. Throughout the next year the administration merely toyed with possible legislative action. It was early 1947 before the White House began a concerted and formal campaign to produce extensive refugee resettlement in the United States.[53]

The president was even willing to limit action in behalf of immigration to Palestine if there were few political rewards entailed. At the same time that he accepted personal credit for forthright efforts on the Holy Land front, he moved to discourage any congressional endorsements for Jewish colonization or nation building in Judea. He registered no qualms about opposing House and Senate actions on the grounds that they might alienate Middle Eastern countries.[54]

A. H. Silver, a close political ally of Robert Taft, had talked to the senator in late October about reintroducing "our resolution" on Palestine—apparently referring to the unsuccessful measure sponsored by Taft and Robert Wagner in 1944. Taft resubmitted his proposal in November and won a Foreign Relations Subcommittee fight to keep the resolution's terminology of a "Jewish commonwealth," not a "Palestine commonwealth."

But within days of that victory, the administration began its counteroffensive. Byrnes began meeting with the Senate subcommittee to seek termination of their deliberations. In early December, Truman

[53] Byrnes to John G. Winant, January 14, 1947, 867N.01/1-1347; memorandum of conversation, January 21, 1947, 867N.01/2147. RG59, NA; *Washington Post*, May 5, 1947, p. 17. By June, 1948, a total of 41,379 persons had entered the United States under Truman's executive order, but by no means were all of them Jewish refugees. Jacques Vernant, *The Refugee in the Post-War World*, p. 482.

[54] *FR*, 1945, VIII, 827.

sent a message to both Taft and Wagner urging postponements until after the Anglo-American committee issued its report. At first it appeared that the president might win his goal. But a week before Christmas, Congress passed a resolution calling for admission of Jews to Palestine to its "maximum of agricultural and economic potentialities" and the establishment of a "democratic commonwealth in which all men, regardless of race or creed, shall have equal rights." [55]

In two communications to the British government Harry Truman shaped much of the subsequent struggle over Palestine. He continued to believe that his requests on immigration quotas had nothing to do with the eventual political settlements in the Promised Land, and he was, no doubt, surprised at some of the reactions to his efforts. Yet he had fundamentally altered U.S. policy. Despite his pretensions of neutrality on the question of Jewish nationalism, he had placed the U.S. government in support of a program which greatly aided the creation of a Jewish state in the Middle East. For the next two and one-half years the whole controversy centered around Truman's appeal to Attlee in the late summer of 1945. It was a fortunate development for Zionists. They could now concentrate their efforts on humanitarian appeals and win support from groups that would never have endorsed the narrow political objectives of the advocates of a Jewish state. Even if the U.S. president could neatly separate political and humanitarian objectives in his own mind, Zionists were well aware that the latter served the former. [56]

Truman's avowed purpose was to aid Europe's displaced persons. He wrote in his memoirs that he was far more concerned with helping uprooooted people than with sponsoring agitation for Jewish statehood. Throughout 1945 he professed indifference toward Jewish nationalists, insisting that he could aid the survivors of Dachau and Bergen-Belsen without passing judgment on the justice of proposed

[55] *New York Times*, December 20, 1945, p. 12. See also Subcommittee on Palestine Resolution—Committee Minutes, November 16, 1945, Record Group 46, National Archives, Washington, D.C.

[56] See, for example, A. H. Silver et al. to Truman, May 2, 1946, Official File 204 (Misc.), Truman Papers.

governments for Palestine.[57] On the surface, such dogged attention to the plight of miserable people, a refusal to discuss long-range political settlements for the Holy Land, appeared both humane and wise. In German camps thousands of desperate human beings anxiously awaited immediate relief. Yet by the summer of 1945 the refugee question had become so entangled with Palestine politics that any successful effort to use Arab territory for resettlement of nonrepatriables required some initial judgments relative to Zionism.

If Chaim Weizmann and his colleagues were right in believing that Jews would never find happiness outside their own Judean commonwealth, advocates of statehood were indispensable allies of mercy and deserved cooperation from any president professing pity for Nazi targets (after all, Zionists sought more than acquiescence; they also wanted protection and advocacy from Truman).[58] Champions of the downtrodden would then face the difficult task of weighing the relative needs of Jewish refugees and Palestinians, of deciding if justice demanded that a new Israel rise from the Holy Land rather than from one of the multitude of other proposed sites. If Jewish nationalists were wrong and Holocaust survivors merely needed some place to go (not a Jewish state), Zionists were really the unwitting enemies of uprooted souls—careless demagogues who placed politics above humanity, kindled Arab fears, and helped cause Moslems stubbornly to support White Paper restrictions on immigration.

If Truman wanted to move thousands from Europe to the Middle East, he had two realistic choices: (1) denounce Zionism, assure Palestinians there would be no Jewish majority in the Holy Land, and thereby hope to relieve Arab fears while winning at least grudging acceptance for some uprooted people, or (2) share the British burden of handling the inevitable bloody resistance from Arabs and devote

---

[57] Truman, *Years of Trial and Hope*, p. 144.

[58] For a sample of Zionist desires in late 1945, see Weizmann to Truman, December 12, 1945, Official File 204, Truman Papers; Stephen Wise to Truman, September 23, 1946, Box 68, Stephen Wise Papers, Brandeis University Library, Waltham, Mass.

his full energies to creating a Jewish state in Palestine. Even beyond the Holy Land, Truman could push for a change in U.S. immigration policy (perhaps he thought he had more influence in London than on Capitol Hill). It is some measure of the force of public opinion that the president, in tragic disregard of his own alleged intentions, chose to do none of the above.

State Department advisers shared the blame for Truman's choices. A president must, and almost naturally does, look at more than just international factors in framing his foreign policy. He must also assess the dominant mood of the American people. If Truman neglected to face the long-term alternatives clearly, so did popular attitudes. Most of the voters wanted to send Holocaust survivors to Palestine without making any decisions on Zionism, and certainly without sharing the British burden in the Holy Land. Yet Loy Henderson and his colleagues seemed to expect the president to operate in a political vacuum and ignore domestic considerations. They failed to take into account the prevailing attitudes and were unable to help the chief executive develop an approach that paid its dues to popular sentiments while recognizing realistic alternatives. Burdened with other problems and trying to make some sense of the conflicting advice on a problem for which he had no expertise, Truman stayed in the middle between White House aides who urged him to ignore Arab feelings completely and a diplomatic corps that often omitted domestic politics from its calculations.

In his conduct of Palestine policy Truman seemed neither to appreciate nor to understand many of the complexities of related issues —refugee problems, Palestinian opposition to Zionism, or even Jewish nationalism. He did realize the necessity of avoiding a crisis situation, and nearly everything he did was to relieve immediate pressures. In fact, he became so entangled in the delicate balancing of conflicting aspirations that he failed to move beyond merely meeting current tensions. He never devised a systematic and consistent policy. His trip to Potsdam had, no doubt, deeply impressed him with the broken existence of uprooted people. Yet late in the year when he sat in his office with State Department chiefs from Near East posts, he may have revealed much of his primary concern. If Palestine could take more refugees, he proposed, it would both alleviate the situation in Europe and "satisfy some of the demands of the 'humanitarian' Zionists."[59]

[59] *FR*, 1945, VIII, 17.

THE ANGLO-AMERICAN
COMMITTEE OF INQUIRY

On a cold January day in Washington in early 1946, six men gathered in Union Station to welcome the incoming train from the north. Four months had elapsed since the Japanese surrender had ended the Second World War, and although peace had slowed the flow of traffic through the great marble railroad hall that stood at the foot of Capitol Hill, it was still a busy place. Six Englishmen stepped from the morning express from New York. The British and the Americans greeted each other with friendly, but reserved, expressions. Together the twelve men were the Anglo-American Committee of Inquiry on Palestine (AACOI), and for the next four months they were to carry on one of history's most extensive investigations of the Holy Land dispute.

In the hours and days to follow, the twelve were together almost constantly. They had lunch the next day with Dean Acheson in Blair House, then met with senior U.S. officials for a round of briefings. Later in the week Harry Truman invited them to the White House. Meanwhile, the State Department had given them special offices deep within the bowels of the old State-War-Navy building that still housed the diplomatic corps.

Truman's administration had actually picked the American members of the committee in late November. Samuel Rosenman had sent the president a list of suggested names, including most of those who eventually served. The chief executive immediately rejected some. Senator Wagner, on Rosenman's original list, was, Truman had scribbled beside his name, "predjudiced [sic]."

In early December the list was completed and released to the press. It included Frank Aydelotte, former president of Swarthmore College; Joseph C. Hutcheson, judge of the Fifth Circuit Court at Houston; O. Max Gardner, former governor of North Carolina; Frank Buxton, editor of the *Boston Herald*; William Phillips, career diplomat; and James G. McDonald, former high commissioner of the League of Nations' effort on German refugees. In London the British announced their own members: Sir John Singleton, judge of the King's Bench in London; Richard H. S. Crossman, a Labourite member of Parliament; Major Reginald Manningham-Buller, a Conservative member of Parliament; Lord Robert Morrison, a Labour peer; Wilfred Crick, banker; and Sir Frederick Leggett, labor conciliator. When Gardner withdrew from the U.S. delegation for health reasons, Bartley Crum, California lawyer, took his place.[1]

In a sense the six U.S. delegates became the American society in microcosm, reflecting the approaches, attitudes, conceptions, and prejudices of the larger population they represented. Their journey through the conflicting claims on promised land became both a symbolic mental pilgrimage, traversing the course along which so many minds were passing in developing opinions on the Holy Land controversy, and a highly influential approach to the problem. When it was all over there were still disagreements among them, but just enough consensus to forge a united front on several key matters. In the process they helped keep attention on the question of admitting one hundred thousand Jews to Palestine and assured that issue continued prominence in the whole controversy.

Bartley Crum had a paradoxical image. He was a Republican corporate lawyer with a reputation for radical associations. Yet much of that notoriety stemmed not from economic philosophy but from an impressive record in defending civil liberties. He had fought against legislation to remove the Communist party from the California ballot, had opposed the deportation of Harry Bridges, and had served under Roosevelt as a special counsel for the President's Committee on Fair Employment of Negroes in Southern Railroads. In the 1930's he had opposed support of Franco's regime and later did the same

[1] *New York Times*, January 5, 1946, p. 7.

for Truman's aid package to Greece and Turkey. Something of a political maverick, he had headed Wendell Willkie's western campaign in 1940 but had supported FDR four years later.

Forty-five years old and the youngest member of the committee, Crum was an energetic and sometimes volatile participant. At one point he threatened to resign because the group failed to issue an interim report, but Truman's personal intervention persuaded him to remain.[2] After the adoption of final resolutions, he vowed to issue his own minority statement favoring partition. Constantly suspicious, he viewed the State Department and the British Foreign Office as coconspirators in a web of intrigue first to keep him off the committee and then to thwart his every effort in behalf of Jewish refugees. Through his friend David Niles, who apparently secured the committee membership for him after Gardner developed a bad case of gallstones, Crum was the most direct link between the administration and the committee.[3]

Crum professed initial neutrality on the Palestine issue but was in fact a strong advocate of positions friendly to Zionist aims. In his view, Jewish settlers in Judea epitomized progressive society. "A new and valid civilization—a 'one world' in microcosm—had been born" in Palestine, he wrote after returning from the Holy Land. Jewish pioneers were revitalizing an ancient land and making the desert bloom. They were even, the Roman Catholic lay leader pronounced, "living according to Jesus," concerned with community good and human rights.[4]

Crum believed that the Jews' claim to the land was valid be-

---

[2] Emanuel Celler to Truman, March 20, 1946, Box 23, Emanuel Celler Papers, Library of Congress, Washington, D.C.; *New York Times*, March 20, 1946, p. 10; Loy Henderson to Joseph C. Hutcheson, February 19, 1946, 867N.01/1-1946; David K. Niles to Crum, February 20, 1946, 867N.01/2-2046; Niles to Henderson, February 20, 1946, 867N.01/2-2046, RG59, NA.

[3] McDonald memorandum I, p. 32, File 14, James G. McDonald Papers, Herbert Lehman Collection, Columbia University Library, New York (this is a diary McDonald kept during his service on the Anglo-American committee); Niles to Matthew J. Connelly, April 16, 1946, Official File 204 (Misc.), Harry S Truman Papers, Harry S Truman Presidential Library, Independence, Mo.; Bartley C. Crum, *Behind the Silken Curtain*, pp. 4–5, 128–130.

[4] Crum, *Behind the Silken Curtain*, pp. 287–292.

cause they were more likely than were their Arab neighbors to create a "genuine political and economic democracy." He was impressed with the prospects that a new Israel could become a showcase society, raising standards for the entire area. "It could bring to the Middle East the good in western civilization—not by domination but by example." He spoke in glowing terms of the movement "back to the land," and the "Sweet Waters of the Jordan." He saw in the Yishuv all of the elements he had long supported for his own society. He even saw a repetition of U.S. history. Armed Haganah terrorists were like Texans expelling Santa Anna, he told Houstonian Joe Hutcheson —or like Boston patriots killing Redcoats.[5]

The California lawyer was a clever and flexible advocate for a Jewish state, ready with replies to any attacks on Zionism. When detractors insisted Holocaust survivors could find little peace in Palestine, Crum countered that any Moslem animosity toward the Yishuv stemmed solely from ambitious demagogues. Average Arabs lived in peace with their Jewish neighbors, he argued. But when Palestinian spokesmen blamed Zionist agitators for any increases in Moslem bigotry and suggested that a Jewish minority would face little difficulty in an Arab Palestine, he was less optimistic about mutual toleration. Islamic prejudices, he concluded, were too deeply rooted in the teachings of Mohammed to allow Jews any hope of living safely in an Arab Palestine. Somehow the probability of Jewish discrimination against an Arab minority seemed too remote for Crum's consideration. When witnesses argued that Zionism meant subjugation of Arabs, Crum spoke only of a Palestinian democracy (not a new Israel) and assured everyone it was all a misunderstanding. Herzl's movement was not ambitious. It sought no more than a Jewish majority in an equalitarian society, he argued. Crum was generally an advocate of partitioning the Holy Land, but when the British recognized part of Palestine as Transjordan, he protested with the same vigor that the Continental Congress once used in lambasting passage of the Quebec Act.[6]

[5] Ibid., pp. 203–213, 233–236, 277–278, 290.
[6] Ibid., 262–283, 295.

Frank Buxton was a Pulitzer Prize–winning newspaper editor from Boston. He entered the investigation with few convictions on the controversy that lay before him but quickly developed a passionate affinity for Jewish ascendancy in all of Palestine. He had secured his position on the inquiry committee partly through the help of Supreme Court Justice Felix Frankfurter (or at least so Buxton assumed), and he maintained a steady stream of correspondence with the justice. Frankfurter was able to help guide his friend down the road to Zion, but it was not such advice alone that generated Buxton's views. More than any other aspect of his investigation, his tour of Poland made an indelible impression on him. In Warsaw and Lodz he encountered undeniable signs of continuing, massive anti-Semitism. Reports of frequent pogroms horrified him. He came out of Eastern Europe deeply disturbed at what he saw. In German refugee camps he encountered even more signs of desperation: "barefooted women, unattended children, horribly dirty quarters." There was no hesitation about his conclusions. "We can't escape the conviction," he wrote Frankfurter, "that there is little place in any part of Europe or anywhere else in the world just now for Jews—except Palestine."[7]

Yet support for lifting White Paper quotas on admissions did not necessarily foster support for Jewish nationalism. Buxton began to sing praises to a broad Zionist program only after he visited Palestine. In Jerusalem he became unreserved in his enthusiasm for Jewish ascendancy in the Holy Land. "How my Vermont father, who used to glory in the land cleared by him and his brothers, would have been amazed at the greater deeds of the Palestinian Jews," he wrote to Frankfurter. "I came away from those farms less cocky and more humble and not quite so certain that American pioneers left no successors."[8]

While Buxton shared many other people's enthusiasm for Yishuv

---

[7] Buxton to Frankfurter, February 4, 1946, Box 40; December 4, 1945, Box 39, Felix Frankfurter Papers, Library of Congress, Washington, D.C.; "Report on Poland by F. W. Buxton," February 16, 1946, File 15, McDonald Papers.

[8] Buxton to Frankfurter, April 4, 1946, Box 40, Frankfurter Papers.

progress, he did not subscribe to the prevailing notions that Jewish civilization bore some missionary responsibility toward less advanced Arabs. In his mind Jews deserved control of Palestine not because they were potential leaven for an underdeveloped Middle East, but simply because they made "superior" use of the land. "Backward" Arabs did not have the right, he argued, to retard the progress of "more successful" Jews.[9] He was even opposed to spending any money on Arab advances. He balked at committee plans for programs for Moslem economic development. Clearly, he regarded Arabs as inferior people—barbaric infidels who, at best, practiced an array of quaintly primitive customs. His most lasting impressions of the Middle East people came not from testimony in the hearing rooms, but from a visit to Ibn Saud ("most engaging old boy I've met," he told Frankfurter). Buxton remembered and recorded his glimpse of the royal harem, the king's offer to find a wife for a bachelor committee member, and the golden dagger and camel's-hair Arabian robe received as gifts from the old monarch.[10]

Buxton opposed partition because it promised too much conflict. He often equivocated, however, about what kind of long-range settlement he did support. "I wanted a strict adherence to the letter and the spirit of the Mandate," he once explained.[11] Yet that position, as he recognized, left him with considerable latitude. Actually, Buxton most likely preferred to keep Palestine intact because he favored Jewish ascendancy over the entire territory.[12]

At any rate, Buxton kept in constant contact with Zionist leaders, continually probing their minds for some notion of what they desired and digressing from their positions only to be more ambitious. Several Zionists became part of an unofficial entourage that followed the committee around Europe and the Middle East, provided Buxton and others with appendages to formal testimony, and kept sympathetic minds well informed about current strategies. At critical junc-

[9] Buxton to Frankfurter, September 10, 1946, Box 40, Frankfurter Papers.

[10] Buxton to Frankfurter, May 28, 1946, Box 40, Frankfurter Papers.

[11] Buxton to I. B. Berkson, January 13, 1948, Drawer 355, McDonald Papers.

[12] Buxton to Frankfurter, April 4, 1946; June 4, 1946; September 10, 1946, Box 40, Frankfurter Papers.

tures Buxton solicited their advice, providing them a status and an access never accorded to any Arab witnesses. Through his correspondence with Frankfurter he kept Jewish nationalists in Washington informed about committee business. At one point he wrote the justice and asked him what Zionist reactions might be to a pro-immigration proposal "accompanied by passages adverse to the principles of Zionism." It was a performance that called into serious question the notion that the AACOI conducted an impartial and disinterested investigation with equal treatment to all witnesses.[13]

James G. McDonald was a former teacher who had dabbled in a variety of jobs since leaving his classroom in 1919 in protest over lack of academic freedom. Most important for his task on the Anglo-American committee was his service as the League of Nations High Commissioner for Refugees from Germany. While filling that post from 1933 to 1935, he came to believe that Jewish nationalism was the best response to Nazi programs of race extermination. Nothing in the decade to follow convinced him otherwise. He saw little purpose for much of what the inquiry was supposed to accomplish. There was no need to measure anti-Semitism in Europe. Its severity was a foregone conclusion. There was no reason to investigate possibilities for refugee settlement outside the Holy Land. The committee's only task, he believed, was to determine how many Jews could gain admission to Palestine. It was a matter of pressing for maximum immigration.[14]

McDonald, accordingly, took little interest in the parade of testimony before the committee except when it reinforced and defended his pro-Zionist convictions. He was openly antagonistic to witnesses who proved unfriendly to Jewish claims. He often dismissed their testimony as an "overstatement" and called Arabs "intransigent," "unyielding," and "uncompromising." McDonald carried home many fond memories of his trip: "swilling" port for several hours in a committee room of the House of Lords; crepes suzette, oysters, and plover at dinner with Bartley Crum; the National Orchestra playing Wagner in a Sunday afternoon London concert; his first trip to the

[13] Buxton to Frankfurter, February 24, 1946; April 4, 1946; June 4, 1946, Box 40, Frankfurter Papers.
[14] *New York Times*, February 26, 1949, p. 7.

Louvre since 1938; and the Dickens chair at the Athenium Club. But
he brought back scant knowledge about the opposition to Zionism.
He remembered more about the art museums ("marvelous Rem-
brandts" and "fine Velasquezes") than about much of the Arab testimony.[15]

McDonald's Zionism was not a rigorously developed political ideology but a vaguely conceived notion that the Mandate and the Balfour Declaration deserved "fulfillment." During the course of his service to the AACOI his only important change in thought was a
refinement of his approach to Jewish nationalism. In conversations
with Crum he began to explore the advantages of partition. In a conference with "one of the most important Americans in London" he
reassured himself that any settlement must not depend "upon either
our Government's military support or upon the broadening of the
United States quotas." In reaction to aristocratic Arab leaders he became convinced that the "feudalistic" Middle East needed the
healthy influence of a Zionist democracy. In his diary he played with
the notion that Jewish domination in Palestine promised the only
hope for peace in the ancient world. Unquestionably, in his mind, Islamic civilization needed guidance from an agent of western culture.
"It has been argued," he wrote, ignoring much of Arab thought, "that
. . . only the Jews . . . will be able to work with peoples of the Arab
world for only they will not be regarded as imperialists or tools of
imperialism and only they will make the just contribution towards
lifting the living standards throughout the Middle East."[16]

Yet despite his favorable disposition toward Zionist success, he
seemed to score poorly as an advocate, at least according to fellow
committee members. "McDonald has a good heart," Buxton wrote,
"but it seemed to me that he would be more effective in an address
to a large assemblage of women than he was in the discussions of
the committee." During a "crucial meeting, where we were all supposed to express our views . . . McDonald said next to nothing." But
apparently the former high commissioner preferred less direct con-

---

[15] McDonald memorandum I, pp. 13, 14–20, File 14, McDonald Papers.
[16] Ibid., pp. 11, 12, 65ff., File 14, McDonald Papers.

frontations with his colleagues. At one point he toyed with the notion of having a newspaper reporter urge Truman to put pressure on a fellow committee member to change his position.[17]

In the late hours of deliberations, when McDonald finally did take a forceful position, it was in behalf of the Jewish Agency. But even then his efforts were clumsy. On April 16 he threatened to withhold his signature from the committee report because, among other complaints, it mentioned the Jewish Agency "only to warn it" for its failure to curb Zionist terrorism. Several hours later he withdrew his objections, telling his colleagues, "I am really more concerned about the success of implementing the 100,000 program than I am with any form of words about the Agency or any other body."[18]

In an important way, though, that surrender epitomized much of McDonald's basic approach to the Palestine question. He believed in complete Zionist success. Like Crum, he anticipated with delight the day when a Jewish-controlled government in the Holy Land would have the power to build dams on the Jordan, drill for oil in the Judean hills, and carry out massive irrigation projects in the Negev. He did want more than mere admission of one hundred thousand Jewish refugees. He really wanted complete authority for the Jewish Agency. But he could be pleased with any increase in power for Zionists. In Paris in early February he confessed to his diary: "It is evident from all that I have learned to date that a good deal less . . . than the absolute demands of the Zionists would be considered a gain." Warming to the subject, he continued: "None the less, it is obvious now that from their point of view it would be strategically a mistake to talk about compromises. . . ."[19]

William Phillips was the oldest American on the committee and the only career diplomat. If he had any previous opinions on the Holy Land and the settlement of displaced persons, he kept them to

[17] Frank Buxton to Felix Frankfurter, May 28, 1946, Box 40, Frankfurter Papers.

[18] "Memorandum on Draft Recommendation," April 16, 1946; "Memorandum to Sir John, Judge Hutcheson, and Other Members of the Drafting Committee," April 16, 1946, File 16, McDonald Papers.

[19] McDonald memorandum I, p. 24, File 14, McDonald Papers.

himself. He had, however, made known his dislike for British colonial authority, especially in India, where he had served as Roosevelt's special representative and had incurred the wrath of British disapproval for his criticisms. He had been ambassador to Italy before the war and, more recently, chief of the OSS in London and Eisenhower's special adviser on European political matters.[20]

Frank Aydelotte was a former Rhodes Scholar and president of Swarthmore College, where he had become a convert to the Society of Friends. Aydelotte was born in Indiana to descendants of French Huguenots. His academic training was in English literature. McDonald called him "romantic and Anglophile." He came to the committee as director of the Institute for Advanced Study in Princeton. He had no special association with either the Palestine question or refugee problems before 1946, and his most notable view on foreign affairs was his advocacy—since at least the late thirties—of an international government.[21]

Both Aydelotte and Phillips were apparently slow to advocate massive Jewish immigration into Palestine. They remained cautious in suggesting any changes in admission quotas. Neither one proposed creation of a Jewish state. Yet both eventually accepted the prevailing committee consensus: Palestine should admit one hundred thousand homeless Jews from Europe. Aydelotte, however, wanted to link refugee settlement to the creation of a Greater Syria that would incorporate the Holy Land into an independent state ruled from Damascus. He argued that such a political settlement would relieve Arab fears over possible Zionist domination and would come closer than any other arrangement to winning Moslem acceptance of the one hundred thousand.[22]

---

[20] Ibid., p. 11, File 14, McDonald Papers; *New York Times*, February 24, 1968, p. 27.

[21] McDonald memorandum I, p. 11, File 14, McDonald Papers; *New York Times*, April 6, 1941, p. 12; August 26, 1941, p. 17; *Time*, March 4, 1940, pp. 42–43.

[22] Aydelotte to Dean Acheson, September 13, 1946, 867N.01/9-1346, RG59, NA; Frank Buxton to Felix Frankfurter, April 4, 1946, Box 40, Frankfurter Papers; Buxton to I. B. Berkson, January 13, 1948, Drawer 355, McDonald Papers.

The chairman of the U.S. delegation and co-chairman of the committee was Joseph Hutcheson, former mayor of Houston and long-time U.S. Circuit Court judge. The Texas jurist was a Presbyterian and self-described "Old Testament Christian." Truman had picked him for the committee after failing to get another Texas attorney, David Simmons, former president of the American Bar Association. For most of his colleagues Hutcheson became the most respected member of the committee, an able chairman who displayed a judicious objectivity. He was "shrewd, very honest, determined to find, if possible, a 'just solution,'" one committeeman wrote. He was "salty" and "independent," wrote another, and had "singlehandedly broken the Ku Klux Klan in Houston."[23]

Although he had not been active in the Palestine debate, Hutcheson exhibited an early antagonism to both Jewish nationalism and large-scale immigration into the Jordan Valley. He spent much of the first month of his investigation toying with various schemes to find European homes for the uprooted. It was wrong, he argued, "for the Jews to accept Hitler's thesis, that Germany and the rest of Europe should be *Judenrein*." In fact, he originally viewed the refugee problem in its broadest terms, equally concerned with both uprooted Jews and homeless Gentiles.[24]

If Hutcheson made any distinctions, it was on a basis other than religion. He was always far more sympathetic with the plight of those who were forcefully uprooted during the war than he was with the "infiltrees" who voluntarily left their homes after the conflict and used displaced-persons camps as way-stations on the road to Palestine. By the middle of February he was convinced, much to his chagrin, that Zionists had concocted an elaborate organization to drain Eastern Europe of its Jewish population, pour the uprooted into U.S. camps in Germany, and agitate for immediate admission to Palestine. "It is quite evident there is a complete system of communication between camps and Poland and that the movement is regulated

[23] McDonald memorandum I, p. 11, File 14, McDonald Papers; Crum, *Behind the Silken Curtain*, p. 5.
[24] Untitled transcript of Hutcheson's remarks to the committee, February, 1946; Hutcheson memorandum, February 13, 1946, File 15, McDonald Papers.

so as not to attract too much attention and opposition," he wrote. In one center he found "everybody was singing or talking about Palestine." With a note of bitter frustration and irritation he concluded, "if some way could be found to get these fanatics into Palestine, it would be temporarily for the good of the world, though what would happen afterwards I don't know." [25]

His initial response was to suggest closing the gates from Eastern Europe to the American Zone in Germany. He wanted to set February 1 as a deadline for accepting people into displaced-persons camps. Anyone who arrived from Poland or elsewhere after that date should be declared an illegal immigrant and "either . . . sent back or required to look after themselves in Germany as refugee Germans are required to do." He could see few who deserved exemption. "Perhaps an exception should be made," he suggested, "of Jews who can show that they really fled from persecution directed at them and cannot safely go back." But the burden of proof lay with the uprooted. It was not enough to "show general violence and disturbances." Any new arrivals who expected special care from Allied authorities should need "strict proof" that they suffered personal discrimination.[26]

Yet so much of what Hutcheson heard in testimony and interviews challenged his opinions. Constant charges of anti-Semitism, especially in Poland, plus the reports of overwhelming refugee preference for Palestine whittled away his determination to eschew all of the Zionist program. By the time the committee met in Switzerland in early April to write its report, his views had considerably mellowed. He told colleagues that he could not "support . . . the view . . . that Jewish immigration had to stop." He could no longer oppose "the whole plan for keeping open a place to which Jews could go." The "miraculous" had happened, Buxton wrote Frankfurter; "the judge" had "seen the light" on present and future immigration policy.[27]

[25] Hutcheson memorandum, February 13, 1946, File 15, McDonald Papers.

[26] Ibid.

[27] Hutcheson to the committee, April 1, 1946, File 16, McDonald Papers; Buxton to Frankfurter, April 4, 1946, Box 4, Frankfurter Papers.

The AACOI's hearings began in Washington in early January. Both the State Department and the White House had wanted the committee to begin work soon after its appointment, but McDonald and others lobbied to wait until Christmas was over. When they got under way, the committee heard Earl Harrison discuss refugee conditions, an array of Jews and Arabs attack each other, Reinhold Neibuhr defend a Jewish commonwealth, and Albert Einstein denounce both British White Paper policy and Zionist ambitions. Through February the inquiry continued in London, Paris, Berlin, Warsaw, and scores of displaced-persons camps. Much of the work came in subcommittees, which fanned out to collect the testimony, inspect facilities, and conduct surveys. Several American members wanted to end their investigation with the European phase. They saw little reason to visit the Near East to hear testimony. Only after numerous proddings from the State Department did they finally consent to full sessions in Egypt and Palestine, with subcommittee visits to other Arab capitals.[28]

After three months of investigation, the AACOI finally arrived in Lausanne, Switzerland, to debate its findings and adopt recommendations. No one on the committee any longer doubted the necessity for sending some refugees to Palestine. The question was now partly a matter of numbers. But there were more fundamental differences than merely disagreements on numbers. In some sense there had been from the beginning, and continued to be, a British-American split on basic approaches. British members, with the possible exception of Richard Crossman, wanted to advocate increased Jewish immigration in a way that would not alienate Arabs. They were, therefore, friendly to suggestions conducive to the eventual creation of a non-Zionist state. Crum, Buxton, McDonald, and Crossman, on the other hand, wanted more than immediate relief for European camp dwellers. They sought policies to produce a Jewish majority in the Holy Land and the realization of a Zionist country.[29]

[28] McDonald memorandum I, pp. 3ff., File 14, McDonald Papers.
[29] Frank Buxton to Felix Frankfurter, February 15, 1946; April 4, 1946, Box 40, Frankfurter Papers.

The split emerged in clearest relief in the debate over a possible repetition of the Balfour Declaration in the final committee report. Major Reginald Manningham-Buller and most of his British colleagues strongly opposed any such restatement. It would be, they argued, provocative to Arabs but of no advantage to refugees. "I cannot think of any useful purpose it would achieve," the major argued, "other than that of possibly placating American opinion." Not one additional refugee was likely to find a home in consequence of its restatement. "I think . . . [it] would have such a serious effect on the Arabs of Palestine and surrounding territories that its repetition would in fact be a bar to actual immigration." Its inclusion, he reasoned, called into serious question the alleged intentions of the United States toward the helpless in Europe. "If I was anti-Jew and pro-Arab," the Conservative M.P. concluded with a note of self-defense, "I would strongly support the repetition of the terms of the Mandate in the clearest terms for I would feel that that would be most likely" to prevent refugees from entering Palestine.[30]

If the major expected his arguments to make a serious dent in the armor of the Zionist sympathizers, he did not understand their intentions. Clearly, Crum, McDonald, and others sought to preserve the promises of the Balfour Declaration as a step toward the creation of a Jewish state. They wanted no part of any tactic that might find homes for the uprooted while sacrificing the struggle for a Jew-dominated commonwealth. In their view, the one hundred thousand were supposed to be the vanguard of a continuing flow of humanity to Palestine, not merely a single emergency relief for the most desperate of Europe's downtrodden.

But the responsibility for articulating much of the pro-Zionist position fell not to one of the committee members, but to a staff adviser, Paul L. Hanna. Hanna was a professor of history from the University of Florida who had established some reputation for expertise in Middle East affairs after the 1942 publication of his study of British policy in Palestine. He joined the committee staff as a spe-

[30] Untitled transcript of Manningham-Buller's remarks to the committee, April, 1946; Bartley Crum, "Notes on Major Manningham-Buller's Memorandum on Immigration," April, 1946, File 16, McDonald Papers.

cial adviser after hearings had already started in Washington, but he had quickly emerged as the key counselor for those positions most friendly to Jewish nationalism. It was he who formulated the pro-Zionist response to Manningham-Buller's suggestion.[31]

Truman and Attlee had supposedly appointed the committee to deal with the problems of uprooted people. With Hanna's help it began to emphasize ways to use the refugees to the best advantage of Zionism. "Jewish immigration," the professor argued, should be an "*essential means* for maintaining and developing the Jewish National Home."[32] He did express some fear that a failure to repeat the terms of the Balfour Declaration might prompt the British to conclude that the committee had endorsed a curtailment of all Jewish settlement in the Holy Land. Yet his anxiety seems feigned. All of the committee members, including Manningham-Buller, were ready to make emphatic their approval of a large emergency quota for Palestine admissions. The major's proposal to exclude the Balfour Declaration overtly threatened Jewish nationalism, not refugees. There is, Bartley Crum admitted, ". . . a grave disadvantage and a great prejudice to the special position of the National Home in any failure to restate the Balfour Declaration and the purpose of the Mandate."[33]

Rumors were widespread in 1946 that the Americans used their economic muscle to coerce the British into accepting the U.S. position. London was seeking a postwar loan from the United States, and the matter still rested in Congress throughout the spring. Several U.S. Zionists had voiced unmitigated opposition to the aid request as long as Great Britain failed to supply complete support for Jewish nationalism. In July, after release of the inquiry report, Averell Harriman, friendly to the loan request, carried on some top secret

[31] P. L. H[anna], "Comments on Major Manningham-Buller's Current Memorandum on Immigration," April 10, 1946, File 16, McDonald Papers.

[32] Ibid. Several delegates commented on the decisive role played by Hanna. Frank Buxton to Felix Frankfurter, April 19, 1946, Box 40, Frankfurter Papers; McDonald memorandum I, pp. 9–10, File 14, McDonald Papers; Joseph C. Hutcheson to Loy Henderson, May 11, 1946, 867N.01/5-1146, RG59, NA.

[33] Crum, "Notes on Major Manningham-Buller's Memorandum on Immigration," April, 1946, File 16, McDonald Papers.

attempts to get the British to appear more favorable to Jewish settlement in Palestine. He told Hector McNeil of the Foreign Office that
an "affirmative statement" from the British was crucial to securing
House approval on the loan.[34]

No doubt the existence of the British loan application had some
effect on the British delegation. Only the most obtuse member could
have failed to realize how seriously some congressmen might have
taken any signs of bold British resistance to U.S. desires for Palestine. It is true that the final report of the AACOI won something less
than full British enthusiasm, a fact that might indicate that at least
some of the English representatives voted for it despite their reser-
vations and objections. John Singleton, the British co-chairman, for
example, delayed the signing of the final report while he made one
last effort to require consultation with the Arabs before any major
increase in immigration was approved. There were even signs of extreme bitterness and frustration in the London delegation. At a final
cocktail party, according to Frank Buxton, Singleton got drunk and
"cut loose on Hutcheson" and other members of the U.S. contin-
gent.[35]

Yet there is no evidence that any direct coercion took place—no
sign that British delegates were willing to bow to all American
wishes. There is, instead, considerable indication that the British
agreed to a plan which appeared to them to be an effective compromise, a tenable approach which promised to satisfy many, but not
all, of their fears concerning possible Arab reactions. The plan was
primarily the work of the American co-chairman, Hutcheson.

The judge had studied the Palestine problem as intensely as any
member of the committee. With a disposition befitting his years of
service on the bench, he had carried to the inquiry the desire to find
a viable, just solution. Independent-minded, he was able to develop

[34] Averell Harriman to James F. Byrnes, July 6, 1946, 867N.01/7-646; John
Balfour to Loy Henderson, June 7, 1946, 867N.01/6-746; RG59, NA. Zionist
groups took no uniform position on the British loan. See Henry L. Selden to
William L. Clayton, July 9, 1946, Series I, Box 2, Palestine Statehood Papers,
Sterling Memorial Library, Yale University, New Haven, Conn.

[35] Frank Buxton to Felix Frankfurter, April 19, 1946, Box 40, Frankfurter
Papers.

positions that were both honest expressions of his own carefully molded thoughts and realistic accommodations to the committee's internal forces. With rigorous devotion to practicality, he worked long hours to reconcile differences and forge a unanimously approved set of recommendations.[36]

Hutcheson's plan included approval for the one hundred thousand admissions to Palestine, a point no one on the committee seriously opposed after three months of study, plus prohibitions against creation of a Jewish state, even by means of partition. "I could not lend my assent," he said, "to . . . colonization of the Jews for the express purpose of obtaining a majority and of depriving the Arabs, by every test the natives of Palestine, of their rights as a majority, and particularly of the benefits which being a majority insures." The judge was equally antagonistic to Arab nationalism. The Holy Land should be "neither an Arab or [*sic*] a Jewish state," he concluded. Any settlement that sought peace had to "remove the fear of Arab and Jew that either is to be dominated by the other." Neither Zionists nor Arab nationalists deserved all they claimed.[37]

In its final form the report bore the heavy imprint of Hutcheson's hand. It specifically excluded Zionist goals. For the immediate future it proposed continuation of the Mandate. An independent Palestine, once it became a reality, should be devoid of "narrow nationalism," fully responsible to its special status as a Holy Land sacred to Jews, Moslems, and Christians. It should become neither a Jewish nor an Arab state.

Partition of the country had won support from only one American member of the inquiry committee, Bartley Crum. While others on the committee may have had their own special reasons for rejecting partition, the report turned it down on purely practical grounds. Geography, the investigators decided, prevented any workable divi-

[36] Hutcheson to the committee, April 1, 1946; "Parallel Recommendations," n.d., File 16; Frank Buxton to I. B. Berkson, January 13, 1948, Drawer 355, McDonald Papers.

[37] Untitled transcript of Hutcheson's remarks to the committee, April 3, 1946; Hutcheson to the committee, April 1, 1946, File 16, McDonald Papers; Hutcheson to Frank Buxton, July 19, 1946, Box 40, Frankfurter Papers.

sion of the land. Indeed, it helped explain why both Moslem and Jews wanted the entire country. The rich coastal plains were too small to survive as an independent economy, while the interior mountains were too poor. Because Palestine was at the crossroads of the Arab world, no part of it could become an exclusively Jewish state without creating major disruptions and inviting serious hostility and trouble.

The U.S. and British delegates concluded that the Yishuv had to bear part of the blame for aggravating Arab opposition and much of the responsibility for dispelling that hostility. The AACOI found a country distinctly divided along religious lines. Moslems had become second-class citizens, enduring the poorest housing, the highest unemployment rates, and the lowest wage scale. They consistently received less pay for the same work than did their Jewish counterparts. Unskilled Arab laborers suffered the greatest imbalance, averaging a little more than half what Jewish workers received. Separate, and clearly unequal, facilities existed for health care and education. More than any other single factor, this disparity between Jewish and Arab standards of living had stimulated the serious friction between the two peoples.

But there was more than the differences between them. Jewish institutions and enterprises had flourished with massive contributions from Europe and America. Arabs had no such benefactors. They grew resentful and felt increasingly threatened. A "vague sense of the power of western capital" had "overwhelmed" them while the foreign investments had passed them by. During the Second World War the Yishuv had become increasingly urbanized, industrialized, and prosperous while Moslems very largely remained rural and poor. The committee did not fault the Jews for their ability to attract outside support, but it did argue that peace in the Holy Land depended upon the Jews' willingness to share the profits. The report concluded: "Taxation, raised from [the entire population], will have to be spent very largely on the Arabs in order to bridge the gap which now exists between the standards of living of the two peoples."

Zionist nationalism and its violent tactics had simply compounded the Arab resentment. The Jewish Agency, its military branch, and the more extreme terror groups were, the committee agreed to say, unjustified in their attacks on British soldiers and Moslem communities. The report even criticized Jewish schools in Palestine for teaching a "fiery spirit of . . . aggressive Hebrew nationalism." If there was any hope for peace, would-be Israelis had to forsake both their violence and their nationalism. Education must cease to be a process of inculcating Jewish youth with Zionist propaganda. With proper government regulations the schools could become instruments in the conciliation between Arabs and Jews.

Beyond the Palestiné dispute the committee directed much of its attention to the problems of displaced persons, separating the refugee question from the Holy Land controversy. The report found that uprooted Jews did not all face desperate conditions that required extraordinary relief measures. While the refugee camps at Belsen in the British Zone of Germany were former Nazi army barracks, the facilities at Bindermickle, Austria, were workers' flats. In southern Italy an entire seaside village housed uprooted Jews. Elsewhere they lived in huts and hotels, apartment houses and cottages. The continent should be able, the investigators concluded, to absorb most of the resettlement. Compensation to pogrom victims must come from the governments responsible for the persecutions. Yet, as the report agreed, a good many refugees did live in wretched conditions. Perhaps as many as one-half million would require admission to non-European countries. Immigration restrictions in Great Britain, the United States, and other countries of the world had to undergo some relaxation. Palestine alone could not absorb the burden. But in perhaps the most celebrated provision of the AACOI report, the twelve men endorse the transporting of one hundred thousand of the uprooted people to the Promised Land and a future immigration policy in Judea that neither automatically excluded nor always admitted Jewish applicants.[38]

Non-Zionists on the inquiry committee could find much to sup-

[38] The entire report was published in *New York Times*, May 1, 1946, pp. 15–21.

port in the final report. It had rejected the creation of a new Israel. Yet Crum, Bruxton, and McDonald could also live with its conclusions, perhaps with some regret that it gave no more to Jewish ascendancy in Palestine but at least satisfied that the sending of one hundred thousand refugees to the Holy Land improved chances for the realization of their ideological goals. The report was the sort of compromise McDonald had discussed in his diary in Paris—an opportunity to get at least something and to acquire it with the unanimous backing of the committee. It would give Crum an opportunity both to praise the rejection of narrow nationalism and to advise Zionist leaders that they could "continue a fight for the achievement of their ideological tenents, principally a Jewish state."[39] Frank Buxton probably spoke for some of his colleagues when he wrote Frankfurter that while he was opposed to some aspects of the documents, he was sure U.S. newspapers would emphasize the one-hundred-thousand proposal.[40]

Like so many others who came into contact with the refugee problem, the six Americans who served on the committee emerged from their experience with deep and abiding sympathies for the plight of Holocaust survivors. The wretched existence of camp dwellers, the signs of continuing anti-Semitism, and the undeniable desire of so many Jews to go to Palestine profoundly affected their attitudes toward the Holy Land dispute. Only Buxton, Crum, and McDonald were pro-Zionists, but the sending of one hundred thousand refugees to Judea had unanimous backing. In the process the committee expressed its tacit agreement with the argument that settlement outside of Palestine would be difficult.[41] None of the American representatives displayed any personal prejudices against Jewish settlement in the United States, but all of them no doubt con-

---

[39] *New York Times*, May 1, 1946, pp. 1–2. Truman was interested in getting a unanimous report and told the U.S. delegates so. Truman to Hutcheson, April 12, 1946, File 17, McDonald Papers.

[40] Buxton to Frankfurter, April 19, 1946, Box 40, Frankfurter Papers.

[41] In an early March report to the committee, the State Department was very pessimistic about the chances for settlement outside of Palestine. Byrnes to U.S. Legation, Bern, March 21, 1946, 867N.01/3-846, RG59, NA.

sciously worked in the shadow of the extensive popular support for U.S. immigration quotas.

For the Zionist members of the committee the promises of a progressive civilization in the Holy Land became irresistibly attractive. Crum, Buxton, and McDonald had impressive records in defending civil liberties. Yet their prejudices against Arab society prevented them from appreciating the Palestinian arguments in behalf of self-determination. Visions of economic miracles in the desert captured their attention and pushed aside any possible misgivings about Zionist ambitions. Those three American delegates tended to focus on the objections of Ibn Saud and to see the controversy as a dispute between the selfishness of a feudal ruler and the needs of an uprooted people. In the process they lost sight of the Palestinians against whom would-be Israelis were really making their claims.

CHAPTER FIVE

TRUMAN AND THE
AACOI REPORT, 1946

J une, 1946, was especially hot and humid in Washington. On some days the still summer heat was so laden with moisture that it seemed to radiate from the Potomac. Not even the shade of the lush foliage of the elm trees could provide much protection from the steaming blanket of warm air. In the government buildings only the monotonous stir of overhead fans prevented the weather from becoming unbearable. Late in the month President Truman had quietly slipped out of the White House without telling reporters, had fled from the steamy city undetected, and had found momentary refuge at the annual Alfalfa Club picnic at Frederick, Maryland. More than once that summer the chief executive spent his weekends at Shangri-La, Roosevelt's old retreat on Catoctin Mountain northwest of Washington. There he could relax, play amateur historian for reporters in an impromptu guided tour of nearby Gettysburg Battlefield, and hope to find some temporary escape from the problems that were beginning to plague his administration: a fight with Congress over continuation of the Office of Price Administration, disputes with the Soviets over arrangements for the Paris peace conference, a Gallup poll that signaled drastically declining popularity for the administration, and the Palestine controversy, among others.

In the midst of workers' strikes in the steel industry, coal mines, and railroads, Truman had hoped to use the Anglo-American inquiry to quiet the pesky Holy Land dispute. He had personally intervened at least twice in the deliberations of the U.S. delegation, once to discourage an interim report because it promised to unleash a major controversy over committee recommendations even before the delegates had completed their work, and later to encourage unanimous committee conclusions that he hoped could settle the matter permanently. When Judge Hutcheson had finally arrived in Washington with the report in his briefcase, Truman appeared to accept the committee's proposed solutions.

But the Palestine controversy would not succumb to the AACOI's treatment. Into the hot summer the Middle East dispute continued to fester and become more complex, an annoying frustration for the beleaguered president. One prevailing interpretation of events contends that the British were responsible for perpetuating the problem, summarily rejecting the committee's conclusions and thereby killing them. Considering the lack of enthusiasm in London for parts of the report, such an outcome might have been expected. Yet the U.S. government, far more than the British government, was primarily responsible for spurning the committee's recommendations. Even in his initial response Truman actually accepted only part of the AACOI statement. By early August he had turned his back on the entire document, including the plans for admitting one hundred thousand refugees to Palestine. In the process he became increasingly cynical about the whole controversy, doing only what political expediency commanded and occasionally making empty gestures of support for massive Jewish immigration to Judea. Strangely enough, Zionist pressures were primarily responsible for pushing the president into such a position.[1]

In 1947, Bartley Crum wrote a book about his experiences on the Anglo-American committee, concluding that the "entire report" had been "cavalierly discarded by Mr. Bevin and Mr. Attlee."[2] All matters considered, reluctance from London would not have been surprising. According to contemporary rumors, most of the British members of the AACOI had been less than enthusiastic about the committee's recommendations. A British staff member allegedly told Crum, "Well, after all we certainly won't implement any such pro-

[1] *Time*, July 1, 1946, p. 20; July 15, 1946, p. 20; July 29, 1946, pp. 13, 16; Truman to Hutcheson, April 12, 1946, File 17, James G. McDonald Papers, Herbert Lehman Collection, Columbia University Library, New York.
[2] Bartley C. Crum, *Behind the Silken Curtain*, p. 282.

gram as this." But the pervasive view ignored actual British responses. With the possible exception of some short delays to create a timing favorable to British negotiations in Egypt, Attlee's government was surprisingly friendly toward execution of the AACOI plan.[3]

Foreign Minister Bevin did insist, however, that all of the recommendations receive equal treatment. Attlee and his cabinet took the understandable position that there was one major potential difficulty in executing the plan: it would be a tricky business to introduce one hundred thousand new Jews into Palestine and still avoid, as the inquiry had committed itself to do, both Arab and Jewish states. In late April the British foreign minister advised the U.S. secretary of state that the Jewish Agency was acquiring large supplies of arms with the help of contributions from Americans. If new immigrants received weapons, he warned, they could become an invading army to impose a Zionist state on hapless Arabs. Attlee sounded a similar theme before the House of Commons. "It is clear," he said, "from the facts presented in the report regarding the illegal armies maintained in Palestine . . . that it would not be possible for the Government . . . to admit so large a body of immigrants unless and until these formations have been disbanded and their arms surrendered. . . . Jews and Arabs . . . alike must surrender their arms." To Zionists these were unreasonable demands. To Attlee's government they were the *sine qua non* for delicately balancing the intricate provisions of a complex plan.[4]

By the spring of 1946, Truman's Palestine policy increasingly relied on the guidance of David Niles, special administrative assistant. For some time White House procedure had routinely referred incoming correspondence on the controversy to Niles. While the chief executive worried about auto industry strikes, John L. Lewis, the Office of Price Administration, and Congress, the aide handled the

---

[3] Ibid., pp. 282–283.
[4] *FR*, 1946, VII, 588, 590; Attlee to Truman, June 10, 1946, 867N.01/6-1046; Loy Henderson to James F. Byrnes, June 10, 1946, 867N.01/6-1046; Averell Harriman to Dean Acheson, April 24, 1946, 867N.01/4-2446, RG59, NA.

Palestine question. When Truman received advice on the Holy Land from the State Department, Congress, or elsewhere, he invariably discussed it with Niles, who was thereby able to cultivate a subtle but powerful influence on the development of policy. Most important, Niles sought to ameliorate the possible impact of Arab protests and threats.[5]

But while Niles rose in influence, James Byrnes had less and less to do with Palestine matters. Most of the secretary's attention focused on Europe and the forthcoming Paris peace conference. To the degree that he acted on the Holy Land dispute, it was in an effort to find a quick, comfortable compromise to a troublesome minor problem. When he spoke of the issue, it was often with either a note of frustration or a sense of disassociation from the matter. In early May he told some reporters, in an "off-the-record" comment, that all "we do is spend a lot of time [just] talking about" Palestine. In August he wrote a leading Zionist that he was going to have nothing to do with Holy Land policy. "I do not [even] know," he confessed, "what the President's views are."[6] The secretary's confession may have been slightly exaggerated, but there is little doubt that he and his department chiefs were not major presidential advisers on the Middle East debate. They continued to service White House needs, executing decisions made in Truman's inner circle. But they did not shape policy in any meaningful way. When State Department leaders suggested any new directions, the president always sought the advice and approval of his own staff before consenting. It seemed that every telegram on Palestine required the endorsement of David Niles.[7]

[5] Letters from various sources referred by memo to Niles, General File; Niles to Truman, May 27, 1946; Truman to Niles, May 23, 1946; Official File 204 (Misc.), Harry S Truman Papers, Harry S Truman Presidential Library, Independence, Mo.; Gordon P. Merriam to Niles, June 4, 1946, 867N.01/6-446, RG59, NA.

[6] "Memorandum of the Press and Radio News Conference, Friday, May 3, 1946," Folder 560, James F. Byrnes Papers, Clemson University Library, Clemson, S.C.; James F. Byrnes to Robert Nathan, August 17, 1946, 867N.01/8-1746, RG59, NA.

[7] Loy Henderson to Niles, February 25, 1946, 867N.01/2-2146; memorandum to Henderson et al., June 26, 1946, 867N.01/6-2646; Henderson to Byrnes,

In Europe, meanwhile, occupation commanders in Germany and Austria were experiencing some anxious moments. Jews from all over the continent were still leaving their homes, seeking refuge in Allied displaced-persons camps, and eventually pressing for passage to Palestine. It was an unsettling progression that played havoc with plans to normalize life in the Old World. Through April and May the War and State departments toyed with the possibility of closing the German border to the influx of new arrivals. General Joseph T. McNarney, commander of the occupation forces, favored the idea. In May, Truman gave theatre commanders discretionary power to stop the influx of Jews into the U.S. zones.[8]

Yet the War Department was clearly reluctant to take such a drastic step. It was worried about its public image if the border closings became a reality and was anxious to have the State Department incur the "initial onus" for the policy. Through May and June the authority to cut the flow of refugees into the U.S. zones remained largely unused. In the weeks following publication of the AACOI report the rate of infiltration climbed sharply, up 50 percent from April, with thousands of people pouring into United States–controlled camps seeking inclusion in the one hundred thousand. Costs rose also, to 2.5 million dollars a month by early June.[9]

In the face of such difficulties War Department and military leaders began for the first time to push actively to get Jewish refugees out of Europe, but they were concerned with more than charity. In a top secret report McNarney warned that the mounting

---

June 10, 1946, 867N.01/6-1046; memorandum for Niles, June 4, 1946, 867N .01/6-446, RG59, NA.

[8] Charles W. McCarthy to Robert Patterson, March 13, 1946, Box 4, Germany File; Patterson to Howard C. Petersen, May 3, 1946, Secretary of the Army (Patterson) Subject File (Safe File), September 27, 1945–July 24, 1947, File "Cabinet Meetings, Agenda Notes, 27 June 47–1 February 46," Record Group 107, National Archives, Washington, D.C. (hereafter cited as RG 107, NA).

[9] Howard C. Petersen to Robert Patterson, July 2, 1946, Secretary of the Army (Patterson) General Decimal File, 1946–1947, Jews; brief for Acheson and Patterson, May 7, 1946, German File, RG107, NA; Charles W. McCarthy to Patterson, July 17, 1946, Box 20; "Suggestion for Off-the-Cuff Comment," n.d., Box 21, Robert Patterson, Library of Congress, Washington, D.C.

"infiltration" was "jeopardizing" his mission. In fact, the general concluded, Jews were arriving "more rapidly than they can be expected
to be removed to Palestine." Equally disturbing, "the preferential
treatment accorded the Jews is engendering an unhealthy attitude
toward them not only in the Germans but also in other displaced
persons and our own troops." McNarney was concerned enough to
write Judge Hutcheson praising AACOI plans for resettlement.[10]

For some time Secretary of War Robert Patterson had been peppering the president with news of occupation woes. In a February
cabinet meeting he told Truman that caring for refugees was a non-
military function that decreased the effectiveness of the army. Several times in the spring Patterson discussed with Truman the food
shortages facing General McNarney in Germany. When Judge
Simon H. Rifkind returned from Europe in April after five months of
service as the army's special adviser on Jewish affairs, the secretary
of war urged the chief executive to meet wth Rifkind and let him
detail the troubles of refugees.[11]

In early May, Major General John H. Hilldring, assistant secretary of state for occupied areas, warned that British "stalling" promised disastrous consequences for U.S. well-being. "Our military and
political interests in Germany and Austria," he wrote, "require that
we press for immediate implementation of the Committee's recommendation." Zionist organizations could help. "Scathing comments
by Jewish leaders and organizations in this country . . . should be directed against the British rather than against both U.S. and British
Government jointly," he advised. "This result," the general conclud-

---

[10] Howard C. Petersen to Robert Patterson, July 22, 1946; Patterson to Petersen, July 1, 1946, Secretary of the Army (Patterson) General Decimal File,
1946–1947, Jews, RG107, NA; McNarney ot Hutcheson, May 13, 1945, File
187, McDonald Papers; Dean Acheson to Petersen, April 29, 1946, 867N.01/4-
2746, RG59, NA.

[11] "Notes on Cabinet Meeting, Friday, February 1st," 1946; "Notes on Cab-
inet Meeting, March 29, 1946," Secretary of the Army (Patterson) Subject File
(Safe File), September 27, 1945–July 24, 1947, File "Cabinet Meetings, Agenda
Notes, 27 June 47–1 February 46," RG107, NA; "Notes on Cabinet Meeting, 5
April 46," Box 2, James V. Forrestal Papers, Princeton University Library,
Princeton, N.J.; Patterson to Truman April 11, 1946, Official File 204 (Misc.),
Truman Papers.

ed, ". . . can be achieved only if this Government pursues an aggressive public policy of needling the British to implement the Committee's recommendation for entry of 100,000 immediately and without reference to future action on any other aspects of the Report."[12]

Hilldring's advice was either enormously influential or prophetic, since both administration and Zionist reactions to the AACOI report followed the general's prescription. Most Jewish nationalists sang endless praise for proposals to end land restriction and to move one hundred thousand settlers into Palestine. Six American members of the Jewish Agency executive wrote Truman their support. But the principle of "no Arab, no Jewish state" incurred unmitigated opposition. An official of the Jewish Agency in Jerusalem complained that Zionist "political aims have been sacrificed to philanthropy." Dr. Baruch Korff, vice-chairman of the Political Action Committee for Palestine, lambasted the AACOI for its anti-Zionist proposals. Both the State Department and the White House received an avalanche of mail from governors, state legislatures, city councils, and private individuals who focused their approval on the immigration program.[13]

Truman's own reactions followed suit. In an important sense it was the president, not Clement Attlee, who rejected the AACOI's recommendations. Truman made no important changes in his position as a result of the inquiry. He merely culled through the final document searching for those provisions which reiterated his earlier views and discarded the rest. Much as Frank Buxton predicted and John Hilldring prescribed, the chief executive focused his attention on the endorsement of one hundred thousand new immigration certificates. "I am very happy," he wrote in a statement released simultaneously with the report, "that the request which I made for the immediate admission of 100,000 Jews into Palestine has been unanimously endorsed. . . ." But the suggestions for "long range political policies" generated no such presidential jubilation. Truman was not

[12] *FR*, 1946, VII, 591–592.

[13] Ibid.; *New York Times*, May 1, 1946, p. 1; Abba H. Silver et al. to Truman, May 2, 1946, Official File 204 (Misc.), Truman Papers; William A. Pittenger et al. to James F. Byrnes, May 24, 1946, 867N.01/5-2446, RG59, NA.

yet ready to give his approval to the entire report. Provisions for Palestine to remain a mandated territory and plans to keep both Jews and Arabs from excluding each other from power required "careful study."[14]

At the very least Truman managed to center attention on the one aspect of the report most offensive to Moslem leaders. Arab response was virtually unanimous in its vehement denunciation of both the AACOI's recommendations and the president's emphasis. Within days, bitter resentments rippled across the Middle East. The Arab Higher Committee in Palestine called for a general strike in protest. In Cairo, newspapers attacked the report as an injustice to Arab rights. Azzam Pasha, secretary general of the Arab League, warned that execution of the plan to bring in an additional one hundred thousand Jews would seriously damage U.S. interests in the Moslem East. Amir Faisal, the Saudi Arabian foreign minister, told a U.S. minister, "I am afraid we Arabs will have to resist, by force, if necessary." Late in May, Ibn Saud refused any further action on proposed air routes or on a pending treaty of commerce and friendship with the United States. From his desk in the State Department, Loy Henderson warned, "we are of course playing with dynamite."[15]

Truman's initial reaction may have stressed the immigration portions of the AACOI report, but the president did not yet reject other provisions of the plan. His words seemed carefully chosen. Intended protection of Arab civil and religious rights in Palestine was "significant." The "large scale economic development projects . . . which would facilitate further immigration and be of benefit to the entire population" were "gratifying."[16] But within three months Truman turned his back on the entire AACOI settlement, including the emergency immigration measures.

By early summer the president found himself in an uncomfortable dilemma. The British, facing growing Zionist terrorism in Palestine, argued that implementation of the AACOI report would require police responsibilities which London did not intend to bear

[14] *FR*, 1946, VII, 589.
[15] Ibid., pp. 599, 604.
[16] Ibid., p. 589.

alone. Any attempt to introduce one hundred thousand people into Palestine, Attlee contended, could kindle a new round of bloodshed and render meaningless any commitment to political neutrality. Yet military planners in Washington insisted that no U.S. troops should be involved in the Middle East, and while Truman might devalue strategic warnings from State Department leaders, he showed no hesitation in accepting the same advice from the Joint Chiefs of Staff (JCS).

The JCS strongly opposed the use of any U.S. soldiers in implementing the inquiry committee's recommendations. "The stability of the Middle East," joint staff planners concluded, "including assurance that the people in this area will not turn to Russia, is a vital element in United States security." If Truman used military means to enforce the report, that stability would be in jeopardy. "The political shock attending the reappearance of U.S. armed forces in [the] Middle East" could generate "serious disturbances throughout the area." North Africa and Asia Minor could "fall into anarchy and become a breeding ground for world war." Clearly, military leaders worried most about rising Soviet influence at the expense of the United States and Great Britain. They imagined a Moslem world turning to the Soviet Union and cutting Britain's Mediterranean lifeline. They spoke with trepidation about a Turkish government weakening its stand on the Dardanelles and becoming no more than a "satellite Russian state." [17]

But the most powerful stimulus for Truman to abandon or weaken his commitment to the entire AACOI report came, ironically enough, from Zionist forces. Many Jewish nationalists had never wanted immigration rights at the cost of sacrificing a new Israel. A. H. Silver began to worry in the spring that he was losing the war while winning the battle. "The present administration," he wrote to Robert Taft, "will preen itself upon having achieved a 'great victory' for the Jews in moving the 100,000 in Palestine." It will, he predict-

[17] "Report by the Joint Staff Planners in Collaboration with the Joint Strategic Survey Committee on J.C.S. 1684," File CCS 092 Palestine (5-3-46) Sec. 2; "Memorandum for the State-War-Navy Coordinating Committee, 21 June 1946 (SWNCC)," Record Group 218, National Archives, Washington, D.C.

ed, "make good campaign material in 1946," but it "will [also] have
given the Zionist movement a death blow." Stephen Wise was less
blunt but still less than overjoyed about the prospects of refugee relief that did not foster a new Israel. David Ben-Gurion had told the
AACOI that "statehood was now more necessary than the 100,000
refugees." And Jewish Agency officials spoke contemptuously of any
possibility that "philanthropy" might interefere with Jewish nationalism.[18]

What worried Silver and other Zionists most was the drift of
events toward the appointment of another Anglo-American committee to complete plans. While Truman continued to issue proclama-
tions of support for the one-hundred-thousand program, the British
government, cabinet members, military leaders, and the State Department began to consider ways to implement the AACOI's recommendations. Even if London and Washington rejected most of the
AACOI report and pushed for no more than massive resettlement of
refugees, technical experts needed time to make arrangements for
the transfers. Besides, Truman had a commitment to consult Jews
and Arabs before undertaking any plan. Initially the president wanted no more than two weeks for such consultation before the United
States pushed ahead, but in deference to British requests he decided
to allow a month.[19]

Accordingly, in June both London and Washington appointed
representatives to carry out final negotiations. Truman assigned
three cabinet members, the secretaries of war, treasury, and state,
to the task, with alternates conducting the actual discussions with
Great Britain. Henry F. Grady chaired the U.S. delegation and represented the State Department. Goldthwaite H. Dorr served for the
War Department, and Herbert E. Gaston, the Treasury Department.
In theory the new Anglo-American committee was supposed to find
ways to implement the AACOI plan. In fact, it faced restrictions

[18] Silver to Taft, July 17, 1946, Box 648, Robert A. Taft Papers, Library of
Congress, Washington, D.C.; *FR*, 1946, VII, 591; S. S. Wise to Truman, July
29, 1946, Official File 204 (Misc.), Truman Papers; Fred J. Khouri, *The Arab-
Israeli Dilemma*, p. 35.
[19] *FR*, 1946, VII, 607.

which made that task virtually impossible. Severely limited options eventually forced some improvisation.

Truman instructed Grady, Dorr, and Gaston to concentrate on the logistics of moving one hundred thousand people into a tiny, disputed country. Meanwhile, both the president and the JCS warned the negotiators that there must be no commitment of U.S. troops.[20] Yet the British, faced with inevitable violent reactions in the Holy Land, were certainly unwilling to allow any refugee movements without U.S. assistance in policing Palestine. With his concentration on immigration to the exclusion of all other recommendations, Truman was deviating from the AACOI report while insisting that it must be the basis for a final settlement.[21]

In late June, Henry Grady and Goldthwaite Dorr arrived in Washington and began work in a small temporary office in the Mills Building, across the street from the State-War-Navy Building. Herbert Gaston, the third negotiator, had not yet received his appointment and would join his colleagues only after they flew to London to meet their British counterparts. For two weeks Grady and Dorr spent the hot summer days poring through diplomatic reports trying to learn as much as possible about the Middle East crisis.[22]

Both of them were determined to work within the confines of the earlier AACOI proposals, eschewing establishment of a new Israel, placing heavy emphasis on non-Palestinian solutions for refugee problems, and advocating major economic development programs for the Arab world while pushing for settlement of one hundred thousand Jews in Palestine. But with the Joint Chiefs of Staff prohibiting any solution that might include use of U.S. troops, Grady and Dorr stressed those aspects of the AACOI plan which might win at least some Arab acquiescence to emergency refugee relief. Dorr in

---

[20] "The Reminiscences of Goldthwaite Dorr," Oral History Collection, Columbia University, pp. 201–202; Dean Rusk to Robert Patterson, July 9, 7946, General Decimal File, 1946–1947, Committee on Palestine, RG107, NA.

[21] Byrnes had advised Truman that before "any decision could be taken to admit 100,000 additional immigrants . . . , the illegal Jewish armies must be suppressed" (*FR*, 1946, VII, 601–603).

[22] "The Reminiscences of Goldthwaite Dorr," Oral History Collection, Columbia University, pp. 185–186.

particular was convinced that joint economic projects between Jews and Arabs in Palestine could lessen chances of conflict. To that end he secured for the committee an adviser from the Army Corps of Engineers, C. A. Hathaway, to formulate plans for water-power development.[23]

Before leaving for London, Dorr and Grady pressed Truman for his blessings for both economic development and the possibility of bringing displaced Jews to the United States. In a White House meeting in early July the president seemed receptive, at least to suggestions of economic aid. He said he was willing to push for loans from either the International Bank or the Export-Import Bank to finance "sound projects." He talked with enthusiasm and some knowledge about irrigation programs and dam building for Mesopotamia. But he was more reluctant to make any promises about refugee admissions to the United States. Only after considerable urging did Truman authorize Grady and Dorr to tell the British that he was willing to push for fifty thousand non-quota admissions to the United States in return for Palestine's acceptance of the one hundred thousand.[24]

Early on Thursday morning, July 12, Grady, Dorr, and the newly appointed Herbert Gaston left Washington on a flight for England. The three carried with them detailed plans for moving the one hundred thousand out of Europe as quickly as possible—plans that had the specific endorsement of occupation commanders on the continent. The problem was now a matter of securing final authorization from the British.[25] Once negotiations began, the British delegates proved to be highly cooperative. Norman Brooks, who headed the British group, displayed constant sympathy for U.S. requests on

[23] Ibid., pp. 191–192, 201–202; Goldthwaite Dorr interview with author, July 11, 1974, New York.

[24] *FR*, 1946, VII, 645, 647; "The Reminiscences of Goldthwaite Dorr," Oral History Collection, Columbia University, pp. 204–205; Dorr interview with author, July 11, 1974, New York.

[25] *FR*, 1946, VII, 646; Dorr interview with author, July 11, 1974, New York; John H. Hilldring to Robert Patterson, July 8, 1946, 867N.01/7-846; memorandum of the Board of Alternates to the Cabinet Committee on Palestine, n.d., 867.01/7-946, RG59, NA.

refugee measures, but he and the Attlee government still faced one overwhelming problem: how best to introduce so many Jews into an Arab country, avoid a Zionist takeover, and still maintain some semblance of legal order.[26]

Zionist terrorism increased through the summer. The Haganah, the military organization of the Jewish community, took credit for bombing Palestine bridges and the blame for destroying coastal radar stations. The Irgun Zvai Leumi and the Stern Gang, both extreme Jewish nationalist forces, kidnapped and murdered British soldiers. In late July the Arab High Committee in Palestine cabled London that unless the British government took action to stop the terrorism, it would call on the Arab people to defend themselves.[27]

London authorities, meanwhile, grew thin on patience. In the early morning hours of a late June Saturday they began retaliation. British troops seized Jewish Agency headquarters on King George Road in Jerusalem. In the days that followed, soldiers arrested more than one thousand Jewish leaders. Armored cars and truckloads of British troops rumbled across the Holy Land. In the first week of July, thirty-one young members of the Irgun came to trial for firearms violations and faced lengthy sentences upon conviction. Mandate courts had already condemned several terrorist gunmen to death. Clashes between Jews and British soldiers were inevitable and, when they came, deadly. Five people fell in the last week of June alone. In London a correspondent for *Time* cabled a somber assessment to New York: "Britain is on the verge of an Anglo-Jewish war in Palestine."[28]

Yet the United States kept pushing for British agreement to a September completion of the one-hundred-thousand program. In Washington and New York, U.S. Zionists maintained their own transatlantic pressure on the British. Huge crowds gathered in

[26] Dorr interview with author, July 11, 1974, New York; "Adventures in Diplomacy" (manuscript), p. 159, Box 5, Henry Grady Papers, Harry S Truman Presidential Library, Independence, Mo.

[27] *Time*, July 1, 1946, pp. 29–30; July 8, 1946, pp. 30–31; *New York Times*, June 17, 1946, p. 1; July 24, 1946, p. 1.

[28] *Time*, July 1, 1946, pp. 29–30; August 5, 1946, pp. 33–34; *FR*, 1946, VII, 639–640.

downtown Manhattan, displayed a Union Jack that bore a super-imposed swastika, and called for opposition to the British loan. Jew-ish war veterans marched on the White House with much the same message. Grady, Dorr, and Gaston constantly insisted on speedy refugee settlement in Palestine.[29]

At first Brooks argued that there was no way to complete the admissions within two months. Then in the second week of negotia-tions he finally consented to set such a goal, never realizing that within twenty-four hours events in Palestine would nearly shatter his promises. That same day, Irgun terrorists bombed the King David Hotel in Jerusalem, killing ninety-one people. The violence sent shock waves around the world. Zionist leaders in the United States denounced it. When Brooks came to the meeting the next day to report the events to his colleagues, he told them that among the dead were British field representatives who were there to arrange for the transfer of refugees from Europe to Palestine.[30] The terror had seriously strained his capacity to remain committed to any quick resolution of the one-hundred-thousand program. "Before," he told the Americans, "I thought it would be difficult to move so many into that troubled land. Now, it is nearly impossible—but we will do it!"[31]

In part, Brooks kept his earlier commitment to the refugee settle-ment because of the emerging agreement between U.S. and British delegates on long-range political arrangements. In the first session in London, Brooks and his cohorts had trotted out an old plan left over from the AACOI hearings. Sir Douglas Harris of the Colonial Office had devised a scheme for a Palestinian federal government com-posed of two semiautonomous states (Jewish and Arab) and a cen-tral authority temporarily under British auspices. The Americans had arrived in England with plans to propose a binational state. Yet several considerations had compelled them to forsake their own schemes in favor of the Harris proposals. Most important, ironically,

---

[29] *Time,* July 15, 1946, p. 29.
[30] Dorr interview with author, July 11, 1974, New York; *FR,* 1946, VII, 648, 651.
[31] Dorr interview with author, July 11, 1974, New York.

Grady and his colleagues became convinced that a federal plan had the best chance of winning Zionist acceptance. The Americans had learned that Jewish Agency leaders now favored partition. To Grady and Dorr, in particular, the Harris plan appeared to be a step in that direction.[32]

Within a week of their arrival in London the Americans had committed their support to a federal arrangement. In the days to follow, negotiators molded the details. When it was all over, they had given the central authorities (the British) control over Jerusalem and the largely uninhabited, but potentially rich, Negev. They had assigned to the Jewish state slightly less than its population merited but had left it with the Plains of Sharon and Esdraelon that included much of Palestine's richest agricultural regions. The Arab state, with 46 percent of the population, got 40 percent of the land, nearly all of it hilly pastures. The plan called for immediate admission to the Jewish area of one hundred thousand of Europe's destitute. Once that emergency relief was over, each state would set its own immigration limits in consultation with British officials and with an eye on economic absorptive capacity. To enlarge that capacity, the negotiators agreed to an extensive program of economic development, not only for Palestine but also for surrounding regions.[33]

No one on the second Anglo-American committee even remotely suspected the kind of reaction their plans would receive. They anticipated some opposition from all corners but expected eventually a measure of general acquiescence. Yet no such result emerged. Zionists in Great Britain and the United States quickly decided to oppose the recommendations. Defenders of Jewish nationalism sprang into action, beseeching the president to reject the Grady plan.[34]

[32] "Adventures in Diplomacy," p. 160, Grady Papers; *FR*, 1946, VII, 648–649; Dorr interview with author, July 11, 1974, New York.

[33] *FR*, 1946, VII, 651–667. Postal and Levy are, at best, misleading when they contend that Jews were confined to 17 percent of Palestine and excluded from the rest under the Grady plan. Under the plan, Jews would have continued to live in all areas of the country. Postal and Levy, *And the Hills Shouted for Joy*, p. 89.

[34] Grady first learned of possible difficulty in a teletype conference with Washington on July 26, 1946. Record of teletype conference, July 26, 1946,

A little after noon on Friday, July 26, Senator James M. Mead, an old defender of Zionism, and James McDonald met with Truman to discuss the subject. The next morning they met again, this time with Senator Wagner. For his part Truman was apparently reluctant to forsake so easily several months of preparation. He was anxious to win early settlement of the one hundred thousand and then to close the matter. Zionist suggestions that he reject the Grady plan embittered and angered him. He lashed out at Mead, McDonald, and Wagner, accusing McDonald of showing little concern for the refugees. He would not allow the former AACOI member to read a one-page statement of his views. But McDonald refused to surrender. In language that would become standard, he called the plan an attempt at the "ghettoizing of the Jewish community in Palestine." Truman responded, McDonald later said, with "what in a person of lesser office would be regarded as annoyance."[35]

Early in the next week Zionist pressure on the chief executive reached a fever pitch. On Tuesday, Truman faced the heaviest assault on the Grady plan. At ten o'clock in the morning Emanuel Celler and a delegation of New York congressmen arrived at the White House. For nearly a month they had sought an audience with Truman only to face constant rebuffs. David Niles had finally arranged the meeting, and the congressmen now had more than general Palestine policy to discuss. They came to denounce the Grady proposals.[36]

Celler spoke for the delegation. He warned that if Truman endorsed the new Anglo-American plans, Democratic party fortunes would suffer, noticeably in New York. Furthermore, the president

---

867N.01/7-2646, RG59, NA. The Washington side of the conference is reprinted in *FR*, 1946, VII, 670–671.

[35] Memorandum, McDonald to Truman, July 27, 1946, File 395; McDonald to Mead, July 29, 1946, File 259; McDonald to Truman, July 29, 1946, File 395, McDonald Papers; Presidential Appointments, 1945–1948, Files of Matthew J. Connelly, Truman Papers; James G. McDonald, *My Mission in Israel, 1948–1951*, p. 11.

[36] Herbert H. Lehman to Truman, July 30, 1946; Presidential Appointments, 1945–1948, Files of Matthew J. Connelly; memorandum for Matthew J. Connelly, June 19, 1946; Celler to Connelly, June 25, 1946, Official File 204 (Misc.), Truman Papers; Celler to Robert Wagner, June 3, 1946, Palestine Box, Robert F. Wagner Papers, Georgetown University Library, Washington, D.C.

would sacrifice the election for no real gains. Provisions for financial assistance to Palestine, Celler pointed out, required congressional approval. Defeat in the House was virtually inevitable.

Truman was visibly impatient throughout the meeting, inattentive and apparently anxious to end the session as soon as possible. He appeared to be nervous, constantly shuffling the papers on his desk. Suddenly he interrupted Celler. He told the congressmen he realized they faced reelection, but he had no time to hear their woes. His concern was with national problems. Then, abruptly, he terminated the conference.[37]

Two hours later the president met with cabinet members over lunch and discussed Palestine policy. Sometime that day he decided to abandon the Grady plan. He was simply unable, Dean Acheson told the British ambassador in Washington, to get the "necessary backing" to support it. Grady and his colleagues learned of the decision after they flew to Paris to talk with Byrnes. The president "hopes," Acheson telegraphed them, "further study might produce [a] plan which would be likely of public acceptance in this country." In the White House, Truman could only despair. "I have about come to the conclusion," he wrote McDonald on Wednesday, "that there is no solution."[38]

Since 1946 Zionist commentators have insisted that the opposition to the Grady plan stemmed entirely from fear that the settlement gave Arabs veto power over the admission of displaced persons to Palestine. They have charged that the British intended to delay initiation of large-scale Jewish immigration until after winning Arab endorsement, thereby deliberately pursuing a permanent postponement.[39] Yet a close reading of the Anglo-American accord and the

---

[37] Celler to Truman, July 31, 1946; Presidential Appointments, 1945–1948, Files of Matthew J. Connelly, Official File 204 (Misc.), Truman Papers; *New York Times*, July 31, 1946, p. 5.

[38] Memorandum of conversation, July 30, 1946; Acheson to Grady, July 30, 1946, 867N.01/7-3046, RG59, NA; Truman to McDonald, July 31, 1946, File 395, McDonald Papers.

[39] James G. McDonald to David K. Niles, July 31, 1946, File 283, McDonald Papers; Nahum Goldman et al. to Truman, July 8, 1946, Official File 204 (Misc.), Truman Papers.

diplomatic communiques concerning its meaning strongly suggests that British intentions were far more positive and that the Grady proposals may have provided the only chance for an early completion of the one-hundred-thousand program without major bloodshed.

Realistically, London and Washington had two broad options in pursuing refugee settlement in Palestine. They could either force the admissions without Arab acceptance or try to gain some degree of Moslem acquiescence. Without U.S. willingness to make military commitments, the British were left with sole responsibility for compelling Arab cooperation. With considerable reason, the British worried about the prospects of a bloody conflict in which they either withdrew, leaving Jews and Arabs to unthinkable internecine warfare, or stayed and suffered attacks from both sides. London was simply unwilling and perhaps unable to remain in Palestine, allow the admission of one hundred thousand refugees, and then sufficiently repress all forceful Arab opposition or additional Jewish aggrandizement. As the Grady report recognized, there was "a degree of sustained and determined resistance of either Jews or Arabs beyond which no policy could be enforced." Attlee's government understandably sought an approach that might win "a measure of acquiescence from the Arabs and Jews."[40]

The Grady plan specifically endorsed procedures adopted earlier for moving one hundred thousand Jews to Palestine and recommended initiation of that relocation as soon as London and Washington "decided to put the consitutional proposals into effect." It also stipulated that admissions should "proceed at the maximum rate consistent with the clearance of the transit camps in Palestine." It did call for conferences between Americans, British, Jews, and Arabs as an "essential preliminary."[41] But those conferences were intended to ease tensions, not stop the relocation process.

Certainly most U.S. officials, including perhaps the president, believed that Great Britain planned only some way to smooth the process of admitting the refugees to Palestine. James Byrnes, who had

---

[40] *FR*, 1946, VII, 666–667.
[41] Ibid., pp. 661–667.

told reporters in May that "what you really need is just to put . . . [the refugees] somewhere," hoped to finish the matter quickly. He wrote Truman from Paris suggesting that the chief executive announce acceptance of the plan. Ambassador Averell Harriman constantly reassured the president that the British had every intention to "give the green light on the 100,000 at the earliest possible moment." He cabled Truman that he was "convinced [the] President can rely on the good faith of [the] British Government to move with the greatest speed." Truman himself apparently told Grady that the ·plan was the "best of all the solutions proposed for Palestine."[42]

Even if London planned delays or had no hope of winning Arab cooperation, Truman's rejection of the settlement did not include any way to circumvent British and Arab procrastinations. The only way Washington could force the use of Palestine for emergency refugee relief was to make military commitments to police the inevitable conflict in the Holy Land. Yet Truman and his advisers had wisely decided to avoid sending any U.S. troops into the squabble. In short, if the president's sole goal was quick resettlement for the destitute of Europe, he had, in accepting the Grady proposals, everything to gain and nothing to lose.

Yet if the Anglo-American accords promised the best hope for early solutions to refugee problems, why did some Zionists oppose them so vigorously? It seems likely that Jewish nationalists condemned the Grady settlement precisely because it did hold considerable promise for refugee relocation, but, as Rabbi Silver so ably put it, that act of relocation would "have given the Zionist movement

---

[42] "Memorandum of the Press and Radio News Conference, Friday, May 3, 1946," Folder 560, Byrnes Papers; *FR*, 1946, VII, 671–673; Harriman to Acheson, July 27, 1946, 867N.01/7-2746, RG29, NA; "Adventures in Diplomacy," p. 163, Grady Papers; Dorr interview with author, July 11, 1974, New York. Grady told Byrnes the "British have definitely and emphatically agreed to issue certificates for one hundred thousand as soon as they are convinced [they can do so] . . . without military force" (Record of teletype conference, July 26, 1946, 867N .01/7-2646 RG59, NA). There is little reason to accept the charge of Howard Sachar that Truman was "hardly more impressed by the Morrison-Grady Report than were the Zionists." Sachar uses the term *White House* rather than *Truman* and might come close to the truth if he is reporting the sentiments of presidential advisers. But he is at best misleading. See Sachar, *History of Israel*, p. 273.

a death blow." Certainly not all of Herzl's followers placed creation of a Jewish state above immediate resettlement for the downtrodden. But some leading advocates of a new Israel did oppose a plan of refugee admissions to Palestine because it confined the area of Jewish control. They seized the initiative and convinced Truman to denounce the Grady plan. Rejection certainly promised no speedier way to find homes for the uprooted. Endorsement for the Anglo-American proposals risked nothing except Zionism.[43]

In the months following the rejection of the Grady plan, Truman grew increasingly cynical and sarcastic about the Palestine issue. He had entered the debate a year before with good intentions toward aiding uprooted people, convinced that his proposals for the one hundred thousand represented a reasonable compromise between extreme Jewish nationalism and Arab opposition. He had, no doubt, expected some appreciation from Zionist leaders. Instead, the fruition of his efforts had encountered stiff, almost bitter, opposition from Herzl's disciples. The president was clearly frustrated when he wrote a friend, "the Jews themselves are making it almost impossible to do anything for them." When Bernard Baruch suggested in late October that the chief executive appoint a special ambassador to handle Palestine policy, Truman shot back: "sometime when you have Atomic Energy and everything else disposed of I'd be glad to discuss the situation with you. Right at the present time I have other things to think about which are in need of immediate solution."[44]

Truman did continue some token attention to the one hundred

---

[43] In early 1947, Jewish Agency leaders in London apparently rejected still another proposal to push for the one hundred thousand without Zionism. Foreign Minister Ernest Bevin told Jewish Agency representatives that he believed he could get Arab approval for the one hundred thousand if "thereafter Arabs would have a say regarding future immigration." The Zionists rejected the "Arab veto." Gallman to James F. Byrnes, March 7, 1947, Palestine Papers, McClintock File, RG59, NA.

[44] Harry Truman, *Memoirs: Years of Trial and Hope, 1946–1952*, p. 153; Truman to Baruch, November 8, 1946; Official File 204 (Misc.), Truman Papers. A year later Truman was apparently still licking his wounds. According to James Forrestal, the president told a cabinet meeting in August, 1947, that he "had stuck his neck out on this delicate question once, and he did not propose to do it again" (James Forrestal, *The Forrestal Diaries*, ed. Walter Millis, pp. 302–304).

thousand. In the middle of August he asked the Grady committee delegates and the Hutcheson commission members to meet together to try to resolve their differences. He maintained contact with Attlee about the refugee question. Yet he refused to send a representative, or even an observer, to planned meetings of the British, Arabs, and Zionists in London.[45] Even without Washington's blessings and participation, the British had scheduled a September conference to fulfill promises of consultation with both sides in the Holy Land dispute. Neither Jews nor Arabs found much to favor in the Grady proposals, but Attlee had doggedly pursued a settlement. Even when Jewish Agency representatives failed to appear at opening meetings, the prime minister delivered his remarks to the assembled Arab delegates. But no Americans were present.[46]

In Europe, meanwhile, the refugee burden was reaching a crisis level. Population of the Jewish displaced-persons centers approached one hundred thousand. State, war, and navy secretaries finally agreed in July to close the borders of U.S. occupation zones and limit the growth of the camps. Yet the tide of humanity pouring out of eastern Europe continued to surge toward Austria and Germany. With Palestine at least temporarily closed and American immigration restrictions still intact, Secretary Patterson and General McNarney could hope only to transfer some of the uprooted people to Italy and other European countries.[47]

But for Truman, if there were no satisfactory Palestine solutions that could affect refugee conditions, there were at least approaches that might bear political fruit. As the president turned away from any realistic pursuit of his one-hundred-thousand goal, he found increasing favor with policies that could serve Democratic party fortunes. With the approach of the November congressional elections, Zionist partisans mounted considerable pressure on the chief execu-

[45] Joseph C. Hutcheson to Frank Aydelotte et al., August 2, 1946, File 187, McDonald Papers; *FR*, 1946, VII, 682, 691, 701.

[46] *FR*, 1946, VII, 682, 688, 691, 692–693, 696.

[47] Patterson to Dean Rusk, August 8, 1946, Box 20, Patterson Papers; Howard C. Petersen to Patterson, July 2, 1946, Secretary of the Army (Patterson) Decimal File, 1946–1947, RG107, NA; Resume of Meeting of Cabinet Committee on Palestine, October 9, 1946, 867N.01/10-946, RG59, NA.

tive. Bartley Crum began lobbying Democratic National Chairman Robert Hannagan to aid in the campaign. Even David Niles joined the effort, apparently providing a letter for Crum to send Hannagan and then doing his own pleading to the president. Niles warned Truman that Republican Thomas Dewey planned to make a pro-Zionist statement and that unless the president did likewise, Democrats would suffer badly in November, especially in New York.[48]

Truman had tried to please Jewish nationalists by advocating immigration increases to Palestine—in the process disavowing any commitment to a particular political settlement. But his efforts had satisfied few of Herzl's disciples. Now he was willing to escalate his offers. In August when the Jewish Agency officially hinted a willingness to accept partition, Truman urged the British to make the Zionist proposal the basis for negotiations. Fearing any move that might suggest lack of friendship to Jewish nationalism, the White House consistently refused to see an anti-Zionist Jewish leader, Lessing Rosenwald, until after the election.[49]

The president saved his supreme gesture, however, until Yom Kippur on October 4. Truman had decided to move beyond his standard endorsements of immigration increases. But he apparently wanted to avoid any appearance of sudden changes in policy. In a carefully worded statement the chief executive said that a partition of Palestine and the creation of an independent Jewish state in part of the country, as Zionists were proposing, would "command the support of public opinion in the United States." It would also be, Truman concluded, the kind of solution to which "our Government could give its support." Neatly timed to coincide with the most sacred of Jewish holidays and to reap the greatest political benefits, the Yom Kippur statement was the first time the president had even approached advocacy of a new Israel. It came on the heels of a Gallup poll that showed Tom Dewey holding a commanding lead over his Democratic opponent in the New York gubernatorial race.[50]

[48] Stephen Wise to Truman, September 23, 1946, Box 68, Stephen Wise Papers, Brandeis University Library, Waltham, Mass.
[49] *FR*, 1946, VII, 682.
[50] Ibid., p. 703; *Time*, October 14, 1946, p. 23. Truman insisted that his

It was a political statement designed for domestic consumption and promising little hope of winning immigration relief for the refugees. In fact, Truman began to concentrate much of his attention on other ways to achieve immediate aid for displaced persons. On Yom Kippur he also addressed himself to major changes in U.S. immigration laws. Previously he had merely suggested giving the uprooted most of the slots within existing quotas. Now he favored significant increases in immigration outside the regular limits. No doubt he was partly moved by the argument that more admissions to the United States would help persuade Arabs to diminish their objections in Palestine, but Truman was also increasingly resigned to the conclusion that any hope for early resettlement of refugees had to depend on more than the Holy Land option. He would play Palestine policy largely for the sake of its domestic political value.[51]

October statement was merely a "reiteration of the policy I have been urging since August 1945 . . ." (Truman to Emanuel Celler, October 10, 1946, Box 23, Emanuel Celler Papers, Library of Congress, Washington, D.C.).

[51] Truman to Walter George, October 8, 1946, Box 68, Wise Papers; Robert Divine, *American Immigration Policy, 1924–1952*, p. 113.

CHAPTER SIX

OIL DIPLOMACY AND THE
PALESTINE QUESTION

Roosevelt and Truman may have lacked a strong commitment to the creation of a new Israel, but both presidents recognized the broad range of national interests in the Middle East. They regarded the Moslem world as a prime target for the expansion of U.S. influence. Both administrations sought major concessions from Arab rulers, especially around the Persian Gulf: oil charters, air rights, pipeline routes, trading opportunities, and establishment of communication facilities and military bases. It was the existence of such ambitions that partly prompted State Department leaders to oppose pro-Zionist policies and provided the diplomatic branch with its most potent argument against aid to the Jewish nationalists.

Interest in the Arab Middle East centered initially on the oil resources and transportation and communication routes through the area. Arabian petroleum had been growing in significance for several years, especially with the decline in U.S. reserves. As early as 1943, Harold Ickes, the petroleum administrator for war, wrote Roosevelt warning of a likely severe crude oil shortage before the end of the next year. In the months to come, Ickes shared his alarm with key cabinet members. Civilian and military leaders quickly developed an acute concern. Geological surveys and other technical data suggested that prospects were dim for finding replacements for dying wells in the Western Hemisphere or for developing synthetic fuels. War and Navy department chiefs feared that the country might not be able to fight future global battles on the scale of World War II. At least they had reason for serious concern and little inclination to be reckless. As Secretary of the Navy James Forrestal noted in late

1944, "in a matter of this kind, the Navy cannot [afford to] err on the side of optimism."[1]

Several U.S. firms had petroleum concessions in Arab countries. Socony Vacuum and Standard of New Jersey shared approximately 23.75 percent ownership of the Iraq Petroleum Company. They also had partial interest in Qatar and areas along the Trucial States coast. Gulf Oil Company and the Anglo-Persian Oil Company evenly divided control of drilling rights in Kuwait, while Standard of California and the Texas Company (Texaco) had exclusive privileges both in Saudi Arabia and on the island of Bahrain. Despite the leases, military leaders could never guarantee control of the fields in case of another war. But they did encourage increased use of the Arabian oil in order to reserve supplies in the Western Hemisphere for a future conflict.[2]

State Department planners were also concerned with securing pipeline routes, communication privileges, and air rights. In the first two years after the end of World War II, American spokesmen negotiated for such concessions from Lebanon, Syria, Transjordan, Saudi Arabia, Iraq, and Egypt.[3]

Yet for the Truman administration the Middle East was more than just one region of potential private profit. To key policy makers the area became the vital region in the protection of U.S. security. By 1946 military chiefs were preparing for a possible war with Moscow. If a fight with the Soviets came, Washington wanted to be in control of Arabian oil and the Suez Canal. Strategic planners envisioned disastrous consequences if the Soviets gained domination over either key asset. One typically pessimistic policy statement saw

[1] Memorandum for James F. Byrnes, August 25, 1946, Forrestal File, Record Group 80, National Archives, Washington, D.C. (hereafter cited as RG80, NA); Fred Searls to Byrnes, August 13, 1945, Folder 620; William D. Leahy to Roosevelt, June 8, 1943; Harold Ickes to Roosevelt, n.d. [ca. June, 1943], Folder 95(1), James F. Byrnes Papers, Clemson University Library, Clemson, S.C.; *FR*, 1943, IV, 756, 921–930; 1944, V, 756.

[2] *FR*, 1947, V, 551–556, 613–614, 627–667; memorandum for James F. Byrnes, August 1, 1945; memorandum for James Forrestal, n.d., Forrestal File, RG80, NA.

[3] *FR*, 1945, VIII, 52; 1946, VII, 29; 1947, V, 556–557, 761–814.

only doom in the wake of any Soviet advances. A "process of deterioration" would force the United States "back to the Atlantic," a "retreat to the Western Hemisphere" that would mean a "war of attrition . . . spell[ing] the end of the American way of life."[4]

U.S. leaders were determined to maintain a forward line in the Middle East. Every inch of territory between Soviet positions and the Persian Gulf became an essential buffer in some future war. Thus, as the Joint Chiefs of Staff explained, northern Iran had significance far beyond its own mineral resources. It offered "opportunities to conduct delaying operations . . . to protect United States controlled oil resources in Saudi Arabia." Long before Dwight Eisenhower enunciated his domino theory, strategic planners regarded every piece of the Middle East as equally significant and worried that unless they maintained friendly ties with each country in the area, the entire U.S. position there might crumble.[5]

While Washington fretted over relations with all of the Arab world, one country, Saudi Arabia, was paramount in the diplomatic and military planning, both because of the predicted size of its petroleum reserves and the U.S. monopoly on them, and because its monarch, Ibn Saud, led one of the two major factions in Middle East politics. A close look at U.S. policy toward that desert kingdom revealed much about the way the Palestine question and petroleum diplomacy interacted with each other in the minds of U.S. officials. Ibn Saud's attitudes on Zionism became a key ingredient in shaping State and War department positions. Within the Saudi-American relations lay much of the pattern for Washington's response to complaints against Jewish nationalism. By 1947 the considerable strategic concerns were having a heavy impact on Truman's Palestine policy. But, ironically, experience in oil diplomacy was prompting some minds to look with hesitant favor on the creation of a truncated Jewish state.

While U.S. petroleum concessions in the Near East were numer-

[4] *FR*, 1947, V, 512–523, 530, 561–563, 575–576, 577.
[5] Ibid., pp. 530, 579–580; John Hickerson to George C. Marshall, December 4, 1947, 711 90/12-447, RG59, NA.

ous, none was more important than the 1933 Saudi Arabian grant to Standard of California and the Texas Company. To develop the field, the two firms had created a jointly owned subsidiary (first called the California Arabian Standard Oil Company, or CASCO, and then renamed in 1944 the Arabian American Oil Company, or ARAMCO). When the war began in Europe in 1939, only token production existed. Yet some estimates placed the country's potential at 30 percent of the world's total supply.[6]

But interest in the desert country centered on more than its fuel resources; it was in the path of important air routes to India and the Far East. Army Air Corps commanders first expressed an interest in flying over Ibn Saud's country in February, 1942. Supplies moving east from Morocco to Karachi had to skirt enemy territory and follow a circuitous path to Khartoum, then north to Cairo, before making the final flight to India. If the planes could travel directly over Saudi Arabia, they could eliminate one sizable detour. In late August, Ibn Saud finally agreed to nonstop flights for both U.S. and British transport aircraft, carefully specifying a route that stayed clear of inhabited regions.[7]

After two years of flights across the desert sands to the Arabian Sea and beyond, the War Department began to tender more ambitious requests of the government in Riyadh, the king's capital. The United States had constructed an airfield on the island of Abadan on the coast of Iran but had reluctantly surrendered that facility to future British domination after the Anglo-Iranian Oil Company enlarged its concession in Iran and actually purchased the land on which the field was located. By late July, 1944, Americans wanted to

---

[6] By March, U.S. corporations controlled approximately 43.6 percent of the known reserves in the Middle East. Memorandum for James Forrestal, March 19, 1947, Forrestal File, RG80, NA; U.S., Congress, Senate, Special Committee Investigating Petroleum Reserves, *American Petroleum Interests in Foreign Countries, Hearings*, 79th Cong., 1st sess., 1945, pp. 23– 24, 31, 73, 341, 379–380.

[7] *FR*, 1942, IV, 567–575; Nils E. Lind, "A Summary of Views on United States Relations with Saudi Arabia," attached to G. L. Jones to Loy W. Henderson et al., May 15, 1946, 711.90F/5-1546.

replace the Abadan field with one at Dhahran, Saudi Arabia. Such an installation could further reduce the flying distance to Karachi, provide a much-needed fuel stop, and enable planes to carry more cargo. Also, it would be located in the heart of the major oil district.[8]

Washington officials had ambitious plans in Saudi Arabia. They sought nothing less than the further extension of an informal empire of ownership and trade abroad, coupled with the spread of military outposts. In their view the United States could secure all it wanted if it could avoid the restraints of traditional imperial arrangements, have the opportunity to bid for the favors of Ibn Saud, and thereby enjoy the blessings of an "Open Door." But because the U.S. plan depended on the initial Arab acceptance of U.S. economic activity in the area, policy makers were sensitive to anything that might alienate Moslem leaders. False moves in Palestine seemed most likely to damage the vital friendships and even produce reassignment of oil charters. Through the early forties Washington strategists worried about the rivalry of their chief wartime allies, Great Britain and the Soviet Union.[9]

Several State Department leaders, including Cordell Hull, Loy Henderson, Wallace Murray, and others, suspected at times that the British were deliberately stirring up anti-American sentiments among the Moslems in order to improve the British position. Although the Soviets had no troops in Arab countries, no negotiators, and no other signs of attempting to exclude Texaco and Standard from Arabian oil, most Washington thinkers simply assumed that Moscow was waiting for an American mistake in Palestine and an opportunity to push capitalist enterprises out of the Middle East.[10]

---

[8] *FR*, 1944, V, 661–670.

[9] A thorough reading of the published documents in the *Foreign Relations* series reveals a pattern of constant devotion to and faith in "equal access" and concern about British and Russian rivalry. See, for example, *FR*, 1943, IV, 943–947; 1944, V, 8–37; 1945, VII, 10–18. See also Roosevelt to James M. Landis, March 6, 1944, Box 119, James M. Landis Papers, Library of Congress, Washington, D.C.

[10] Memorandum to Cordell Hull, June 11, 1943, Folder 95(1), Byrnes Papers; *FR*, 1944, V, 585, 618, 627, 633, 656.

The "Russian threat" appeared to many American minds to be the best reason for the United States to block creation of a new Israel. "We may be sure," Averell Harriman concluded from his ambassador's chair in Moscow, "that the Soviets will use this issue [Palestine] to increase Soviet influence."[11] Wallace Murray, director of the Office of Near Eastern and African Affairs, pictured Soviets advancing, with Arab welcomes, through Iran, into Iraq, and on to the shores of the Persian Gulf, where they would be in striking distance of the oil fields of Kuwait, Bahrain, and Saudi Arabia. He became so worried about a pro-Zionist declaration in Congress that in late October, 1944, he began insisting that even in the midst of the presidential election campaign the matter required the immediate attention of the president.[12]

Yet for all the talk during the war about both British and Soviet competition in the Middle East, the United States was already in the process of eliminating one of its rivals through the time-honored method of amalgamation. Fears of British encroachments were gradually giving way to the building of an Anglo-American coalition to pursue Arab oil. While jealousies and resentments continued to fester just below the surface, and some minor officials refused to go along, basic policy moved relentlessly toward cooperation. By 1945, Washington had managed to eliminate most of its differences with London and to coopt the British into a series of agreements from which the United States could emerge in a dominant position.[13]

But eventual cooperation with the British did not signal any commitment to include the Soviet Union in the division of Arabian oil. In fact, it was the basic U.S. opposition to Soviet participation in the petroleum development that stimulated much of the alliance with the British. As one State Department subordinate wrote to another

[11] *FR*, 1944, V, 622–623, 646–648.
[12] Ibid., pp. 634–635.
[13] Memorandum of conversation, November 28, 1945, 711.90F/11-2845; Ted Achilles to John Hickerson, July 30, 1945, 711.90F/7-3045, RG59, NA; "Meeting of the Secretaries of State, War, and Navy," November 20, 1945, James V. Forrestal Diaries, Box 1, James V. Forrestal Papers, Princeton University Library, Princeton, N.J.; *FR*, 1947, V, 505, 524, 550–552, 604–605, 619.

in 1945, "We should take whatever action is necessary to protect our oil concession vs the British or any others. [But] if we fight one another, the Russians will find it easier to throw us both out."[14] Some officials, including Truman, did mention on occasion the possibility of including Moscow in the Middle East oil arrangement. They talked about U.S. and Soviet interests "dovetailing" in the area. But the language of cooperation eventually gave way to the ideology of antagonism to the communist power. In 1944 and 1945 policy makers increasingly referred to Britain as a partner and the Soviet Union as the enemy.[15]

To a large degree the continued rivalry with Moscow, rather than the cooperation achieved with Great Britain, stemmed from the growing inclination to moralize about Open Door principles, to regard them as more than strategies in the play for empires, and to think of them as righteousness institutionalized. Diplomatic chiefs, who began with the assumption that they must help remake the Arab world in the image of the United States because the transformation would make that area more susceptible to U.S. economic penetration, became convinced that they were also benefiting Moslem civilization. Washington officials could easily view their own economic quest as an ideological struggle for justice and peace. With their devotion to the Open Door and their assumption that the Soviets were unlikely to abide by the U.S. principles, conflict was inevitable.[16]

"We have been supporting," Loy Henderson explained to General Harry H. Vaughan, military aide to President Truman, "the policy of the open door in the Near East. . . ." That policy, he went on, was beneficial "to us in our commercial relations and in the end to world peace." Without even mentioning the Soviet Union, Henderson made it clear that he viewed the struggle for U.S. dominance in Asia Minor in ideological terms. As the "peoples of the Near East

[14] Jack D. Hickerson to Ted Achilles, n.d., 711.90F/7-3045, RG59, NA.
[15] *FR*, 1944, V, 8–40, 622–624, 646–648; 1945, VIII, 10–18, 49–63.
[16] William Eddy to James F. Byrnes, September 13, 1945, 711.90F/9-1345, RG59, NA; *FR*, 1946, VII, 1–6.

. . . move forward, politically, economically, and socially," he explained to Vaughan, "it is important that this movement should be in the direction of western democracies rather than in the direction of some form of autocracy or totalitarianism, which would render sympathetic understanding and cooperation between that part of the world and the United States more difficult." To protect its own position, Washington must take steps to acquaint Arabs with "our way of life."[17]

Later that same day, George Wadsworth, minister to Syria and Lebanon, told Truman himself that a U.S. failure in the Middle East was more than the loss of economic and military advantage. If the Moslems "turn to Russia . . . [they] will be lost to our civilization."[18] Earlier the State Department Coordinating Committee had noted that the "Middle East is and will remain one of the principal testing grounds of the ideals for which the war is being fought and of the world security system now being constituted." U.S. planners must recognize that "throughout most of this region the Western democratic, free enterprise system, represented in the main by the British, is now in competition with the authoritarian, closed economic system represented by Soviet Russia."[19] In the eyes of many oil diplomats, they were fighting for both economic well-being and world peace with justice. It is not surprising that they attached so much significance to maintaining friendships with the Arab countries.

Harry Truman and many Zionist commentators have charged that State Department antagonism to Jewish statehood stemmed from anti-Semitism within the diplomatic corps. Yet there was little, if any, evidence to support such a conclusion. Critics of the Near Eastern Office simply assumed that if Loy Henderson opposed a new Israel, he also opposed aid to downtrodden folks. Such an insensitive

[17] *FR*, 1945, V, 10–11.

[18] Ibid., p. 14. It was Wadsworth who also suggested at the same time (late 1945) that "there need be no conflict between us and Russia in [the Middle East]." By early 1946 Gordon Merriam better reflected the trend in State Department thinking when he wrote that Wadsworth's ideas were "dated." Soviet "policy and methods in the Middle East" made the Soviet participation unacceptable. *FR*, 1946, VII, 6.

[19] *FR*, 1945, VIII, 37.

attitude, defenders of Zionism concluded, could come only from religious prejudice. But the diplomats did not disregard the plight of uprooted people. They simply saw no reason to tie the refugee problem to the Holy Land controversy. In fact, the foreign-policy leaders urged Truman to support more U.S. settlements for the displaced Jews, hardly the position of bigoted officials. Some State Department people were even willing to advocate increased immigration to the Holy Land if Truman agreed to guarantee Arabs there would be no Zionist commonwealth.

Henderson and his associates probably did have some favoritism toward Arab claims in Palestine. But such attitudes hardly count as anti-Semitism (at best a strange term to use in picking sides between two Semitic peoples). The antagonism to Herzl's disciples came from an honest conviction that Zionists had no right to impose their government on unwilling Palestinians (there were, after all, Palestinian Jews who also opposed establishment of a new Israel). Indeed, even if the State Department wallowed in antagonism toward Jews, that feeling alone could not account for efforts against Zionism. As public polls indicated, many Americans harbored all of the old prejudices against Jews while favoring Jewish settlement and political ascendancy in Palestine.

If any one predisposition dominated State Department thinking, it was not anti-Semitism but a virile form of anti-Communism. The thought of Soviet advances terrified the diplomatic corps. Fear of the "spreading stain" with its threat to the Open Door overshadowed all other considerations.[20]

Both the Roosevelt and Truman administrations had at their disposal considerable economic power in the Middle East. In 1941 the United States slowly began a lavish campaign to win the favor of Ibn Saud. Oil company officials and government leaders agreed that

[20] Ibid., 1944, V, 598–599, 610–611, 614–615; 1945, VIII, 10–18, 734–736; Gordon Merriam to Wallace Murray, June 15, 1945, 867N.01/6-1545; James Moose to James F. Byrnes, August 28, 1945, 867N.01/8-2845; Loy Henderson to Byrnes, June 12, 1946, 867N.01/6-1146, RG59, NA; William Yale to Merriam, July 30, 1945, Palestine Folder, William Yale Papers, Harvard University Library, Cambridge, Mass.

the old monarch in Riyadh was the key to the future of U.S. involvement in Saudi Arabia. Anything that threatened the king held ill omens for oil charters and aviation grants. Essential aid could keep him in power and possibly guarantee access to the petroleum deposits and the airfields. A policy of befriending and even maintaining the Moslem ruler originated with Texaco and Standard, but it eventually became the responsibility of the Roosevelt and Truman administrations. Under a variety of guises both presidents did what seemed necessary to keep Ibn Saud on the throne and consolidate the U.S. position in the desert country.[21]

World War II created the first test for U.S. tactics. Europe's conflict eventually boiled over beyond the continent and touched the affairs of the Arab world. In the two years following Hitler's invasion of Poland, Saudi Arabia's chief source of foreign exchange, the anunal Moslem pilgrimages to Mecca, declined drastically. By 1941, Ibn Saud's government faced severe financial difficulties. The monetary crisis threatened to create a national economic depression and spark widespread bitterness against the head of state. Unrest might topple the monarch and, with him, the U.S. concession. To deal with the emergency, CASCO began making advanced payments on future oil, hoping the money could help the king avoid an overthrow.[22]

But while subsidies to Ibn Saud might have been good investments in posterity, they were also costly. With the development of the Lend-Lease program, however, CASCO officials saw a way to get U.S. taxpayers to assume financial responsibility. Texaco and Standard, the two parent companies, hired an agent to convince the administration to channel Lend-Lease supplies through the British to Riyadh. Roosevelt responded affirmatively to the overture and scribbled a note to Secretary of Commerce Jesse Jones: "Will you

21 Memorandum for James Forrestal, March 31, 1947; memorandum for James F. Byrnes, August 25, 1945, Forrestal File, RG80, NA; Loy Henderson to Dean Acheson, September 28, 1945, 711.90F/9-2845, RG59, NA.

22 Memorandum for James Forrestal, March 31, 1947; memorandum to Roosevelt, April 16, 1941; J. A. Moffatt to Roosevelt, April 16, 1941, Forrestal File, RG80, NA; "United States Policy Toward Saudi Arabia," August 25, 1945, 711 .90F/8-2545, RG59, NA.

tell the British I hope they can take care of the King of Saudi Arabia. This is a little far afield for us."[23]

Through 1942, London understood that part of its aid from Washington should go to Riyadh. By 1943, however, oil industry leaders began to fear that the British might receive all the benefits from the U.S. generosity. Accordingly, they sought to make Ibn Saud eligible for direct Lend-Lease assistance. Once again the president was responsive to their requests. In February, Roosevelt declared that "the defense of Saudi Arabia is vital to the defense of the United States," thereby fulfilling the single prerequisite for giving Lend-Lease materials to the Riyadh government.[24] In the years to come, the aid package included trucks, irrigation machinery, food, military equipment, and a multimillion-dollar program of treasury assistance. Under that program the United States agreed to provide the silver and minting for fifteen million riyals, the basic Saudi Arabian coin.[25]

Actually, even before the beginning of formal Lend-Lease arrangements with Riyadh, the Roosevelt administration was busy courting Saudi Arabia with other forms of assistance. In early 1942, as a primary part of the effort to win the original air routes over the Arab country, the State Department sent Riyadh a team of agricultural and engineering experts headed by Karl S. Twitchell, a mining and hydraulic engineer. The Twitchell mission spent seven months and traveled ten thousand miles, criss-crossing the desert to conduct experiments, take soil samples, and formulate advice on agricultural development. Improvements in food production were apparently high-priority items in the mind of Ibn Saud, and the United States was willing to cater to the king's emphasis. In 1944 the Foreign Economic Administration assumed responsibility for the land development project at Al-Kharj. Seven experts on dry farming from the Department of the Interior conducted an experimental program in

[23] Exhibit No. 13, Special Committee to Investigate Petroleum Resources, Forrestal File, RG80, NA; James M. Landis to Edmund Morgan, Box 31, Landis Papers; *FR*, 1941, III, 624–627.

[24] Memorandum for James F. Byrnes, August 1, 1945, Forrestal File, RG80, NA; Byrnes to Roosevelt, February 17, 1944, Folder 95(1), Byrnes Papers; *FR*, 1941, III, 643–645; 1943, IV, 854–860.

[25] *FR*, 1941, III, 632, 636–637; 1943, IV, 860–920; 1944, V, 670–760.

desert cultivation that eventually won the praise of the monarch. The whole program was a mere trickle in comparison to the capacity of the U.S. economy but a sizable largesse for the still primitive arid country.[26]

Beyond the association to channel early Lend-Lease aid to Riyadh, the first important Anglo-American alliance in dealing with Saudi Arabia was the decision in late 1943 to share equally in the shipping of military supplies to Ibn Saud. Under that agreement the United States and Great Britain began supplying rifles, Bren machine guns, and reconnaissance cars—at least enough to maintain "internal security" but not sufficient for any extensive national defense. In 1944 London and Washington developed a joint subsidy in other areas, dividing the responsibility for over two million dollars' worth of sugar, rice, cereals, and other foodstuffs.[27]

From 1943 to late 1944 the Roosevelt administration considered one additional tactic to protect the oil leases. When Harold Ickes wrote the president warning him about the dim future for U.S. petroleum reserves, he suggested that the government create a company for the purpose of buying control of CASCO. Backers of the plan argued that such official participation in the Arabian concession was the best way to insure permanent U.S. access to the oil deposits and justify Washington's efforts to protect a foreign mineral concession. In the summer of 1943, Jesse Jones and the Reconstruction Finance Corporation created the Petroleum Reserve Corporation (PRC) to execute Ickes's plan.[28]

Texaco and Standard executives certainly welcomed the prospects of government aid in courting Arab leaders and in financing

[26] Parker T. Hart to Gordon P. Merriam, May 13, 1946, 711.90F/5-1346; *FR*, 1943, IV, 844, 861, 863–864, 935; 1944, V, 675, 707, 709–710, 736–738; 1945, VIII, 878, 907–909; "Joint Communication to Saudi Government Concerning American-British Joint Supply Program for Saudi Arabia in 1944," attached to D. Short to William S. Culbertson, October 8, 1944, Box 25, William S. Culbertson Papers, Library of Congress, Washington, D.C.

[27] *FR*, 1943, IV, 1–2, 45, 844; 1944, V, 719–722; 1945, VIII, 999.

[28] James F. Byrnes to Roosevelt. January 17, 1944; "Proposal," January 17, 1944; Harold Ickes to Roosevelt, n.d.; memorandum to Henry L. Stimson, July 11, 1943; William D. Leahy to Roosevelt, June 8, 1943, Folder 95(1), Byrnes Papers; *FR*, 1943, IV, 921, 925–932.

new refineries in the Middle East, but they gave no support to the schemes for public ownership of the oil concessions. Both parent firms and the American Petroleum Institute unleashed a public campaign to discredit Secretary Ickes and the PRC. Despite initial support from Roosevelt, Ickes and his cohorts eventually lost the struggle to the delaying and diversionary tactics of the oil industry and its chief administration supporter on the issue, Cordell Hull. In a "compromise" that actually followed CASCO's script, the PRC and Ickes finally settled in 1944 for government ownership and financing of a proposed pipeline from the Arabian Peninsula to a Mediterranean port. When that plan died, the PRC's role in Middle East oil policy came to a virtual end. By the time Truman became president, U.S. diplomatic efforts in Saudi Arabia were permanently in behalf of private investments in the fuel reserves.[29]

In the last months of the war in Europe, U.S. planners began to consider the future of their policy in Saudi Arabia. War, Navy, and State department leaders carried on an extensive consultation within their own ranks and with each other before the new secretary of state, Edward Stettinius, sent the White House a set of recommendations in December, 1944. It called for forty-three million dollars in aid over a five-year period and an effort to secure an Export-Import Bank loan for the Riyadh government. Washington planned to supplement the Saudi Arabian budget, construct roads, train pilots, and build railroads. Diplomatic chiefs were so anxious to fund Ibn Saud that the U.S. minister in Jidda, William Eddy, even suggested that a loan be made indirectly through National City Bank if Congress was unwilling to give its blessings.[30]

By the beginning of the new year, State, War, and Navy department leaders were clearly assuming responsibility for formulating aid programs for Saudi Arabia and then seeking both White House

---

[29] James F. Byrnes to Roosevelt, January 25, 1944, Folder 71(1); A. F. Carter to Byrnes, January 27, 1944; F. A. Davis to Michael J. Deutch, November 3, 1943, Folder 95(1), Byrnes Papers; *FR*, 1941, III, 624–627, 629–632; 1943, IV, 935–937; 1944, V, 10–20.

[30] Memorandum for James F. Byrnes, August 25, 1945; memorandum for Byrnes, August 1, 1945, Forrestal File, RG80, NA; Henry L. Stimson to Cordell Hull, October 23, 1944, Box 22, Forrestal Papers; *FR*, 1944, V, 744–760.

and congressional support. In early 1945 the State-War-Navy Co-ordinating Committee (SWNCC) endorsed both immediate and post-war assistance to Riyadh. Lend-Lease provided the machinery through which the executive branch could easily supplement Ibn Saud's budget and encounter virtually no legislative resistance. No Congress was likely to vote against funds "vital to the defense of the United States." But peace would obviously deny use of the war program and the argument of immediate military necessity. In March, SWNCC leaders met with congressional spokesmen in the office of House Speaker Sam Rayburn and outlined the financial situation in Saudi Arabia. They secured a promise of help from the legislators. Two months later Dean Acheson carried the message to Senate Majority Leader Alben W. Barkley, Finance Committee Chairman Walter George, and Naval Affairs Chairman David Walsh.[31]

Roosevelt had indicated in January that he wanted the State Department to proceed with aid plans. In February the president had met with Ibn Saud at Great Bitter Lake. But when FDR died in April, the process of convincing the White House had to begin anew. Truman first learned about the details of the policy in a late May memorandum from Grew and in a subsequent meeting with Acheson and Under Secretary of the Navy Ralph Bard. It took no more than a map of Middle Eastern oil areas to convince the new chief executive to approve postwar aid to Ibn Saud and promise to help persuade House and Senate leaders to follow suit. Truman assigned Fred Vinson, director of the Office of War Mobilization and Reconversion, to the task of coordinating efforts on the matter. He also pledged to negate any opposition from Secretary Ickes. In the months to come, Vinson, State Department people, petroleum industry leaders, military chiefs, and legislators struggled with various formulas for an aid package.[32]

[31] Ralph K. Bard to James Forrestal, May 26, 1945, Forrestal File, RG80, NA.

[32] John L. Sullivan to James Forrestal, July 25, 1945; Carl McGowan to Mr. Sullivan, June 22, 1945, Forrestal File, RG80, NA; *FR*, 1945, VIII, 861–863, 900–902.

In July, Congress passed a Lend-Lease appropriation bill that provided five million dollars in assistance as part of a continuing joint effort with the British to aid Saudi Arabia. It also assigned three million dollars to a supplemental program of purely U.S. assistance and enough silver to mint another ten million riyals. Yet that generosity from the legislature did not indicate that the State Department had won its battle of influence in the Senate and the House. Lawmakers were still unwilling to provide anything more than wartime assistance. A comprehensive plan for long-range supplements to Riyadh simply lacked the necessary congressional backing. In May, Senator Barkley and his colleagues had warned Acheson that it would be difficult to secure postwar aid. They had expressed a hope that the assistance could be "done with as little legislation" as possible. In June the State Department had postponed indefinitely any requests for congressional approval for peacetime assistance to Ibn Saud.[33]

Hesitation to aid Saudi Arabia matched an equal reluctance to spend money for other governments. Lawmakers emerged from World War II facing a variety of requests from allies for financial help. Yet the legislators constantly displayed a stinginess with U.S. money and were slow to grant any loans or grants. The uncooperative attitude on Saudi Arabian relief was more reflective of this general reluctance to approve foreign aid than it was of any lack of interest in Arabian oil.[34]

Administration leaders had decided to concentrate on methods of aid that did not require direct congressional endorsement. (Actually, the War Department had already pioneered in the techniques of disguising assistance to the desert kingdom. In 1944 the army sent a military mission to Saudi Arabia and early the next year began using it as an intermediary for a road-building project.) Initially, in 1945, the White House and the State Department hoped to get as much life as possible out of the Lend-Lease program. Even when Japan surrendered in August, Truman continued war aid to Saudi Arabia

---

[33] *FR*, 1945, VIII, 896.
[34] For more on this point, see George C. Herring, *Aid to Russia, 1941–1946*.

while terminating it in most areas of the world. Through the fall and into the winter several million dollars in military equipment passed to Arabian hands—first guns, armored cars, and trucks and then ammunition and maintenance tools. As late as January, 1946, Truman was still giving his approval to "completion" of the Lend-Lease support for Ibn Saud's government. The "chief consideration," Minister in Residence Eddy explained, "is [the] political importance of fulfilling promises to Arab Govt at this . . . time." [35]

Yet the days of Lend-Lease were obviously numbered. If the Truman administration expected to continue its subsidy to Riyadh without congressional approval, it needed a new device. Throughout the summer of 1945 the State Department considered two alternatives. Under one plan, ARAMCO would sell petroleum to the U.S. Army and Navy. ARAMCO would then produce, transport, and refine the oil for the American military at cost. A second scheme called for an Export-Import Bank loan to the Saudi Arabians. In return, ARAMCO was supposed to maintain a "substantial reserve of oil in the ground" for the future use of U.S. armed forces. [36]

By October the architects of policy had decided to pursue the second alternative, but without any specific arrangements for the military purchase of oil from ARAMCO. In early January, 1946, the board of directors of the Export-Import Bank approved twenty-five million dollars' credit for Saudi Arabia. That loan carried with it strong controls over Ibn Saud's national budget, a stipulation the monarch found unacceptable. After several months of negotiations, the bank and the king finally agreed to ten million dollars' credit, secured with future oil royalties from ARAMCO, for the purpose of buying from the United States a host of needed products: cereals, grains, sugar, textiles, agricultural tools and machinery, automotive equipment, and office supplies. Throughout much of the next year Ibn Saud sought a second loan from the United States for public works projects, including railroad building, but ARAMCO, rather

[35] *FR*, 1945, VIII, 954.
[36] John L. Sullivan to James Forrestal, July 25, 1945; Carl McGowan to R. Bard, May 31, 1945, Forrestal File, RG80, NA; R. Keith Kane to Forrestal, March 16, 1945, Box 22, Forrestal Papers.

than the government, finally provided five million dollars for transportation development.[37]

For their aid to Saudi Arabia the Roosevelt and Truman administrations expected and secured some specific returns. In May, 1945, the Arab king agreed to the construction of an airfield at Dhahran and to U.S. military and commercial use of the facility for three years after the end of the war, but he insisted that the base become Saudi Arabian property at the close of hostilities. By 1946 the United States controlled the budget of the Riyadh government, set national priorities, decided what kind of transportation system the country should have, and determined the capacity of its military (enough strength to put down internal revolt, but little ability to engage in war with its neighbors, either defensively or offensively). Despite occasional complaints over construction procedures, the king allowed completion of the Dhahran airfield.[38]

Yet even with the aid to Ibn Saud's government, many strategists remained unsure that Saudi Arabia was securely in the U.S. fold, especially in light of the continuing agitation over Palestine. The immediate evidence was inconclusive. Any signs of U.S. friendship for a new Israel usually sparked a heavy assault from Riyadh. Soon after publication of the AACOI report in May, 1946, one source reported to the State Department that "Ibn Saud has sent some of his best lawyers to Paris to get in touch with the French and the *Russians*."[39] ARAMCO officials told representatives of the United States that they were worried lest Truman continued to endorse the sending of one hundred thousand Jews to Palestine.[40]

But on at least two occasions Ibn Saud led Washington to believe that the Holy Land question actually meant little to him personally. In July, 1946, the king told Minister J. Rives Childs that his "greatest regret," so the envoy reported, "was that the President had not con-

[37] *FR*, 1945, VIII, 954, 960, 999; 1946, VII, 739–750.

[38] *FR*, 1945, VIII, 841, 868–869, 890–894; 1946, VII, 739–742, 747–750; 1947, V, 1329–1335.

[39] William Sands to Byrnes, June 20, 1946, 867N.01/6-246 [italics in original], RG59, NA.

[40] Hart to James F. Byrnes, June 17, 1946, 867N.01/6-1746; Cecil B. Lyon to Byrnes, July 1, 1946, 867N.01/7-146, RG59, NA.

sulted him concerning the proposal for 100,000 Jewish immigrants *in advance* of American commitment."[41] Three months later, while General Benjamin F. Giles was in Saudi Arabia to negotiate Trans World Airlines operations of air service in the country, the monarch told him that "neither Aramco, TWA, or any other American company had anything to fear from Saudi Arabia." The charge d'affaires reported that the ruler said, "I am talking big because everyone else is and it seems to be the most effective course, but in the end Palestine will not affect my relations with the Americans."[42]

Ibn Saud did in fact continue to "talk big" on occasion. But there was an unmistakable drift in the king's concerns away from Palestine and toward other matters. Despite U.S. worries about the possibility of friendship between Moscow and Riyadh, the old monarch, like ruling elites elsewhere, feared Soviet influence and the spread of Marxist ideology with its implicit challenge to his autocratic rule. More than once he shared with U.S. representatives his antagonism to "communist propaganda."[43]

He worried also about rivals in the Arab world, principally the Hashemite family. In his rise to power earlier in the century, Ibn Saud had consolidated his own kingdom on the Arabian peninsula at the expense of the Hashemites, who had been rulers of the Hejaz and sherifs of Mecca and Medina. Now his old enemies, still in power in Syria and Jordan, were seeking to establish a Greater Syria that might include Iraq, Transjordan, and all or part of Palestine, forming a considerable base from which to menace Saudi Arabia. In early 1947, when Crown Prince Saud arrived in Washington for an official visit, he shared his father's concern with the White House and the State Department.[44]

Opposition to a Greater Syria and the general struggle with the

[41] J. Rives Childs to James F. Byrnes, July 6, 1946, 867N.01/7-646 [italics added], RG59, NA.

[42] Merritt M. Grant to James F. Byrnes, September 30, 1946, 711.90F/9-3046, RG59, NA.

[43] See, for example, J. Rives Childs to James F. Byrnes, June 17, 1947, 711.90F/6-1747, RG59, NA.

[44] Memorandum of Truman's conversation with Faisal, December 13, 1946, 867N.01/12-1345, RG59, NA; *FR*, 1947, V, 739–740, 1336–1337.

Hashemites were actually major elements in Ibn Saud's anti-Zionist rhetoric. As ruler over the holy cities of the Moslem world, he had enormous prestige. But it was a prestige with obligations. He had to champion Arab causes. In late 1947 the king explained to Minister Childs: "I occupy a position of preeminence in the Arab world. In the case of Palestine I have to make common cause with other Arab states. Although [they] . . . may bring pressure to bear on me I do not anticipate that a situation will arise whereby I shall be drawn into conflict with friendly western powers over this question."[45]

But Ibn Saud had also made common cause with the United States. By 1947 he depended upon both U.S. private capital and governmental grants to sustain his regime and develop his oil fields. The British, who had once held an honored place in his court, were now among the feared as probable allies and agitators of the Hashemites. The king even told Americans that he worried about an "open door" that might give British, French, and other oil interests access to development of Arabian petroleum. He relied most on ARAMCO, perhaps because it had the resources of some governments without the apparent political ambitions.[46]

Obviously, Washington's Palestine policy remained something of an embarrassment to Ibn Saud. He felt some continuing necessity to pose as the defender of "Arab rights," but he wanted no conflict with the United States over the creation of a new Israel. Several times he suggested ARAMCO might ameliorate part of the difficulty by changing national registry to Canadian or some other affiliation, a course petroleum industry executives threatened to follow if Washington continued on the road to Zion.[47]

If ARAMCO became a Canadian firm, it might save Ibn Saud some embarrassment in his dealings with the oil company, but it certainly would not eliminate all of the problems connected with reactions to the rise of Jewish nationalism. For one reason, anti-Zionism

---

[45] *FR*, 1947, V, 1336.

[46] Ibid., 1946, VII, 740–741; 1947, V, 634–635.

[47] Memorandum of conversation, November 4, 1946, 867N.01/11-446; Parker T. Hart to James F. Byrnes, June 17, 1946, 867N.01/6-1746, RG59, NA; *FR*, 1947, V, 665–668, 1329–1342.

elsewhere in the Middle East appeared to be more deeply en-
trenched. In Syria and Iraq, opposition to a new Israel edged toward
blind fanaticism. Prime ministers and parliaments in those countries
could ill afford to trifle with public emotions on the issue. The prospect that Washington's policy might generally alienate much of the
Arab Near East was, in itself, enough to cause consternation among
certain strategists, some of whom talked with horror about the possibility that "under Russian leadership the dark skinned Eastern world
would . . . meet the Western world . . . with aggressive strength in
the days to come."[48] Both Secretary of the Navy James Forrestal and
Under Secretary of State Robert Lovett displayed a concern that
the General Assembly might experience a "lash-up between the Asi-
atic peoples and those of the Middle East on a color-versus-white
basis."[49]

But there were even more specific reasons for immediate concern. By the fall of 1946, Gordon Merriam, chief of the Division of
Near Eastern Affairs, had developed an elaborate scenario of heavy
losses from any policy that embraced Zionist goals. U.S. support for
the creation of a Jewish state, he wrote to Loy Henderson, could
cause a "serious break with the British [because they would find
the United States so unreliable]. . . . A serious break with the Arabs
. . . the Near East to turn increasingly toward the USSR. . . . [and]
risk of losing a part of the world which we are endeavoring to preserve for western influence by a strong attitude in Greece, Turkey,
and Iran. There is no use in strengthening the arch if we are going
to kick out the pillars."[50]

ARAMCO officials were certainly not satisfied. During much of
1947 they were in the process of trying to secure an additional concession from Arab countries. A sister company, Tapline Corporation,
with the same two parent firms, hoped to build a thirty-inch oil pipe-

---

[48] Myron C. Taylor to Truman, May 15, 1946, Official File 204 (Misc.),
Harry S Truman Papers, Harry S Truman Presidential Library, Independence,
Mo.

[49] Forrestal, *Forrestal Diaries*, pp. 306–307.

[50] Merriam to Henderson, October 15, 1946, Misc. Historical Documents Relating to Truman, Truman Papers.

line from Saudi Arabia to a Mediterranean terminal. The project required not only Ibn Saud's approval, but also the consent of the other countries through which it would pass. After successful completion of negotiations with Riyadh in July, Tapline officials faced considerable difficulty with Syria. Even government approval did not insure completion of the project. In late 1947 violence born of resentments over Zionism forced suspension of the pipeline construction.[51]

Yet U.S. dollar diplomacy had certainly managed to appease the objections of Ibn Saud. In late 1946 and early 1947 there was some renewed hope in policy-making circles that other corners of anti-Israel sentiment were equally prone to acquiesce. If Riyadh was less than sincere about its anti-Zionism, perhaps opposition elsewhere to partition might be equally insincere. In November, 1946, Dean Acheson summarized for the British the department's assessment of probable Arab attitudes toward partition. He concluded that only Syria was likely to furnish "bitter and determined opposition." In the case of Saudi Arabia, "If the situation is skillfully handled," he wrote, "we hope that there will be no actual break. . . , because they have so much to hope for both economically and otherwise from good relations with us."[52]

By late 1946 most diplomatic thinking began to view matters in a new light. An imposed settlement could produce Arab resentments. But continuing conflict over the issue invited unknown trouble. It might be better, State Department wisdom was slowly concluding, to settle the dispute then, even if by partition, and weather the inevitable storm than to endure more years of turmoil and uncertainty. Department officials hoped the crisis from Moslem protests would be brief.

Oil diplomacy had a curious impact on the course of U.S. policy toward Palestine. It provided the major stimulus for anti-Zionist positions. But in some sense that may have been an unfortunate circumstance for Palestinians seeking to maintain their own homeland.

[51] *FR*, 1944, V, 8–9; 1947, V, 668, 1335–1340.
[52] Memorandum of conversation, November 23, 1946, 867N.01/11-2346, RG59, NA.

As long as the objections to Jewish nationalism focused on the whims of Ibn Saud, there was likely to be little discussion of the legitimate fears and misgivings of the residents of Judea, few prospects that many would notice the Arab willingness to accept some refugees, and no chance for non-Zionist Jewish leaders in Palestine, like Dr. Jules Magnes, to make much impact on public opinion in the United States. In many minds the struggle over promised land was a contest between the downtrodden survivors of the Holocaust and the ambitions of rich oil potentates. Palestinians became forgotten folks in the process.

CHAPTER SEVEN

PARTITION

In the small hours of the morning of July 12, 1947, two young British intelligence sergeants, Clifford Martin, 21, and Mervyn Paice, 20, emerged from a café in Nathanya, Palestine. As they walked down the dark main street, Irgun Zvai Leumi gunmen took them captive. Within a few hours British authorities were searching for the kidnapped pair, and the town was under martial law. But extensive investigation revealed nothing. Nearly three weeks passed without any word from the victims or their Zionist captors. Then at 2:00 A.M. on July 31, patrolling soldiers found the bodies of Martin and Paice hanging in a woods some distance from Nathanya. After an initial check with mine detectors revealed nothing, a British captain advanced cautiously to lift one of the dead men from the gallows. A bomb inside the body exploded, destroying the corpse and wounding the captain slightly in the face.[1]

To many people the Nathanya incident was part of a pattern of violence that was slowly shaping both U.S. and British policy in Palestine. Zionist terror was sparking an increasing number of Arab reprisals as both sides escalated their way through a year of bloodshed and bombings. By late summer, Jews were killing Jews as Haganah and Irgun forces clashed. Jewish Agency leaders initially denounced the Nathanya murders and vowed to help Mandate authorities curb the killings, but they retracted their commitment after the British arrested several prominent Jews in Jerusalem. Jewish ter-

---

[1] Memorandum, August 3, 1947, attached Robert Macatee to P. Meriour, August 4, 1947, 867N.01/8-447, RG59, NA; *Time*, August 11, 1947, p. 34.

ror squads blasted Arab businesses and bombed the Cairo-to-Haifa railroad. Eight days of fighting in August left thirty-two dead. In October, Moslem ambushers killed two Jews in Kfar Sirkin. Four days later, Haganah gunmen retaliated against two Arabs. That same month, anti-Zionist extremists in Jerusalem began the systematic bombing of consulates of those nations deemed too friendly with Herzl's disciples. In England, neo-Fascist leader Sir Oswald Mosley used the fate of "unfortunate British lads in Palestine" to incite a wave of British anti-Semitism.[2]

Twelve hours before the Nathanya abductions, another drama had begun to unfold with equal significance for the Palestine question. In the afternoon of July 11 an old Chesapeake Bay ferryboat, the *President Warfield*, now renamed the *Exodus 1947*, slipped out of Sète, France, on the Mediterranean coast. It flew a Honduran flag, and each of its 4,554 refugee passengers carried a visa to Colombia. Eleven days later the crowded steamer arrived at its intended destination: Haifa, Palestine. Actually, it was not the only such ship leaving European ports for the Holy Land in 1947. The former excursion boat was part of a fleet of vessels carrying the uprooted to Judea, hoping to embarrass British authorities and create the impression "in the world that all Hebrews are on the move." Faced with a growing number of immigrants pushing into the waters off Palestine, British authorities had been interning them on the island of Cyprus. Crowded together in the detention centers, thousands of pitiful Holocaust survivors had become shocking but eloquent testimony to the need for refugee resettlement somewhere. *Exodus* sponsors, most of them private American contributors, hoped to tax British capacity to block infiltration and dramatize the closed door in the Promised Land.[3]

British naval vessels had little difficulty intercepting the creaky,

---

[2] *FR*, 1947, V, 1388; *Time*, July 14, 1947, p. 26; August 18, 1947, pp. 31–32.

[3] "Memorandum on the Project of the Exodus to the Members of the Hebrew Committee of National Liberation," April 7, 1947, Series I, Box 2, Palestine Statehood Papers, Sterling Memorial Library, Yale University, New Haven, Conn.

overloaded ferry as it entered Palestinian waters on July 18. At first the captain refused to allow a landing party from two British destroyers to come aboard. But the patrolling ships rammed the refugee boat, squeezing it between their bows. British Tommies stormed onto the captured ship amidst a barrage of corned beef and potato tins. Within twenty-four hours Mandate authorities had unloaded the human cargo in Haifa, placed the refugees on three British boats, and shipped them back to France.[4]

In the weeks that followed, the ill-fated former *Exodus* passengers became an international sensation. When they arrived at Port-de-Bouc, France, they refused to debark, and the Paris government would not force them to do so. Some threatened suicide. In frustration, British officials issued an ultimatum: the Jewish refugees must either go ashore in France by 6:00 P.M., August 22, or face forceful debarkation in the British zone of Germany. When the deadline came, only a few passengers responded. The rest stayed on in hopes of arousing world opinion. By the time the tattered band of humanity arrived in Hamburg in September, their cause had attracted important support. Thousands of letters flooded the U.S. government. In England the *Manchester Guardian* called London's handling of the affair "unpremeditated folly."[5]

Exodus 1947 and the Nathanya incident became symbolic of the extent to which Jewish nationalists and other advocates of refugee relief were willing to go to achieve their goals. One group, the American League for a Free Palestine, now seized much of the initiative from older organizations and pursued a bold program. Ostensibly Zionist in its sentiment, the league capitalized on resentment against British rule in Judea, humanitarian sympathies for the uprooted, and sufficient public confusion about its own position to put together a broad coalition of views. It talked of "Palestinian independence," implying support for a nonsectarian state, but it also advocated "Hebrew nationalism." Most important, it provided decisive action in behalf of both displaced persons and Jewish ascendancy in the Prom-

[4] *FR*, 1947, V, 1139; *Newsweek*, September 1, 1947, pp. 31–32.
[5] *Time*, September 1, 1947, p. 18.

ised Land. The league had contacts with the Zionist underground in Palestine. It had raised nearly one million dollars and had organized a clandestine campaign to carry displaced persons to the Holy Land.[6]

To many league supporters, chances for refugee settlement anywhere except Palestine faded every month. Truman still took few steps in behalf of changes in U.S. immigration laws. Anti-Semitism in the United States appeared to be so virulent that some administration advisers hesitated to use the Jewish situation in Europe in appeals to Congress for quota increases. The White House seemed more intent on playing politics with posts in the Immigration Service than on any real efforts to find U.S. homes for the uprooted. From Germany, meanwhile, came word that "we are in the most critical condition in preventing wholesale famine" in the U.S. and British zones. Available rations are producing "slow famine," Secretary Patterson reported: "Occupation has no chance of success if these conditions continued."[7]

It was increasingly apparent that troubles over Palestine would not go away voluntarily. Pressures for admitting more Jewish refugees were becoming immense. Resistance to Zionism was just as dedicated. Violence in the Holy Land threatened to spark a major war that could easily mushroom into a regional conflict between Jews and Arabs and, in the process, seriously damage imperial well-being. From the State Department's perspective, instability was a formidable enemy to U.S. interests in the Middle East.[8]

In the course of 1947 the foreign-policy chiefs moved toward

[6] Guy M. Gillette to Arthur H. Sulzberger, n.d. [ca. August, 1945]; memorandum on conference with Earl Harrison, August 21, 1945, Series I. Box 1; Peter Bergson to the Paris Office of the Hebrew Committee of National Liberation, December 3, 1947; confidential newsletter, May 23, 1946; Y. Ben-Ami to J. Barough et al., May 19, 1947, Series I, Box 2; memorandum of Gillette to Anglo-American Committee of Inquiry, January 3, 1946, Series I, Box 6, Palestine Statehood Papers.

[7] James F. Byrnes to John G. Winant, January 14, 1947, 867N.01/1-1347, RG59, NA; Robert Patterson to George C. Marshall, June 13, 1947, Secretary of the Army (Patterson), General Decimal File, 1946–1947, Jews, RG107, NA.

[8] See, for example, J. Rives Childs to Gordon Merriam, H. S. Villard, and Loy Henderson, June 3, 1946, 867N.01/6-346, RG59, NA.

finding a compromise solution. Settlement now seemed essential. Yet resolution of the dispute appeared unlikely unless imposed from the outside. By October the United States had decided to support the creation of a small Jewish state in Palestine. But that decision was only indirectly a result of the rising tide of Zionist pressure. It grew primarily from the hopeful expectation that partition might be able to win a measure of acceptance from both sides in the Holy Land conflict and quiet the storm in the Middle East. It came in part because diplomatic chiefs thought they saw an opportunity to have the United Nations impose the solution, thereby shielding the United States from any responsibility or resentment. Thus, Washington's commitment to division of the land emerged from hesitancy and indecision and only after months of frustrating failure to find any other solution.

Attlee's London Conference on Palestine in August and September, 1946, paid few positive dividends. Both the Jewish Agency and the Arab Higher Committee refused to attend the meetings. The Arab League sent representatives but would not abandon its opposition to additional Jewish immigration into the Holy Land. In frustration the British decided in October to adjourn the sessions until after the twenty-second Zionist Congress, which was scheduled for December. By January, 1947, the Palestinian Arabs had consented to participate in the second phase of meetings, but Zionists still refused to engage in any formal conversations with their competitors for the Promised Land. Foreign Minister Bevin could do little more than shuttle exchanges between the Arabs and the Jews. No real progress was forthcoming.[9]

Both sides were unyielding. Arabs insisted that their September proposals for immediate independence, full protection of civil rights for the Yishuv, and an end to refugee admissions become the basis for any settlement. Zionists initially refused to make any proposals but claimed they would consider a partition scheme if someone else suggested one. In late February, Bevin told David Ben-Gurion and Nahum Goldmann that he could probably secure Arab consent for

[9] *FR*, 1947, V, 1000–1002, 1008–1011, 1024–1026.

the admission of one hundred thousand refugees and a large measure of local autonomy for Jewish areas of Palestine. In return there had to be no threat of an unlimited Jewish immigration that might eventually produce a Zionist state. Both Goldmann and Ben-Gurion rejected the opportunity for emergency settlements and refused to consent to any scheme that might give Arabs "veto" power over steps leading to the creation of a new Israel.[10]

By early February Bevin was growing weary of the lack of progress toward a settlement. He wrote Byrnes that he was seriously thinking of turning the whole matter over to the United Nations without any recommendations, a course the United States opposed. He intended to make only one more attempt to find a solution. Great Britain was proposing to move toward complete independence for Palestine within five years. In the period of transition the British would guide the disputed territory toward a large measure of local autonomy. Thereafter, international arbitration would determine immigration policy. At the end of four years, Palestinians would determine in a plebiscite what kind of government they intended to have. Neither side accepted the British solution. Arabs wanted immediate independence. The Jewish Agency wanted the British to stay in Palestine but to create the conditions conducive to Zionism's success.[11]

In Washington, meanwhile, the State Department kept a watchful eye on developments but took no action. When George Marshall became secretary of state in January, 1947, he deliberately avoided involvement in the London Conference, telling reporters he had to be "very careful" in making any comments about the "delicate negotiations." A week later Dean Acheson and Loy Henderson did assume a momentary initiative after the British, Zionists, and Arabs appeared to reach an impasse. While Truman and Marshall were away

10 W. J. Gallman to George C. Marshall, March 8, 1947, Palestine Papers, McClintock Files, RG59, NA; *FR*, 1947, V, 1058.
11 *FR*, 1947, V, 1033–1037, 1044–1048; H. S. Villard to George C. Marshlal, February 18, 1947, 867N.01/2-1847; Marshall to Ernest Bevin, February 17, 1947, 867N.01/2-1747, RG59, NA.

from Washington, the under secretary and the Near East Office director decided to urge the British to admit three thousand refugees each month (twice the planned rate) while work continued toward a permanent political arrangement. But neither Acheson nor Henderson made any public gestures. They quietly dropped their immigration request after London rejected it.[12]

Through most of the winter Truman had had little to do with Palestine matters. In November the White House had announced that Secretary Byrnes was assuming direct responsibility for the problem. The president did address two letters to Ibn Saud, one in late October and the other on January 24, 1947. Both communications, products of the State Department, were conciliatory in tone but made no apologies for supporting the one-hundred-thousand program. The president failed, however, to take the initiative on the London Conference.[13]

By late February, Jews and Arabs were packing their bags, preparing to leave London. The conference was over. Two years of negotiations and commissions had failed to produce a settlement. Events in the Holy Land grew progressively more complex. Acheson wrote, "1947 is going to be a bad year in Palestine and the Middle East, with increasing violence and grave danger to our interests in that area."[14]

There had always been one major alternative to any Anglo-American settlement of the Palestine controversy. The United States and Britain could assign the matter to the United Nations. The prospects of seeking arbitration in the new world organization had actually first occurred to State Department planners in 1945. In the first months after the end of the World War, Loy Henderson had repeatedly voiced some hope that at least the major powers could reach agreement on the Holy Land question. When Truman first called for enlarged immigration quotas into the Holy Land, he ar-

[12] *FR*, 1947, V, 1032, 1042, 1049–1052.
[13] Ibid., pp. 1011–1014.
[14] Ibid., pp. 1048–1055.

gued that the final political settlement in Palestine should come from the United Nations.[15]

British officials had often voiced similar positions. In Attlee's initial response to the Harrison report in 1945 the prime minister had told Truman that he planned to submit proposals to the world organization as soon as possible. In the original invitation to create the AACOI the British suggested to Washington that the inquiry could prepare recommendations for the United Nations. London's operation of a mandate was, of course, first under the auspices of the League of Nations and then under United Nations authority. As early as October, 1945, Foreign Minister Bevin told his U.S. counterpart that he favored establishment of a trusteeship in Palestine.[16]

Yet Washington's and London's initial enthusiasm for United Nations involvement in a Palestine accord began to cool rapidly in late 1945 and early 1946. In December, William Cargo of the Division of Dependent Areas Affairs suggested that the United States should neither oppose nor encourage General Assembly discussion of the controversy. By May, Secretary Byrnes spoke with some concern when he told Truman that unless the United States aided in implementing the Anglo-American report, "some other state may refer the matter to the Security Council at any moment." In July, Attlee echoed the secretary's concern. Obviously, both the United States and Great Britain were now far more reluctant to see United Nations action than they had been a year before.[17]

But the following year of frustrating inabiilty to find a solution, the growing violence in Palestine, and U.S. refusal to assume any military responsibility in the dispute took their toll on British resistance to United Nations involvement. Truman's rejection of the Grady plan, coupled with continued Zionist demands for control of Judea, virtually insured that London would eventually turn to the world organization. But when Attlee announced in February, 1947, his intention to do so, State Department leaders were unprepared to

[15] Harry Truman, *Memoirs: Years of Trial and Hope, 1946–1952*, p. 140; *FR*, 1945, VIII, 709, 717–719, 741, 748, 759, 776–781, 797.

[16] *FR*, 1945, VIII, 741, 774, 779–781.

[17] Ibid., 1946, VII, 600, 602, 612–623, 643, 711.

react. Dean Acheson was acutely aware that the United States really had no firm proposals to make. He worried that unless the administration crystalized its own position, the "Russians will take the ball and start off with an immense propaganda advantage" or, equally regrettable, "Congress will undertake the [lead] . . . with rather disastrous results." [18]

Architects of U.S. policy were not even sure they wanted United Nations consideration of Palestine. To the men who viewed political change and instability with considerable alarm, the world organization was too unpredictable, capable of unthinkable solutions, and certainly not an automatic ally of Anglo-American interests. Despite past differences with London, State Department policy makers still felt more comfortable with the Holy Land in the hands of their trans-Atlantic partners than they did at the mercy of the General Assembly or the Security Council. Accordingly, Washington urged the Attlee government to offer the United Nations some guidelines for its review of the dispute. [19]

In March the administration began assuming the British role in the Greek Civil War, aiding the royalist government and believing that the rebels were, in part, agents of Moscow. As Truman prepared to intervene unilaterally in the internal affairs of another country, diplomatic chiefs sought to avoid a United Nations investigation. A special session to consider Palestine might easily expand its agenda, Robert McClintock of the Special Political Affairs Office told a State Department colleague, "to include other, and possibly to us, embarrassing items." [20] It would be best, he told reporters confidentially, to avoid any unscheduled General Assembly meetings while "the Greek-Turkish matter was still hot." Even Security Council review of the Zionist-Arab dispute was fraught with pitfalls. "There is no telling," McClintock concluded, "what variety of forms it might as-

[18] Ibid., 1947, V, 1049; Acheson to George C. Marshall, January 22, 1947, 867N.01/1-2247, RG59, NA.
[19] George C. Marshall to Ernest Bevin, February 17, 1947, 867N.01/2-1747, Palestine Papers, McCormick Files, RG59, NA; *FR*, 1947, V, 1036, 1048, 1052–1059.
[20] McClintock to Dean Rusk, March 19, 1947, Palestine Papers, McClintock Files, RG59, NA.

sume." Through most of March the U.S. diplomats managed to avoid any action, rejecting Secretary General Trygve Lie's suggestion that he appoint a special committee to investigate the situation but failing to advance their own alternative.[21]

Yet the misgivings over United Nations involvement gradually gave way to the notion that the world organization might be able to serve a purpose for the United States. Before March ended, U.S. representatives were urging Great Britain to ask for a special meeting of the General Assembly for the purpose of creating an ad hoc committee to investigate Palestine and formulate recommendations for the regular September session.[22]

In part it was a course born of necessity. London clearly intended to assign Palestine to the world organization. Washington had to make the best of the situation. At the same time, it apparently began to occur to some State Department chiefs that the United Nations might be able to accomplish what the United States could little afford to do. It could possibly impose a solution. If the General Assembly assumed responsibility for a settlement and thereby diluted and deflected Moslem resentments away from the United States, it might even be feasible to allow the creation of an abbreviated Jewish state.[23]

Foreign-policy leaders in Washington now fought to insure that the special session confined itself to the creation of an *ad hoc* committee to investigate the Palestine dispute and make recommendations to the regular fall meeting of the General Assembly. In early April the State Department contacted the foreign offices of fifty-two nations and lobbied for a limited agenda. When the session opened on April 28, advanced preparation paid handsome rewards. Every attempt to expand the area of consideration, including an Arab bloc effort to debate immediate termination of the Mandate, fell to the U.S. opposition. Much as the Truman administration prescribed, the

[21] Robert McClintock to Dean Rusk et al., March 28, 1947; McClintock to Rusk, March 12, 1947, Palestine Papers, McClintock Files, RG59, NA.
[22] *FR*, 1947, V, 1020, 1060, 1062, 1063, 1067.
[23] Ibid., pp. 1063–1068, 1086–1088, 1199–1200.

assembled delegates created the United Nations Special Committee on Palestine (UNSCOP), with eleven "neutral" nations as members: Guatemala, Czechoslovakia, India, Iran, Netherlands, Peru, Sweden, Uruguay, Yugoslavia, Australia, and Canada.[24]

Creation of UNSCOP helped place the Palestine matter in a temporary limbo but did not permanently relieve the United States of all responsibilities in the dispute. Immediately the administration faced a decision about the degree of its own participation in the work of the special committee. While the State Department momentarily considered offering advice, Secretary of State Marshall thought otherwise. In June he announced to his colleagues that the best policy was no policy; the United States must avoid association with any particular solution. Final settlement should emerge as a United Nations scheme, not as an "American plan."[25]

Through the summer UNSCOP ploughed through the ground so often turned in international investigations. Despite a boycott from the Arab Higher Committee, the group spent much of June and July listening to testimony in Jerusalem. In August a subcommittee visited refugee camps in Europe. Some of the delegates were on the docks at Haifa when *Exodus 1947* arrived. Late in the month they filed their report. But there was no single set of conclusions. The members unanimously agreed to several items, including early termination of the Mandate, protection of holy places, maintenance of economic unity in Palestine, and the inability of the Holy Land to solve all of the refugee problem. Most of the controversial points, however, appeared in two separate judgments, reports of a majority and a minority.[26]

Seven of the eleven committee members endorsed the partition of Palestine into an Arab state, a Jewish state, and an international city of Jerusalem. At the same time, they called for economic union among all the areas. The plan left Great Britain in control of the entire country for a two-year transitional period beginning on Septem-

[24] Ibid., pp. 1068–1085.
[25] Ibid., pp. 1103–1105.
[26] Ibid., pp. 1107–1112, 1113–1116, 1123–1131, 1135–1136.

ber 1, 1947. It allowed 150,000 immigrants to enter the future Zionist commonwealth during the two-year period after that date. The minority report, on the other hand, proposed establishment of an independent federal state after no more than three years.[27]

The United Nations proposals at least temporarily relieved the United States from direct involvement in the settlement of the Palestine controversy. As George Marshall had prescribed, there was, it was hoped, no longer any image of an "American" plan of settlement. But the secretary's approach obviously faced a severe test in the weeks ahead. When the General Assembly met to debate the UNSCOP recommendations, Washington could not escape the eyes of the world. Arab capitals and Zionist organizations alike would carefully analyze the U.S. response. Bitterness and disappointment from some corners were virtually inevitable. Marshall simply hoped to minimize the recrimination as much as possible.

Actually, the State Department had been for some months preparing itself to accept the majority report. Beginning in November, 1946, the diplomatic corps had engaged in a debate with itself about the merits of dividing Palestine. In reaction to Truman's Yom Kippur statement, Leslie Rood of the Near East Division had prepared a lengthy analysis of partition and its merits relative to other possible solutions. Division, he concluded, meant struggles over borders. Both the bi-national approach and the provincial autonomy plan, however, encompassed the impossible task of getting Arabs and Jews to cooperate with one another after the settlement. Conflicts were inevitable as long as Jews pursued their efforts to become a majority of the population and Arabs sought to resist domination. "Partition has the advantages," he wrote to his colleagues, "of automatically solving the immigration and land transfer problems, and obviating the need for Arab-Jewish cooperation with a single government. Constitution making difficulties encountered in most solutions are eliminated." Even if Arabs did not accept the surgery, the Jewish Agency's recent endorsement of division insured it a measure of success. "Once the boundaries are drawn the community accept-

[27] Ibid., p. 1143.

ing the plan can assume control in its own area unaffected by the non-acceptance of the other community."[28]

In his last months in office as under secretary of state, Dean Acheson had edged toward favoring partition. As with Rood, the move stemmed from purely strategic considerations rather than from any sudden conversion to Zionism. He told the British ambassador to Washington in late January that splitting Palestine had both domestic political advantages in the United States and the promise of the least resistance from the disputing parties. Acheson wanted to settle the troublesome conflict with a minimum of friction, but he had no ideological devotions to any particular resolution of the matter. Partition appeared increasingly attractive because it was "likely that the opposition to such a solution would be vocal rather than physical. . . ."[29]

Yet for much of 1947, Acheson, in his reluctant support for partition, was still in a distinct minority within the State Department. While nearly everyone called for the admission of at least one hundred thousand refugees to the Holy Land, prevailing wisdom in most corners of the foreign policy staff favored the establishment of a trusteeship in Palestine and the eventual creation of a single state, neither Jewish nor Arab. In late May, Warren Austin, the U.S. ambassador to the United Nations, wrote Secretary Marshall endorsing unitary independence within five to ten years. A State Department position paper in early June took much the same stand. Loy Henderson was the most vocal and vehement in his defense of such an approach, and in his attack on partition he forecast ruin for U.S. oil interests in the Middle East if Washington flirted with the creation of even a truncated Jewish state.[30]

Through the summer there was a good deal of confusion and indecision within the department about what kind of policy the United States should pursue. When UNSCOP filed its conclusions, Wash-

[28] "Partition of Palestine," November 18, 1846, 867N.01/12-346, RG59, NA.

[29] Acheson's remarks may have been more than personal opinion and actually may have carried presidential approval. Memorandum of conversation, January 21, 1947, 867N.01/1-2147; memorandum of conversation, January 27, 1947, 867N.01/1-2747, RG59, NA.

[30] *FR*, 1947, V, 1086–1088, 1096–1102, 1120–1123, 1281–1282.

ington still had made no firm commitments. Diplomatic leaders in the administration and in Congress were becoming preoccupied with Cold War tensions. Apprehensions over Russia stalked their every step, creating enormous hesitancy and perplexity in developing Holy Land policy. They worried most about the possibility that wrong moves in Palestine might produce a rapprochement between Arab capitals and Moscow. But the foreign affairs chiefs also fretted over the possibility that Jewish immigrants arriving in Judea from eastern Europe might be Soviet agents. A few searched for reassuring signs that the Jewish settlers were really good anticommunists. Others puzzled over Stalin's likely position and concluded that he was inevitably going to oppose creation of a Jewish state in Palestine. In May, when Andrei Gromyko, the Soviet ambassador to the United Nations, indicated possible support for participation, the United States was unprepared to react.[31]

In the midst of such uncertainty, Zionists tried to insure a more favorable administrative climate for their cause. In late July, David Niles moved to implant a sympathetic voice in a key spot. He urged Truman to appoint Major General John H. Hilldring to the U.S. delegation to the United Nations for the sole purpose of handling Palestine matters. Ironically, Henderson had suggested creation of such a position. Niles now sought to use it for Zionist goals.[32]

Hilldring was an old advocate of shipping Holocaust survivors to the Holy Land. While he undoubtedly had some affection for Jewish ascendancy in Judea, he always reserved his greatest concern for refugee conditions in Europe and the implications they had for the Cold War. The general wanted to revive both West Germany and Japan as part of a *cordon sanitaire* around the bastion of communism. Sending Jews to Palestine would aid the economic recovery of Germany. It would also eliminate a lingering source of social tension in the former Third Reich.[33]

---

[31] Memorandum of conversation, October 3, 1947; Loy Henderson to Robert Lovett, October 6, 1947; Robert McClintock to Dean Rusk, October 29, 1947, Palestine Papers, Rusk Files. RG59, NA; *FR*, V, 1072–1073, 1081–1083.

[32] John Snetsinger, *Truman, the Jewish Vote, and the Creation of Israel*, pp. 54–55.

[33] *Newsweek*, August 4, 1947, p. 38.

After Truman appointed Hilldring to the United Nations delegation, the general became an important voice in the final move toward acceptance of the majority report. Yet his impact on the high policy counsels was small in comparison to the growing State Department conviction that partition deserved passage because division seemed to offer the best chance for a quick resolution of the controversy. In fact, one prominent line of thinking argued that the majority report was the best way to prevent a major Jewish push to gain the entire Holy Land, a prospect that promised chaos and violence and resulting harm to U.S. interests. "If the Participation Plan fails of acceptance at this assembly we shall be involved in a most unpleasant mess," Robert McClintock wrote to the under secretary. "Arabs will give no credit whatever . . . while the Jews, particularly in our own country, will make every effort by clandestine means and otherwise to bring more of their number from the DP areas in Europe to Palestine. . . . Since the impetus . . . [would] be largely American our relations with the Arab world . . . [would] grow if anything worse."[34]

Most instrumental in fostering such a perspective was Secretary of State George C. Marshall. He apparently concluded that the United States could not continue to ignore the growing demands of Zionists. Incessant agitation from Jewish nationalists might spark a major war and set into motion an uncontrollable chain reaction, all to the detriment of U.S. imperialist interests. But he also realized that any appeasements of would-be Israelis threatened to drive Arabs into a rapprochement with the Soviet Union. Beginning in the late spring, he pushed the notion that a United Nations solution might be able to end the years of turmoil, satisfy minimum Zionist demands, and leave the Arabs with no serious reason to blame the United States.[35]

In September meetings with the United Nations delegation in New York, Marshall crystallized his strategy. U.S. representatives would remain silent on the matter during the early days of the fall session, encouraging broad discussion and appearing to weigh the

[34] McClintock to Robert Lovett, October 20, 1947, Palestine Papers, Rusk Files, RG59, NA.

[35] *FR*, 1947, V, 1096–1101, 1103–1105, 1285–1287.

unfolding debate. After the opening round of deliberations, the U.S. delegation would announce its backing of the majority statement. To soothe inevitable Arab resentments, Washington would refrain from actively campaigning for adoption of its own position but would push for amendments to the partition plan, principally boundary changes in the Negev that would give more territory to the Moslems. The original UNSCOP partition scheme planned to leave a large Arab minority in the Jewish state and give the Zionists control of a much larger percentage of Palestine than their population merited. Contemplated U.S. changes proposed to correct the imbalance.[36]

The delegates were, however, not yet willing to make their commitment to an abbreviated Jewish state unalterable. If it became clear that the partition proposal could not garner an endorsement from the necessary two-thirds of the General Assembly, they were prepared to adopt a "switch position" that could elicit the required support. More than any other consideration, the desire for a solution imposed by the United Nations animated the U.S. policy.[37]

Marshall realized that his plans to win Arab acquiescence to the United Nations decision required the most careful balancing act. Any sudden blessings by the United States for partition could spark a new round of Arab protests. The secretary of state had to move cautiously. On September 17 he made his first public statement on the matter, telling the General Assembly that his government looked with favor on those UNSCOP proposals carrying unanimous or majority approval. Most observers, including the Arab delegations, interpreted the speech as an endorsement for the creation of an abbreviated Jewish state. But when Marshall and Hilldring met with Moslem leaders a week later, the two men assured the Middle East delegates that the United States remained uncommitted. The State Department clearly wanted to convey a posture of impartiality to suggest that Washington was still engaged in a genuine quest for a workable solution. They hoped that such soul-searching might win them some grudging respect from the Arabs.[38]

---

[36] Ibid., pp. 1147–1151, 1159–1162, 1173–1174.
[37] Ibid., pp. 1162–1163, 1166–1170.
[38] Ibid., pp. 1151–1153, 1159–1162, 1173–1174.

Through September and into early October, Marshall and his colleagues played out the deception. On October 10, Ambassador Herschel V. Johnson of the U.S. delegation finally unveiled the true U.S. position. Copies of the statement had already gone to the six Arab governments the night before. Zionists were pleased. Arabs were angry.[39]

Harry Truman wrote in his memoirs that he gave the orders for Ambassador Johnson's speech favoring partition. In a technical sense the president did make the decision, approving the statement formulated in the diplomatic office. But the chief executive was not really a key ingredient in the U.S. move toward endorsement of the majority report. At least he was not a prime mover in the months immediately preceding the fateful announcement, and he had not taken an active role since his Yom Kippur statement of the previous October.[40]

Truman had actually rebuffed several attempts to induce his support for Jewish ascendancy in Palestine. In early August he wrote Rabbi Wise that he was finding it "rather difficult to decide which [side] . . . is right." Furthermore, he told the Zionist spokesman, "a great many other people in the country are beginning to feel just as I do." Two days later he complained to a cabinet meeting that he had stuck his neck out on the question once and did not propose to do it again. Even when Robert Hannagan began pressing the president for a pro-Zionist statement that might aid Democratic National Committee fund-raising efforts among Jews, Truman demurred. When Hannagan made his final appeal in early October and invoked the pressure of major contributors to the party coffers, the president simply counseled that "everything would be all right" if Jewish nationalists would "keep quiet."[41]

On one occasion Truman did initiate contact with the State Department about a Palestine-related matter, but even then he accept-

---

[39] Ibid., pp. 1180–1181.
[40] Ibid., pp. 1177–1178.
[41] Truman to Wise, August 6, 1947, Official File 204, Harry S Truman Papers, Harry S Truman Presidential Library, Independence, Mo.; James Forrestal, *The Forrestal Diaries*, ed. Walter Millis, pp. 304, 309, 323.

ed his diplomats' plans for the situation. In late August he stopped Under Secretary of State Robert Lovett after a cabinet meeting and asked him about possible responses to British plans to return *Exodus 1947* passengers to Germany. Lovett assured the president that the State Department was doing all that it could. Formal protests were inadvisable because they would have the "effect of freezing the British in their position." Informal expressions of concern had already gone to London, Lovett explained. Truman concurred.[42]

Far from taking any vigorous steps in behalf of partition, Truman apparently did not even see the Johnson statement until immediately before its delivery. He then had only enough time to warn against too much U.S. responsibility for execution of the majority report. In the weeks that followed, State Department leaders formulated basic policy and kept the White House informed on no more than the general outlines of their decisions. The president remained completely outside a good many significant debates within the United Nations. He said nothing about the important maneuverings over economic union, seemingly unaware of Jewish Agency attempts to diminish the relationship between the two states.[43]

Even Truman's celebrated intervention in behalf of Jewish control over the Negev was indecisive. Under the majority report the fertile but largely uninhabited triangle of land in southern Palestine belonged to the future Zionist state. But Marshall, in his efforts to placate Arab resentments, hoped to reassign it. When news of the State Department intentions surfaced, Jewish nationalists protested loudly. After a White House visit from Chaim Weizmann, Truman called the United Nations delegation in New York to suggest that they might want to leave the Negev in the hands of the Jews.

At least the president left the impression with Weizmann that he was issuing orders to that effect. In reality the chief executive was less emphatic. He first talked to Hilldring, who clearly favored Zionist control of the area. With reinforcement from the general, Truman urged ultimate acceptance of the borders delineated by the original

---

[42] *FR*, 1947, V, 1138–1140.
[43] Ibid., pp. 1177–1179, 1202–1215, 1222–1242; office memorandum, October 9, 1947, Palestine Paper, Rusk Files, RG59, NA.

majority plan. But when Lovett telephoned Washington later in the day to check signals, Truman said he had "not at all intended to change the Department's instructions." His only concern was to see that the United States did "not stand out as a useless minority."[44] After Lovett explained basic strategy, the president seemed satisfied. He authorized the under secretary "to go ahead . . . as contemplated."[45]

Actually, plans to reassign the Negev were already close to dead letters even before the president's call to Hilldring. Earlier in the day Henderson had authorized the New York delegation to "gracefully" drop the amendments after the subcommittee deliberations, where they were expected to face defeat. In fact, Marshall's strategy had never concerned itself with really obtaining Arab control for all of southern Palestine. The secretary and his colleagues were merely interested in making public gestures in behalf of their position. It was all part of an attempt to appear as friendly as possible to the Moslems while accepting the Jewish Agency's solution to the Palestine dispute. Even without Truman's call to New York, the delegates and department officials realized there was little chance of getting sufficient support in the United Nations committees. They wanted merely to be able to say, as they eventually did, that they had tried.[46]

When Truman did take an unalterable stand, it was in opposition to direct U.S. responsibility for enforcement of the partition decision. He constantly insisted, as the Joint Chiefs of Staff recommended, that there be no U.S. military involvement in Palestine. He also objected to economic commitments to the settlement except through the auspices of the United Nations. The president did not want the United States to participate on a commission to implement division of the Holy Land. He would accept a part in such a body, he told Lovett, only if the Soviet Union was likely to be a member.[47]

[44] Memorandums for the file, November 19, 1947, Palestine Papers, Rusk Files; C. Bohlen to Robert Lovett, November 19, 1947, 867N.01/11-1947; note apparently from Lovett at bottom of 867N.01/11-1947, RG59, NA.

[45] Note by Lovett on conversation with Truman in C. Bohlen to Lovett, November 19, 1947, 867N.01/11-1947, RG59, NA.

[46] *FR*, 1947, V, 1217, 1249–1252, 1255–1269, 1271–1278.

[47] Dean Rusk to Robert Lovett, October 9, 1947; Robert McClintock to

He remained equally opposed to any efforts by the Unted States to secure other votes for the majority report. The original State Department plans had called for an abstention from any lobbying efforts, and the architects of diplomacy had arduously stuck to their formula despite growing criticisms and even some serious reevaluation from within their own ranks. Truman shared Marshall's desire to avoid any primary U.S. responsibilty for passage of a partition plan. Creation of a Jewish state must be the handiwork of the United Nations, where Arab resentment might recognize, as the president wrote to Ibn Saud, that "the vote of the United States counts for no more than the vote of any other counrty, large or small."[48]

More significant than any presidential contribution was the drive toward a quick settlement. Truman himself had ably expressed administration sentiments when he told Hilldring that he did not want anything to "upset the Apple-cart." While Marshall and his associates had originally decided to support partition largely because it was the majority position and, therefore, appeared to have the best chance for passage in the General Assembly, the reasons for accepting division of Palestine appeared even more compelling as the debate unfolded. One of those reasons was that the Soviet Union's decision to endorse the majority position increased chances for passage and helped entrench U.S. concentration on that particular solution.[49]

By late October, United States commitment to partition was so strong that State Department officials gave little thought to accepting a proposed Arab compromise that included a good deal of Jewish autonomy in Palestine. Faced with both Soviet and U.S. backing for the majority plans, several Middle East governments had apparently decided to make a counteroffer. Nuri Pasha, head of the Iraqi delegation, had worked through Prince Faisal, Ibn Saud's son, to

Rusk, October 9, 1947; October 15, 1947, Palestine Papers, Rusk Files, RG59, NA; *FR*, 1947, V, 1177–1178, 1283–1284, 1302.

48 Truman to Ibn Saud, November 19, 1947, 867N.01/11-1947, RG59, NA. Marshall did decide in late October to "line up" votes for the U.S. amendments to the majority plan and proposal for implementing partition. *FR*, 1947, V, 1198–1199.

49 Memorandum for the file, November 19, 1947, Palestine Papers, Rusk Files, RG59, NA; *FR*, 1947, V, 1180–1182, 1188–1192.

persuade the king to assume the initiative. In essence, the Arab leaders informally invited the United States to meet with the monarch for the purpose of devising a compromise solution. While the State Department's Near Eastern division was most responsive to the overtures, other diplomatic chiefs were not. In Washington and New York the momentum for settlement was running on one track. Commitment to partition seemed unalterable.[50]

In the process that led to United Nations endorsement of partition, Truman's contribution was far less significant than the decisions of several other Americans. Many Americans individually and in groups did make decisive contributions to the process. Friends of Zionism in the United States left their mark on the proceedings, especially on the final vote to adopt the majority report. In June, Senator James Murray invited Emanuel Celler, Freda Kirchwey (editor of *The Nation*), and a few others to meet with him to plan ways to secure United Nations action favorable to Zionism. Support for Jewish nationalism is important, he wrote the New York congressman, on "moral and human grounds, and I believe too that, selfishly speaking, it may have very important political repercussions in our own country."[51] Initial strategy called for pressure on Marshall and Truman. "We must get the message to the President," Celler told Murray, "that his chances for election are greatly impaired unless there is a solution of the Palestine question along traditional American lines."[52]

Ultimately, however, Celler and his cohorts aimed at delegates to the General Assembly and the ballot on partition. By November they were pushing hard. Four days before the final vote, a group of twenty-six prominent Americans, including several representatives and senators, sent telegrams to the United Nations delegations of Haiti, Greece, Luxembourg, Argentina, Colombia, China, El Salvador, Ethiopia, Honduras, Mexico, the Philippines, and Paraguay. Meanwhile, Celler conducted his own separate campaign. He tele-

[50] George Wadsworth to Herschel V. Johnson, October 21, 1947, Palestine Papers, Rusk Files, RG59, NA; *FR*, 1947, V, 1172, 1175, 1192.
[51] Murray to Celler, June 5, 1947, Box 23, Emanuel Celler Papers, Library of Congress, Washington, D.C.
[52] Celler to Murray, July 9, 1947, Box 23, Celler Papers.

graphed the foreign minister of Mexico in early November, expressing concern over rumors of possible abstention in the vote. "It is hoped that wiser counsel will prevail," he wrote, ". . . [and] both logic and political morality combine to make the proposed partition of Palestine necessary."[53]

By November 25 pressure was coming from many directions. Zionists had even managed to enlist some support from within the White House. Matt Connelly, the president's private secretary, joined with J. Howard McGrath to work on Latin American countries, the Philippines, and Siam. Celler sent a wire to Carlos Romulo, the delegate from the Philippines, urging support. The pressure on Manila from congressmen, senators, and even the U.S. delegation in New York was apparently becoming so intense that the president of the Philippines eventually complained to Truman.[54]

Rumors and accusations about additional pressure filled Washington. Robert Lovett reported that two of his aides overheard Bernard Baruch telling the delegate from Paris, Alexandre Parodi, that unless he voted for partition, France would receive no help under the Marshall Plan. Firestone Tire and Rubber Company officials claimed that U.S. Zionists urged them to use their influence in Liberia, where the corporation had extensive holdings. Faris Bey el-Khouri of Syria complained to Loy Henderson that Herschel Johnson was using considerable force on South American representatives. According to Truman himself, the U.S. consul in Haiti had pushed the president of that country for a favorable vote.[55]

Such unofficial U.S. persuasion was not, however, uniformly suc-

[53] Celler to Torres Bodet, November 13, 1947, Box 23, Celler Papers.

[54] Celler to Romulo, November 25, 1947; Celler to India League of America, October 27, 1947; Celler to Connelly, December 3, 1947, Box 23, Celler Papers; Romulo to McGrath, January 19, 1948, Howard J. McGrath Papers, Harry S Truman Presidential Library, Independence, Mo.; Herbert Bayard Swope to Bernard Baruch, November 27, 1947, Box 77, Bernard M. Baruch Papers, Princeton University Library, Princeton, N.J.

[55] *FR*, 1947, V, 1290; Truman, *Years of Trial and Hope*, p. 158; diaries of James Forrestal, December 14, 1947, James V. Forrestal Papers, Princeton University Library, Princeton, N.J.; Truman to George C. Marshall, December 11, 1947, Palestine Papers, Rusk Files; memorandum of conversation, December 3, 1947, 867N.01/12-347, RG59, NA.

cessful. When the Ad Hoc Committee endorsed a partition plan on November 25, Haiti, Liberia, Mexico, and France joined thirteen other countries in abstaining (better than voting against the plan, but not exactly what Zionists expected). The Philippine delegate was deliberately absent.[56]

When the General Assembly began its debate on the twenty-sixth, Arab delegates were optimistic about defeating the resolution. Backers had to increase the margin of approval from the simple majority required in committee to the two-thirds endorsement needed for final passage in the plenary session. But they were apparently losing votes instead. Representatives from both Haiti and the Philippines announced opposition to partition. Weeks of Zionist lobbying seemed fruitless.[57]

Debate continued through the afternoon. Then, quite unexpectedly, Dr. Oswald Aranha of Brazil, president of the General Assembly, announced his intentions to cancel the evening session, move for adjournment, and reconvene on Friday, November 28. Arab leaders were horrified. Too much could happen in two days of continuing pressure from pro-partition forces. The Middle East delegates implored Aranha to abandon his plans. They even offered to surrender their own time in the debate in order to reach a vote on Wednesday. But the assembly president turned a deaf ear to the Moslem requests. He entertained a motion for adjournment, and it passed, twenty-four to twenty-one.[58]

For the next forty-eight hours the competitors fought the final battle over passage. Arabs hoped to crack the Latin American block further. Haiti, Liberia, and the Philippines became the chief targets for Zionist forces. By Friday the Middle East governments feared they were on the edge of defeat. They could do little more than fight for an additional delay and hope for the best. With French support they managed to convince the assembly that it was still possible to find a peaceful compromise. Accordingly, the delegates voted twenty-

[56] Carlos Romulus to Emanuel Celler, December 4, 1947, Box 23, Celler Papers.
[57] Fred J. Khouri, *The Arab-Israeli Dilemma*, pp. 54–56.
[58] Ibid., p. 55.

five to fifteen to postpone the final decision for another twenty-four hours in hopes of stimulating an agreed settlement between Arabs and Jews. That evening the Moslem delegates formulated their final attempt to avert partition. When the assembly reconvened on Saturday morning, they unveiled proposals that bore a striking resemblance to both the minority suggestions and the 1946 Grady plan. It advocated independence for a democratic federal nation modeled after the United States and having two largely autonomous cantons, one Jewish and the other Arab.[59]

But the twelfth-hour Middle East tactics could not withstand the momentum for an immediate decision. Both the United States and the Soviet Union opposed further delays. At 5:35 P.M. on Saturday, November 29, 1947, the General Assembly approved the partition proposal. Thirty-three states voted for the division plan, thirteen opposed it, and ten abstained. Siam was absent.[60]

A combination of factors had produced the support for partition. Washington's and Moscow's agreement on the proposition no doubt impressed many minds. Belgian officials later divulged that they voted yes because they "got the impression" that the United States wanted them to do so. Zionist movements inside several Latin American countries paid handsome dividends. But the crucial pressure came from the United States. Even without Truman's personal participation, congressmen, White House staffers, senators, members of the United Nations delegation, and consuls had performed their own valuable efforts to secure passage of the resolution. Pressure on Haiti, the Philippines, and Liberia finally bore fruit. All three supported partition. If they had collectively voted against it, they would have defeated the resolution.[61]

---

[59] *FR*, 1947, V, 1289, 1293–1294.
[60] Ibid., p. 1291.
[61] Khouri, *Arab-Israeli Dilemma*, p. 56; Robert McClintock to Gordon H. Mattison, December 19, 1947, Palestine Papers, Rusk Files, RG59, NA.

CHAPTER EIGHT

TRIUMPH AND TRAGEDY

By early 1948 it was apparent to many diplomats that the partition plan did not guarantee a peaceful solution to the Holy Land question. Arabs violently resisted its enforcement. Zionists moved to consolidate and expand their control. At first, snipers and secret bombers shattered the peace. Eventually, open warfare raged across Palestine. Gun battles became daily affairs. Every day the fighting left its litter of mortar shells and corpses.

The Haganah, the Irgun, and the Stern Gang quickly seized control of predominantly Jewish areas, while "pioneers" established new settlements in some sparsely populated regions. After two thousand Moslem guerrillas stormed the kibbutz of Kfar Etzion near Hebron in early January, Jewish forces began what the Jewish Agency called "preventive defense." They attacked suspected enemy strongholds in an attempt to force their adversary into a "passive state."

It became a season for brutal savagery. In March, three trucks and an armored car rolled onto Ben Yehuda street in Jerusalem's Jewish shopping district. The drivers, all wearing British uniforms, quietly abandoned the vehicles. Minutes later the equipment erupted with a blast that crumbled nearby shops and hotels, leaving fifty-two dead beneath the rubble. Within a week a Stern Gang bomb retaliated. As a train carrying British soldiers from Cairo passed through an orange grove near Rehovoth, an explosion ripped the cars from their tracks and killed twenty-eight passengers.

Before dawn one April morning, one hundred Zionist commandos swarmed into the small Arab village of Deir Yessin outside Jerusalem. Irgun and Stern Gang members blasted the tiny huts with demolition charges. By noon they had butchered more than two hundred people in the most brutal massacre of the conflict.[1]

Throughout the Middle East, Arab acceptance of the United Nations plans simply never materialized. Opposition was bitter. U.S. installations became frequent targets for the resentment. A Damascus mob broke into a rear window of the U.S. legation in early December, climbed to the roof, and tore down the flag. Another gang stormed and looted the Russian-Syrian Cultural Society in retaliation for the Soviet vote for partition. In Jerusalem, Americans risked serious harm if they ventured beyond the British security zone. For strategic planners in Washington, other signs of Arab displeasure were even more disturbing. Within days after the General Assembly vote on partition, protests forced a halt in construction of the oil pipeline from Saudi Arabia to the Mediterranean.[2]

Protests and resistance developed despite Washington's constant insistence that partition must become a reality. Even strong opponents of the division settlement upheld the program. In early December, Loy Henderson told Iraqi officials that he "could see no other solution than the acceptance by the Arabs of the United Nations solution." Later in the month the State Department sent a round of telegrams to Moslem capitals echoing that sentiment. Furthermore, American diplomats constantly rejected Arab offers for a compromise solution that included a federal system with Jewish and Arab states and admission for one hundred thousand refugees.[3]

If Arab responses to partition were disappointing, British reactions were equally discouraging. Prime Minister Attlee refused any cooperation with the United Nations Palestine Commission, the group responsible for executing the General Assembly recommendations. Years of frustrating inability to solve the Holy Land controversy and irritation over U.S. pronouncements had taken their toll. Foreign Minister Bevin had grown especially annoyed over Truman's occasional willingness to offer advice without assistance. Bevin

---

[1] *FR*, 1947, V, 1322–1329; 1948, V, 607–611; *Time*, January 19, 1948, p. 39; March 1, 1948, p. 19; March 8, 1948, p. 30; April 19, 1948, p. 35.

[2] *FR*, 1947, V, 668, 1307–1308, 1322.

[3] Ibid., pp. 1244, 1293–1294, 1311, 1319–1321; 1948, V, 571.

was in no mood to cooperate with any scheme that included American suggestions. The Foreign Office was also concerned with more substantive matters. Troubles in the Middle East threatened Anglo-Iraqi relations at a critical time. Accordingly, in January, London barred the United Nations commission from Palestine until two weeks before the scheduled departure of the last British soldiers. Furthermore, His Majesty's civil servants could not stay in the Holy Land to run utilities when the Mandate ended without loss of pension rights.[4]

The United Nations was supposed to use its prestige to insure execution of the partition plan. Yet events from Bagdad to London were destroying hopes of such enforcement. Organized Arab opposition, Zionist impatience, and British recalcitrance were creating an untenable situation for the world body. While Jewish nationalists welcomed the General Assembly's endorsement of Jewish statehood, they were not at all anxious to realize the other major part of the November resolution, the sections calling for economic union between the two sectors of Palestine. In early February a special report from the Palestine Commission to the Security Council held out little hope for the realization of the whole plan without armed intervention.[5]

In Washington two distinct factions within the State Department, each with its own allies elsewhere, fought for control of Truman's policy. One group, concerned with maintaining friendships in the Moslem world, wished to abandon any commitment to partition. Some spokesmen, especially in the Near Eastern branch, had always had such opinions. Others reacted to the course of events. Loy Henderson's stoic and patient opposition to the United Nations plan was beginning to gain support, but the arch-enemy of Zionism was leaving most of the attack to new opponents of partition.

George Kennan, who headed the recently organized Policy Planning Staff, took much of the initiative. When the National Security Council decided to study the "security" implications of the General

[4] Ibid., 1948, V, 533–536, 544–545, 562–563, 611–612.
[5] Ibid., pp. 572, 607–609, 613–614, 630–631, 640–643.

Assembly resolution on Palestine, the task of preparing a report fell to Kennan and his colleagues. By January they believed that continued support of partition could damage U.S. interests. Angry Arabs might slow the flow of oil at a time when the Marshall Plan needed a 150 percent increase in Middle East production. Most of all, strategic planners trembled at the thought that either Soviet or U.S. troops would be involved in the enforcement of partition. Any large U.S. participation would, the diplomatic soothsayers concluded, seriously drain national forces, set an unhealthy precedent, and further alienate Near Eastern leaders. Yet, they reasoned, even if Washington refused to contribute anything to policing the division, Moscow would undoubtedly use the opportunity to establish a Soviet beachhead in Asia Minor. "It must be assumed," the Policy Planning Staff argued with Cold War logic, "that Moscow will actviely endeavor to find some means of exploiting the opportunity." Truman could afford neither to take part nor to allow Stalin to go it alone.[6]

Despite the convictions of Kennan and others, however, through most of February the top State Department officials still defended the United Nations resolution. Both Marshall and Lovett seemed determined to salvage the General Assembly recommendations. At the United Nations, Warren Austin was equally dedicated to the division plan. So was Dean Rusk, head of the United Nations Affairs Office. None of them had become Zionists. They simply thought that continued support for partition still promised an early end to the Holy Land fighting and, thereby, best served U.S. interests in the Middle East. Rusk, for example, wanted the United States to intervene militarily because he feared the Soviet Union might be able to exploit continued fighting. Besides, the future secretary of state concluded in April, the "presence of our forces in Palestine might be advantageous from a strategic standpoint, and would give us the opportunity to construct bomber fields in the Middle East."[7]

---

[6] Ibid., 1947, V, 1283, 1313–1314; 1948, V, 545–554, 619–625; James Forrestal, *The Forrestal Diaries*, ed. Walter Millis, pp. 359–362, 364–365; "The Position of the United States with Respect to Palestine," February 17, 1948, Clark M. Clifford Papers, Harry S Truman Presidential Library, Independence, Mo.

[7] *FR*, 1948, V, 797.

While the State Department engaged in a debate with itself, Truman provided no resolution for the dispute. The president was of two minds. Political pressures continued to demand his support for partition. White House advisers constantly urged him to promise all necessary support for partition and to lift an embargo on arms to Palestine. Truman was obviously sensitive to such pleas in an election year. Yet the president was equally reluctant to assume many national responsibilities to see partition become a reality. He had supported the idea in November as a way to avoid involvement. The United Nations was supposed to restore order. Truman was hesitant to contribute U.S. troops to a peace-keeping force or even to encourage the creation of such an instrument. In January he told a press conference he planned to keep U.S. soldiers out of Palestine. When the General Assembly established a committee to implement division, Truman blocked U.S. membership in the group. Throughout the winter, as the chances for a peaceful solution evaporated, the president's commitment to partition waned.[8]

In early January, Truman revealed much of his conception of the Holy Land problem in a White House meeting with George Wadsworth, ambassador to Iraq. The chief executive told his envoy that he had great confidence in Secretary Marshall and could "go along with what the Department might recommend." After two and one-half years in office, the president was clearly frustrated and slightly confused. In his recollections of events *he* had proposed the Anglo-American Committee of Inquiry in 1945. Only British "bullheadedness" and Jewish "fanaticism" had defeated his good efforts and kept Henry Grady from implementing the Anglo-American recommendations, he told Wadsworth. While London and the Zionists still exhibited the same flaws, Truman did not intend to be a party to future failure. He authorized Wadsworth to tell Arab leaders there would be no enforcement of partition by the United States if neighboring countries stayed out of Palestine.[9]

Truman continued, however, to leave Palestine policy largely in

[8] Ibid., 1947, V, 1283–1284, 1302, 1319–1321; 1948, V, 542, 578–579, 592–595, 633–634, 687–696.
[9] Ibid., 1948, V, 592–595.

the hands of Marshall and Lovett. But they had to weigh the implications of the president's continued resistance to U.S. military involvement in the Holy Land. Since problems elsewhere occupied most of the secretary's attention by early 1948, the under secretary searched for some way to salvage the division plan. Yet growing testimony that the scheme was unworkable without force, and Truman's reluctance to help impose partition, made Lovett's task difficult. Neither he nor Marshall was initially able to devise any solution to their problem. As late as February 12 the secretary confessed that he did not yet know what course of action he might favor.[10]

But Marshall could not avoid making some decision. He had three possible ones. He could insist that partition must become a reality, even if it required enforcement and the use of U.S. troops. He could do nothing, in which case there would probably be no United Nations action, only chaos. Or he could insist that the Security Council had the responsibility and authority to restore order but not to impose a division of Palestine. On the morning of February 19, 1948, Marshall and Lovett decided to pursue the last option. Austin would announce the new U.S. position before the Security Council. It was a compromise which left no one completely satisfied.[11]

Truman, meanwhile, continued to give his diplomatic chiefs a free hand. Even before he learned the details of the State Department's revised approach, he assured Marshall that he could proceed without regard to "political factors." When the president finally received a detailed outline of the new plans and a copy of Austin's speech, he quickly approved them. In doing so, he authorized a major change in U.S. policy which constituted a subtle but decisive step away from the partition resolution. Yet Truman did not want to admit that he had altered anything. In the same telegram to Marshall he approved Austin's statement and at the same time insisted that "nothing should be presented to [the] Security Council that could be interpreted as a recession on our part from the position we took in the General Assembly."[12]

[10] Ibid., 533–539, 543, 545, 554–556, 581–583, 587, 612–619, 640–643.
[11] Ibid., pp. 546, 633, 637–640.
[12] Ibid., p. 645.

Yet Truman had every reason to realize that a major shift was under way. In the State Department memorandum that carried to the White House the first news of Austin's impending statement the diplomats had outlined their plans beyond the speech. If opposition to partition continued and the Security Council was unable to secure sufficient acquiescence to avoid "enforcement measures," they intended to ask the General Assembly to reconsider the whole matter. "It would be clear," they wrote to the president, "that Palestine is not yet ready for self-government and that some form of trusteeship . . . will be necessary." [13]

Warren Austin delivered his remarks to a slightly puzzled Security Council on February 24. Reactions varied. Zionists worried that Truman meant to abandon partition. Arabs were generally optimistic, but cautious. Yet there was still some possibility that the United States might continue endorsement of the division plan. If sufficient support existed elsewhere, Lovett intended to cooperate. But he refused to "carry the ball." [14]

When the Security Council turned its full attention to Palestine in late February, however, few countries exhibited any enthusiasm for partition. Rusk notified Lovett on February 26 that "Belgium does not wish to approve partition again." Only the Soviet Union and the Ukraine remained unalterably committed to the division plan. Lovett's dedication slowly drained away. He instructed Austin to vote to implement the General Assembly resolution but to make no "impassioned speeches in its defense." [15]

If the State Department needed additional encouragement to abandon partition completely, it got it from the Central Intelligence Agency late in February. A CIA report on Palestine predicted U.S. losses and Soviet gains in the Middle East if the United Nations used force to establish a Jewish state. [16]

By early March, Lovett and Marshall could no longer maintain their backing for division. On March 5 the secretary told the presi-

13 Ibid., pp. 637–640.
14 Ibid., p. 660.
15 Ibid., pp. 662, 663.
16 Ibid., pp. 666–675.

dent in a cabinet meeting that the Security Council would probably "find itself unable to proceed with partition," in which case "it will refer the Palestine problem to an immediate special session of the General Assembly for fresh consideration." The diplomatic corps now suggested that the United States support the establishment of a trusteeship over Palestine.[17]

On March 8, Truman approved the new policy. All that remained was some decision on when Warren Austin would announce the proposals. For the next ten days Washington waited while Security Council members carried out one last effort to save the General Assembly solution. Yet there was little hope of success. Several Arab delegations suggested an old compromise, including admission of one hundred thousand Jewish refugees and considerable Jewish autonomy in a federal state, but they continued to oppose partition. Jewish Agency representatives were not enthusiastic about specific details of the United Nations plan. They wanted a Jewish state, but under their own terms. In meetings between permanent members of the Security Council, only the Soviets and the French exhibited much support for partition, and that, too, was waning.[18]

Marshall feared a major threat to world peace if the Palestine dispute remained unresolved. On March 16 the secretary instructed Austin to announce the U.S. proposals. But the ambassador was still reluctant to abandon partition completely. He wanted to insert a statement that the proposed trusteeship would "be a temporary measure . . . without prejudice to [a] future settlement." Even then, he delayed his remarks for three days. On March 19 he could wait no longer. "Warren Austin," *Time* magazine reported, "finally dropped the other shoe." [19]

Harry Truman had approved the new U.S. position. Yet he was still uneasy with his own decision. His White House advisers, including Chief Counsel Clark Clifford, had constantly urged continuing

---

[17] Ibid., pp. 676–677, 678–685.
[18] Ibid., pp. 676–737
[19] Ibid., pp. 736–737; *Time*, March 29, 1948, p. 22.

commitment to partition. Clifford, a former Washington lawyer largely responsible for the 1948 election strategy, had sent the president two long memorandums on Palestine in early March. He pleaded with the chief executive to use every "pressure he can bring to bear upon the Arab states to accept partition." Truman was reluctant to disappoint Clifford.[20]

Truman was equally hesitant to disappoint Zionist leaders. He had become irritated over the constant demands of Jewish nationalists and was refusing to see anyone on the Palestine question. But he did agree to meet with Chaim Weizmann after some emotional pleas from his former business partner, Eddie Jacobson. The British Zionist arrived at the White House on March 18. Even though Truman had already approved a change in U.S. policy, he could not break the news to Weizmann. Instead, he apparently assured his visitor that there would be no change.[21]

While the president must have realized his vow was deceptive, he did not know when Austin would deliver his remarks. He had left matters so completely in Marshall's hands that he had given the secretary a virtual carte blanche on Palestine affairs. Truman had no idea that Austin planned to unveil the trusteeship proposal the next day after Weizmann's visit.

After the announcement of the new U.S. position came from New York, the White House was enormously embarrassed. Presidential aides, who had no advanced warning of any changed position and who regarded partition as an article of faith, were perplexed. Clifford sought an immediate explanation from the president. But Truman was unwilling to confess his own part in the drama. Instead, he exhibited "bewilderment and consternation" over Austin's speech. He told his counsel to "find out how this could have happened." Feigning innocence, he said, "I assured Chaim Weizmann that we were for partition and would stick to it. He must think I am a plain

---

[20] *FR*, 1948, V, 687.
[21] Harry Truman, *Memoirs: Years and Trial and Hope, 1946–1952*, pp. 160–163; Clark M. Clifford, "Recognizing Israel," *American Heritage* 28 (April, 1977): 4–11.

liar." When Clifford later reported that both Marshall and Lovett knew of the speech in advance, Truman told his aide, "They have made me out a liar and a double-crosser. We are sunk." [22]

Rather than let his pro-Zionist White House people realize his duplicity, Truman continued to play out the deception. On March 24 the president brought his White House staff and State Department leaders together to reconcile his alleged support for partition with the trusteeship proposal. In the end, Truman took what had been Warren Austin's position all along. The trusteeship would be a temporary arrangement to avoid violence and cool emotions. Partition was still a long-range possibility. [23]

While Washington struggled with itself and Truman sought to cover his own embarrassment, events in the Holy Land were rendering any policy totally meaningless. Great Britain was withdrawing all its personnel from Palestine, with the final departures scheduled for May 15. Zionist forces were preparing to seize power for themselves the moment British authorities left the country. Despite the arms embargo, U.S. organizations continued to supply the Israelis with assistance. Even if Washington managed to eradicate United Nations blessing for the creation of a Jewish state, Jewish leaders in the Promised Land fully intended to complete their drive for statehood. "Come what may," Moshe Shertok of the Jewish Agency told the Security Council, "the Jews of Palestine are determined to obtain the necessary arms and defend themselves." [24]

State Department leaders now directed most of their energy to

---

[22] Clifford, "Recognizing Israel," p. 7. Truman claimed in his memoirs that he did not promise Weizmann anything inconsistent with Austin's March 19 speech. Truman also said that the trusteeship proposal was not inconsistent with his long-range plans for Palestine. Truman, *Years of Trial and Hope*, pp. 160–163.

[23] Clifford, "Recognizing Israel," p. 10; *FR*, 1948, V, 744–746, 748–752; 754–760. Ironically, it was Clark Clifford, one of Truman's strongest defenders, who provided evidence that the President deceived his staff. The central files of the State Department provide evidence that Truman willingly participated in the decision to abandon partition. If Clifford's testimony about what the president said to his staff is correct, the chief executive misled his advisers. My interpretation simply accepts the validity of both Clifford's account and State Department papers.

[24] *Newsweek*, April 12, 1948, p. 31.

achieving a cease-fire. Continued fighting threatened ominous possibilities. Some diplomats envisioned a dark progression of events in which both sides gained allies and the Palestine fighting escalated into a world war. The president seemed equally worried and pledged full support for peace-seeking efforts even if they hurt him politically. He was willing to allow U.S. troops to help maintain a truce as long as they served under the United Nations flag.[25]

But every element of the controversy militated against finding peace. Jews and Arabs hated each other intensely. After the massacre at Deir Yessin, resentment and indignation spread through Moslem ranks. Arabs wanted revenge, not compromise. They were less flexible on the immigration issue than they had been six weeks before.[26]

U.S. efforts did obtain Security Council adoption of a cease-fire resolution on April 17. Yet there was no one to enforce that resolution. Major power rivalries, especially the Cold War between Moscow and Washington, froze the United Nations. Despite Truman's willingness to the contrary, the Defense Department was still reluctant to provide any troops for policing the peace. At the same time, the entire Truman administration wanted no Soviet soldiers in Palestine. Great Britain was determined to end its involvement on May 14. The idea of using French troops died quickly in recognition of deep Arab bitterness toward Paris.[27]

Washington diplomats, nevertheless, kept trying to secure joint Anglo-American responsibility for the peace. In late April, State Department officials thought they were making progress toward a truce, especially with the Jews. But Moshe Shertok dashed those hopes in an April 29 letter to Marshall. The Zionist spokesman insisted that he could not agree to any cease-fire terms that included "the deferment of statehood." [28]

For a while diplomatic leaders believed that a peace faction might emerge from Zionist ranks or that non-Zionist Palestinian Jews

[25] *FR*, 1948, V, 770–777, 797–798, 804–805, 811–812, 877–891.
[26] Ibid., pp. 809–810, 817, 823, 826, 887–890, 915–916.
[27] Ibid., pp. 774, 805, 827, 830, 833, 837.
[28] Ibid., pp. 874–876.

might be able to end the bloodshed. They were pleased with British plans to meet in Geneva with forty prominent Jewish leaders from Palestine in hopes of finding a settlement. State Department hopes fed on rumors of a struggle in the Jewish Agency between the war party of Rabbi Silver and the moderate camp of Goldmann and Shertok. Indeed, there may have been such division in Zionist ranks. In early May, Goldmann told Austin he hoped Marshall might meet with Shertok and Silver and pressure them into a truce. But even if some doves existed, they did not control the movement.[29]

As the deadline for British departure approached, Haganah and Irgun forces took the initiative. On April 27 they drove into Haifa, seizing that industrialized port city of 140,000 Arabs and Jews. Thousands of Moslems evacuated by boat across the bay to Acre. A few escaped inland over the Rushmiya bridge before Zionist forces shut that route. Within a week two thousand Irgun fighters sliced into the Arab city of Jaffa, belying Zionists' claims that they intended to seize no more than the United Nations had given them in November. Much of the population fled in terror along the road to Ramallah. Despite the boastful assertions to the contrary, Arab leaders were incapable of protecting their own people. On the fringes of the Holy Land, Syrians, Egyptians, Saudis, and Jordanians prepared to intervene, but for many Palestinians the Arab League's promises of assistance were small comfort from the terror and chaos around them. Some prepared to leave. In a fashionable Jerusalem neighborhood Arab mothers hid their small children in closets and taped their mouths to avoid detection from marauding bands of Zionist commandos outside.[30]

Faced with growing anarchy, the British simply moved with dispatch to extract themselves from the disorder. Outside government buildings in Jerusalem they burned the records from more than two decades of Mandate rule. From London the *Economist* summarized

[29] Ibid., pp. 823–824, 826, 877–879, 893–894, 920–922, 929–930; Goldmann to Rosenman, May 10, 1948, Clifford Papers.

[30] *FR*, 1948, V, 889–891; *Newsweek*, April 26, 1948, p. 31; May 3, 1948, p. 30; May 10, 1948, p. 28; May 17, 1948, p. 38; *Time*, March 1, 1948, p. 1.

national attitudes: "The British will not carry through any scheme [to maintain peace] single handed. Nine months ago they still might have done so, but the murder of the two young sergeants brought about one of those rare shifts in British public opinion which, once they have occurred, are irrevocable and which no statesman will challenge." It had become obvious that "since neither Britain nor America will enforce a settlement, the Arabs and Jews will, by bloody war, enforce their own." [31]

By early May, British officials began to tell U.S. diplomats that King Abdullah ibn-Husein of Jordan held the key to an eventual resolution of the whole conflict. London hinted that its agents had worked out plans for Abdullah to effect a de facto partition of Palestine. While Zionists secured Jewish areas, the Arab monarch would use the British-created Arab Legion to cut across the Holy Land and annex the Moslem portion to his own kingdom. Arthur Creech-Jones first suggested the idea in a conversation at Warren Austin's apartment on May 2. Four days later the U.S. ambassador telegraphed Washington that he was convinced British policy now rested on such a scheme. Apparently Creech-Jones also told Jewish Agency officials about the plans. On May 10 the U.S. consul in Jerusalem reported that Zionist spokesmen there "hinted broadly" that they had an "understanding" with Abdullah and placed "little stock" in the "bellicose statements" of the Arab monarch. [32]

In the days before May 14, Truman faced "unbearable pressure to recognize the Jewish state promptly," as Clark Clifford told Robert Lovett. A torrent of mail flooded the White House, most of it pro-Zionist. Every sign pointed to deep trouble for Democrats if the chief executive failed to extend diplomatic contact immediately. The party faced not only a loss of voters in key states but an equally devastating decline in financial support as well. Truman had faced similar types of political pressure before on this issue, and he had not always bowed to it. But conditions were different now. It was an

---

[31] Quoted in *Newsweek*, April 26, 1948, p. 31.
[32] *FR*, 1948, V, 971.

election year, and opinion polls already predicted difficulty for the White House incumbent. For a while Truman appeared willing to "run" the "political risks involved." But the situation in the Middle East made such risks increasingly less attractive.[33]

Zionists had presented Truman with a fait accompli in Palestine, or at least so it seemed in accounts he received from his advisers. The president was concerned about what might happen in the Holy Land after British withdrawal. For weeks State Department people had been painting a picture of complete chaos as the Mandate officials left without a United Nations decision on the future status of the country. In early May he learned that Jewish forces already controlled their part of Palestine and had a possible "behind the barn" deal with Abdullah for him to take the rest. Especially after the failure of truce negotiations such an arrangement seemed to be the only reasonable way to maintain authority and order. Besides, it appeared to cost Truman nothing. He did not have to send troops along with recognition. His White House advisers in particular suggested that Zionist forces had taken care of virtually everything. He needed to supply nothing except recognition. Truman had never opposed Zionism. He was just never inclined to give it any aid. But this time assistance was cheap. As Dean Rusk told two of his colleagues, "I don't think the boss will ever put himself in a position of opposing that effort when it might be that the US opposition would be the only thing that would prevent it from succeeding."[34]

White House advisers did play a major role in convincing Truman to issue an immediate recognition. On May 12 the president held a meeting with senior people from the State Department and three of his advisers: Clark Clifford, David Niles, and Matthew Connelly. The diplomatic corps wanted to support Security Council efforts to obtain a truce in Palestine and a commissioner appointed by the General Assembly to manage basic community services. But Clifford argued that truce efforts were unrealistic. He urged the president to announce his intention to recognize the new state even be-

---

33 Ibid., p. 854.
34 Ibid., pp. 967, 973.

fore its declaration of existence. "It is better to recognize now," a Clifford aide scribbled in a note to himself, and "steal a march on U.S.S.R."[35]

For the time, Truman agreed with Robert Lovett's assessment that premature recognition "would be buying a pig in a poke." Yet Clifford continued to push his point. If no recognition could be made before May 14, why not a statement on that day? Clifford apparently hammered home one key point: once the British left, there would be "no government or authority of any kind in Palestine. Title would be lying about for anybody to seize." Truman had always attached much significance to maintaining order in the disputed country. State Department advisers had provided him with little more than legalistic reasons for withholding the recognition. They had never made a convincing case that recognition would even hurt relations with the Arab world. Indeed, the diplomatic corps had helped create the impression that there really was a deal between Zionists and Abdullah to perform surgery on the Holy Land. Given a choice between State Department warnings about undefined threats to U.S. interests and White House advice that immediate recognition could restore order, Truman opted for the latter.[36]

On May 14 the United Kingdom prepared to remove the final vestiges of its mandate authority. In the Tel Aviv Museum, David Ben-Gurion read a declaration of independence for a new Israel. Within minutes the United States became the first country to extend de facto recognition to the newly declared country.[37]

Israel was born amidst hope and promise for several hundred thousand Holocaust survivors. But for as many Palestinian Arabs, Zionism's culmination produced tragic consequences. In the wake of Deir Yessin and in a general climate of violence, Moslems in the Promised Land often fled in terror. Others stayed for a while, only to suffer the pains of war, dislocation, abuse, and discrimination.

Was it possible to compensate Jews for the pogroms without overtaxing Palestinians? Truman and other world leaders could have

[35] Ibid., pp. 972–976.
[36] Ibid., p. 1005.
[37] Ibid., pp. 989–994.

found homes for the uprooted without a new Israel. In fact, the Zionist effort became a major cause of Arab resistance to Jewish settlement in Palestine. It is, however, easy to understand why many Jewish leaders insisted that they must have their own nation. Centuries of Christian bigotry, climaxing in the Nazi nightmare, had conditioned the seed of Abraham to expect the worst when anyone else was in control. Yet the construction of a Jewish state did not require domination of most of Palestine or the displacement and terror of Arabs. Indeed, many Jewish nationalists condemned the aggressiveness and excesses of the Zionist terrorists.

Admittedly, any attempt to solve the refugee problem outside of Zionism required an enormous initiative from Truman. He might have defused the quest for Jewish statehood with stronger efforts and success in behalf of more liberal U.S. immigration laws. But his puny moves in that direction left him most vulnerable to criticism.

Truman did have several chances to accept an Arab compromise that included Palestinian homes for more than one hundred thousand Jewish refugees. From late 1947 until early April, 1948, when Zionists began extensive military campaigns, Moslem leaders repeatedly suggested the creation of a bi-national federal government with two American-style states, one of which would be primarily Jewish with considerable local autonomy. The Arab offer also promised protection of religious liberty. But State Department leaders rejected the plan, partly because Zionists refused to accept it but also because Marshall, Lovett, and the president pinned their hopes on the partition plan.

Perhaps there was no way for a U.S. president to deflect the drive for Jewish statehood. Money from American donors sponsored the growing military capacity of the Haganah and other underground forces. Yishuv leaders were prepared to seize a portion of Palestine even without endorsement from the United Nations. Contributions for the Zionist cause enjoyed such widespread acceptance in Washington government circles that the administration generally failed in its efforts to stop the flow of arms, supplies, and ships.[38]

[38] Department of State records 867N.01, RG59, NA, for 1947 are filled with

Yet even if Truman reconciled himself to the creation of a truncated Jewish state, he still had an opportunity (and perhaps a responsibility, in light of the private American role in sponsoring the Zionist movement) to minimize harm to Arabs. But he never assumed the initiative in seeking a solution, preferring instead to wash his hands of the matter and pretend he had no role to play in either preventing or controlling Jewish statehood. At the time, the administration's 1948 rejection of the United Nations division plan and the earlier refusal to help enforce it appeared to aid Arab efforts. In reality, they meant Zionists would face few effective restraints on their ambitions while Truman dabbled superficially with a trusteeship plan that had too little backing and came much too late. Meanwhile, British authorities abandoned Palestine after years of inept preparation for independence. In so doing they left the dispute to a clash of swords that inevitably wreaked havoc on both sides and brought defeat for one.

Beyond a compromise solution the only chance for a peaceful settlement rested in effective United Nations action. But that would have required cooperation among the major powers, including the United States and the Soviet Union. The Truman administration was not even able to achieve an understanding with the British, let alone the Soviet Union. Even the policy makers who wanted to work through the United Nations did not, in general, see the world organization as an avenue for joint U.S.-Soviet efforts to maintain the peace. They regarded it as a possible instrument for opposing Moscow. In early May, when H. V. Evatt, the Australian minister for external affairs, suggested that Washington and Moscow combine efforts and intervene to restore order in Palestine, Truman rejected the idea as "preposterous."[39] The U.S. recognition of Israel while the United Nations continued to consider cease-fire plans was a crippling blow to the young world organization.

State Department leaders often championed the Arab cause in

---

the details of a considerable attempt on the part of the State Department to stop the flow of private military aid to the Zionist underground in Palestine.

[39] *FR*, 1948, V, 987.

Palestine, but they were only incidentally concerned with aiding Holocaust victims without displacing Palestinians. They spent far more time and effort in trying to forecast Soviet plans than they did in attempting any solution to the refugee problem. Fear of Soviet challenges to the emerging Anglo-American hegemony in the Middle East became so dominant that many State Department leaders began to see every Jewish refugee from eastern Europe as a possible agent for world communism. Diplomatic chiefs first alarmed themselves about the "threat" in late 1947. By January, 1948, they envisioned a well-organized cadre of Soviet sympathizers infiltrating the ranks of the uprooted and winning passage to Palestine. State Department captains had compiled a miserable record in predicting Moscow's response to the Palestine question, but they kept trying.

Justice for Arab and Jewish claims was not, of course, an item of top priority for the president. In the early days of his administration Truman did view Jewish immigration to Palestine with a sympathy he never completely lost. Yet that disposition played only a small part in shaping his subsequent policy toward Zionism. Far more significant was the chief executive's concern about stability in both Europe and the Near East. The president responded first to the situation in the Old World because he believed that the refugee problem seriously aggravated continental troubles and invited Soviet advances. In the Middle East the Missouri Democrat sought to appease Jewish leaders while avoiding the contentious goals of Zionism. He valued the oil resources and the strategic concessions of the Arab world and wanted to send one hundred thousand Jewish refugees to Palestine—not as an encouragement to Jewish nationalism, but in hopes of keeping Herzl's movement from the hands of ambitious and disruptive elements.

Over the next three years Truman never altered his perspective or changed his priorities. The fate of Palestine always came second to more basic goals. By 1946, however, the president had constructed, with the advice of his White House staff and military leaders, some basic standards for any solution to the Holy Land dispute. Those minimum requirements still had nothing to do with the merits or weaknesses of the Zionist claims. They stemmed from the chief executive's reading of political and strategic realities. Truman insisted that U.S. diplomacy seek a resolution that (1) did not involve the use of U.S. troops; (2) avoided the introduction of Soviet military presence in the Middle East; and (3) did not alienate American Zionists. He was apparently convinced that his prerequisites could protect both domestic and international interests.

Initially the president thought his one-hundred-thousand program had all the necessary ingredients without any of the forbidden elements. When he discovered that it failed to satisfy Jewish nationalists, he was quite willing to escalate the offer, even to the point of subtle endorsements of partition. At the same time, the chief executive maintained his opposition to the use of U.S. soldiers in Palestine. Throughout the United Nations debate he believed that if U.S. troops stayed out of the Holy Land, he could befriend Zionism without seriously alienating Arab leaders. If the army participated in any settlement, the Missouri Democrat reasoned, Moslem recrimination was likely to be extensive, and Moscow could use the presence of the United States as an excuse for sending its own personnel. When it became apparent that partition was impossible without stern enforcement and U.S. participation, Truman abandoned the division plans even at the risk of incurring political losses at home.

Despite the celebrated differences to the contrary, the president actually shared a basic Palestine perspective with his State Department. Both Truman and his diplomatic corps wanted a policy ultimately acceptable to Arab capitals. They initially disagreed only on how far the United States could afford to go without alienating the Middle East governments. Near Eastern division experts began the Truman era convinced that Washington should do nothing to foster an increase in Jewish strength in the Holy Land. Loy Henderson and his colleagues believed that support of a trusteeship in Palestine represented a minimum concession to the Moslems. A few in the State Department never changed their views. But much of the foreign policy wisdom, including that of Secretary Marshall, eventually concluded that Arabs would acquiesce to division if partition acquired United Nations endorsement. If Truman disagreed with State Department advice by late 1947, he did so on the side of caution.

Secretary Marshall and others were reluctantly willing to commit U.S. soldiers to enforcement of partition. The president was not.

Truman's policy in Palestine raises some basic questions about the impact of public opinion on U.S. diplomacy. There is little reason to believe the president formulated his approach from the direct pressures of popular attitudes. Yet the voters made an impact. Fear of national reactions kept Truman from pressing for a U.S. solution to the refugee problem. With no alternative, the chief executive clung tenaciously to the idea of sending Holocaust survivors to Palestine. Equally significantly, the president shared the cultural perspective that caused so many to smile on Jewish ascendancy in the Holy Land. With reinforcement from public discussions of the matter the Missourian could easily believe that Jews really did make superior use of the land and that they could become welcomed missionaries of Western progress.

In his management of Palestine matters Truman bowed to direct public persuasion only once. His rejection of the Grady plan stemmed solely from Zionist pressures. In turn, that decision produced momentous consequences. It virtually insured that Great Britain would eventually withdraw from Judea, leaving Jewish nationalists with the opportunity to seize control for themselves. Yet it took more than public attitudes to turn the president's head. It took a well-organized lobby to command White House attention. In fact, there is no reason to believe popular opinion demanded any action on the Anglo-American proposals. Most polls indicated strong support for Jewish settlement in Palestine but considerable indifference toward establishment of a new Israel.

Truman's handling of the Palestine controversy also raises some important questions about the contributions of the United States to the creation of Israel. Certainly the advocacy of the one-hundred-thousand program helped center attention on humanitarian considerations rather than on the less appealing political goals of Zionism. Truman's veto of the Grady plan killed a scheme that spelled doom for Jewish statehood. Yet neither move provided the Jewish nationalists with any direct assistance in moving uprooted people to Palestine or in the establishment of government machinery. Even passage of the United Nations partition resolution provided no concrete aid to Herzl's disciples. At most, the General Assembly vote meant there would be no action to prevent Zionist domination of Palestine. It gave the movement leaders precious time to consolidate their power before British withdrawal. While de facto recognition provided nothing of substance, it did pave the way for the later de jure recognition and the first U.S. military aid to Israel.

Perhaps the most significant American contribution, however, came from private sources. Without a concerted administrative effort to produce a non-Zionist solution, pro-Zionist elements seized the initiative from the government. Money from benefactors in the United States helped pay for the massive campaign to ship Jewish refugees to Palestine. It bought weapons for the underground fighters. It enabled Jewish nationalists to create the enormous instability that eventually forced some concessions from both the U.S. government and Arab leaders. It gave advocates of statehood the military strength to gain control of Palestine. Without the financial aid, success would have been unlikely. With it, Israel defeated her enemies and won domination over much of the Holy Land.[40]

[40] The Palestine Statehood Papers at the Sterling Memorial Library, Yale University, contain what is probably the most extensive documentation of private American aid to the Zionist underground.

W

hen Zionist leaders announced the creation of a Jewish state, Arab governments from Cairo to Damascus labeled the Israelis rebels and sent troops to crush the uprising. Arab League spokesmen insisted that Palestine be neither Jewish nor Moslem but a united commonwealth respecting the religious rights of all. They ultimately recognized an all-Palestine government with its capital in Gaza.

But the Truman administration insisted that the Egyptians, Jordanians, Syrians, and others who entered the Holy Land were invaders. As the fighting reached full-scale war, Washington sought United Nations help in establishing a cease-fire. Both the State Department and the White House wanted to pacify the situation quickly. Continued fighting threatened the stability so important to U.S. interests in the Middle East. Diplomatic leaders now pushed for a settlement that included continued existence for Israel, a trusteeship for Jerusalem, and some unspecified status for the rest of Palestine.

In June, 1948, the world organization finally secured a cease-fire. While the move was ostensibly neutral, it actually provided vital aid to the Israelis. When the fighting stopped, the Zionist army was suffering. While both sides broke the truce, the Israelis managed to benefit most from the lull in the war. They imported both arms and manpower during the peace. Private contributors in the United States supplied much of the financial backing. When the killing resumed in July, the once beleaguered Zionist forces were able to take the offensive.

With encouragement from the United States, the United Nations continued through the summer of 1948 to seek a settlement. In May the General Assembly appointed Count Folke Bernadotte of Sweden to mediate the dispute. By late June, Bernadotte had molded a peace proposal that included a federal union involving both Palestine and Transjordan. There would be two largely autonomous states, one Jewish and one Arab. Bernadotte called for some revisions in the old partition boundaries. He assigned the hotly contested Negev to the Arabs and western Galilee to the Jews.

Both sides in the Middle East dispute denounced the terms, but Great Britain and the United States initially endorsed them. Israelis objected to provisions reducing the size of the Jewish state. Arabs wanted a united Palestine. In time, however, even the U.S. president rejected the Bernadotte plan. Pro-Zionist opposition to the proposals made it difficult for Truman to maintain his support in an election year.

In September a Zionist terror squad murdered Bernadotte in Jerusalem, and peace seemed most elusive. The United Nations established a Conciliation Commission, and Ralph Bunche, an American, assumed Bernadotte's duties. But the Israelis were determined to gain as much territory as possible, and the Arabs were equally determined to prevent them from doing so. Zionists wanted to make sure they got the Negev and prepared to take it militarily. Beginning in early September they ignored the terms of a second truce and moved troops into strategic positions for a final assault on Egyptian strongholds. After goading the Arabs into an incident, they began "Operation Ten Plagues," a major offensive in the South.

At the United Nations, meanwhile, the British and Chinese introduced a resolution calling for an end to the fighting. Secretary Marshall initially gave U.S. support to the peace effort, but because it required Israel to give up newly conquered territory, friends of Zionism in the United States again pressured Truman. A few days before the election the president withdrew his government's backing from the resolution. On October 28 Israel once more took advantage of the U.S. political situation and the stalemate in the United Nations with a push to seize all of western Galilee. The Zionist leaders used tactics they had perfected against the Egyptians. They first accused Arabs of breaking the truce and then refused to allow the United Nations to investigate the charges. In late December they struck again, this time against Egypt.

When the General Assembly divided Palestine in November, 1947, most Zionists hailed the settlement and Arabs rejected it. After a year of conflict, however, Israelis ignored the partition plan and pushed for additional territory while Cairo and other capitals talked of returning to the original division borders. In January, 1949, the Egyptians and Israelis began peace negotiations on the isle of Rhodes, with Ralph Bunche acting as mediator. In the next few months he secured a series of armistice agreements to end the war. Meanwhile, Zionist forces continued to make advances, especially around the Gulf of Aqaba and in central Palestine. When the conflict ceased, Israel controlled far more territory than the original United Nations partition resolution ever intended. Jordan took most of the rest of old Palestine.[1]

Armistice agreements ended the war in 1949, but they brought no peace. For a generation to come, Arabs and Israelis continued to fight. Above all other causes, the Zionist seizure of the Holy Land and the displacement of Palestinians stimulated the conflict. A year of fighting left nearly one million people homeless. As the armies of Zion advanced into predominantly Arab regions in 1948, whole villages often fled in panic, especially after the terror of Deir Yessin. There were two hundred thousand refugees by May 15, 1948, when the British left the Holy Land. During the war that followed, the Israeli army, in the name of security, deliberately uprooted nearly that many more, often ordering people from their homes and then

[1] The bibliography includes a good many accounts of the Arab-Israeli conflict and U.S. policies that form the basis for the summary in this epilogue. The following works were especially helpful: Fred J. Khouri, *The Arab-Israeli Dilemma*; Howard M. Sachar, *A History of Israel: From the Rise of Zionism to Our Time*; Maxime Rodinson, *Israel and the Arabs*; Nadav Safran, *The United States and Israel*; and J. Bowyer Bell, *The Long War: Israel and the Arabs since 1946*.

destroying those dilapidated villages deemed unfit for settlement. Indeed, Count Bernadotte had concluded in the summer of 1948 that "almost the whole of the Arab population [had] fled or [been] expelled from the area under Jewish occupation."[2]

Furthermore, Israeli policies toward both the refugees and the Arabs who remained in Palestine helped feed the conflict. Zionist leaders expropriated Arab lands, froze bank accounts, and generally refused to allow the refugees to return home. In times of crisis the policy grew even harsher, often resulting in "preventive arrests" and sometimes harassments and brutality. Despite the mistreatment, however, the refugees did not carry on an organized war against Israel in the years immediately following 1948. Although some individuals occasionally staged deliberate raids, most of the early conflicts resulted from innocent mistakes. The armistice left borders that did not always coincide with traditional boundaries. Confusion on both sides was inevitable. Refugees seeking to return home to reclaim land, move property, or rescue relatives often incurred trouble from Israeli authorities.

Yet not all of the conflicts were accidental. The Zionist victory and subsequent displacement of a million people left harsh feelings. Palestinians were reluctant to forget. Some never gave up their determination to return home and overturn the Zionist regime. The troubles usually followed a distinct pattern. Small bands of disgruntled Arabs would conduct their own private war of retaliation, raiding Jewish settlements. Then Israel would eventually respond with massive strikes against neighboring Arab countries. Especially after 1951, Prime Minister David Ben-Gurion directed large reprisal attacks on a "two blows for one" basis.

In a sense, renewed fighting between Israel and the Arab countries was inevitable, given the policies and intentions of both sides. While Egypt, Jordan, Lebanon, and their neighbors gave little early aid to Palestinian commandos (actually curbing refugees from entering Israel and thus causing conflict), they did apply economic

[2] Khouri, *Arab-Israeli Dilemma*, p. 124.

sanctions against the Jewish state. Egypt refused to let the Israelis use the Suez Canal or the Gulf of Aqaba, in part to protest the seizure of land at the northern end of the gulf after the armistice.

Yet the Egyptian policy was not the major source of conflict. The practice of punishing the Arab countries for the deeds of Palestinian commandos eventually produced far more trouble. Indeed, Cairo was willing to submit both its Suez and Aqaba policies to the World Court or even end the blockade if Israel agreed to accept United Nations requirements on the treatment of Palestinian refugees. Especially after a February, 1955, Israeli attack on the Gaza Strip, Egypt was determined to strengthen its military and aid fellow Arabs.

But perhaps the chief source of conflict was the intention of many Zionist leaders to take even more land from the Arabs. One faction of Jewish nationalists had always rejected partition and called for seizure of additional territory. That group found increasing support in the early 1950's from people who wished to crush the Palestinians entirely. In the name of both security and ancient religious beliefs, the Zionists pushed toward the old limits of Palestine and even beyond.

In 1955 Israelis moved into the demilitarized zone on the border with Syria. When small skirmishes followed, they raided a Syrian town, killing fifty-six residents. Yet when war finally came between Israel and her Arab neighbors, it erupted in the wake of international events that had little direct relationship to the struggle over promised land. After Gamal Abdel Nasser came to power in Egypt in 1952, the Eisenhower administration subsequently promised economic aid to help build the Aswan Dam across the upper Nile. But when Nasser purchased military goods from the Russians, Secretary of State Dulles cancelled the assistance in July, 1956. One week later, Cairo announced intentions to nationalize the Suez Canal, pay off stockholders (most of whom were British or other Europeans), and use income from the waterway to pay for the dam.

Both London and Paris prepared to go to war against Egypt. The United States was angry with Nasser but took no action. The British and French moved troops into the eastern Mediterranean, and Nasser pulled forces out of the Sinai to protect Cairo and Alexandria. Israel decided in October to exploit the situation. With the hope that the presidential campaign in the United States would keep Eisenhower quiet, Jewish forces struck into the Sinai Peninsula.

But the Americans reacted quickly. They introduced a resolution into the Security Council calling for an Israeli withdrawal from Sinai. The British and French, however, vetoed it. Washington finally won approval in the General Assembly for a plan to have the United Nations supervise the border in the Sinai and along the Gulf of Aqaba in return for Israeli withdrawal from newly conquered territory. While both sides eventually accepted, and Israel withdrew from all but a small portion of occupied land, only Egypt allowed United Nations Emergency Forces (UNEF) on her territory.

Bitterness and persecutions became the chief results of the war. Arabs in Israel and Jews in Egypt found life especially difficult. The Cairo government stepped up its harassment of Jewish citizens, while Tel Aviv did the same to Moslems under its jurisdiction. Perhaps the most tragic incident occurred at the village of Kfar Kassem when Israeli border police killed nearly fifty Palestinians who failed to obey a curfew they knew nothing about.

In the years to come, border conflicts continued to exist, but they were relatively few in number. Major elements in the Zionist state still wanted all of the Holy Land, including the West Bank, Sinai, and the Golan Heights, and the Palestinians hoped to retake their homeland. Yet no serious threat of war developed until after a clash in April, 1967, over disputed land along the Syrian border. Israel staged a major reprisal raid on Syria a few days later, and Palestinian commandos increased their attacks on the Jewish state. Meanwhile, the Egyptians prepared to respond in case of an Israeli attack on Syria. On May 18 they requested that the UNEF leave Egyptian territory in the Sinai. Secretary General U Thant complied.

Nasser was apparently reluctant to go to war. He was aware of his own military weakness and fearful of U.S. support for his enemy. Yet pressure from Arab nationalists forced him to respond to attacks on Syria. In May he once more closed the Gulf of Aqaba to Israel.

Jewish leaders were apprehensive. The old advocates of taking all of Palestine now found support from those who worried over access to the Gulf of Aqaba and blamed the Arab governments for the commando raids. Seemingly, war with Egypt could satisfy ancient ambitions, thoroughly crush the Palestinians, and win permanent access to the Suez and Aqaba. Cairo knew that war was likely but refused to back down. While the Egyptians denied responsibility for the Palestinian commandos, they defended the guerrilla raids and reminded the Israelis that the Zionist movement utilized terrorism in its own drive for power in the forties. Nasser continued to blame Palestinian unrest on the Jewish mistreatment of refugees.

For a while a diplomatic effort by the United States to find a compromise solution appeared to have some chance for success. But before any plan could win acceptance, the Israelis attacked Egypt on June 5. Within days they also bombed Syria, Jordan, and Iraq. Within a week they had taken control of Sinai, the Golan Heights, and the West Bank, including all of Jerusalem. The June war achieved most of the old Zionist territorial ambitions, but it did not end the Palestinian unrest. In fact, it did the exact opposite. As the Israelis swept into Arab land, they created a quarter of a million fresh refugees. The Palestine Liberation Organization was born in 1969, a child of the conflict. Commando raids from the uprooted became more frequent. Israel responded to each attack as she had in the past, escalating the fighting with each reprisal.

For twenty-five years both the Security Council and the General Assembly consistently condemned Zionist expansion, the Israeli reprisal policy, and the treatment of the Palestinian refugees; 1967 was no exception. In November the Security Council passed the British-sponsored Resolution 242, which called for "withdrawal of Israeli armed forces from territories occupied in the recent conflict." Yet the Israelis ignored the United Nations criticism. For reasons of security, religion, and economics, Zionist leaders held on to the newly conquered territory. Even Arab hints that they would recognize the Tel Aviv government and stop economic warfare against it did not dissuade Jewish leaders from their plans to keep the gains of war.

With no prospects for Israeli compliance with Resolution 242 and little hope that either the United States or the United Nations would apply sufficient pressure on the Zionists, Arab leaders contemplated military action against their enemies. On October 6, 1973, Egyptian tanks and infantry crossed the Suez Canal and pushed into occupied Sinai. Eleven days later the oil-producing Arab states announced a petroleum boycott against the United States. For the fourth time in twenty-five years there was war over the Holy Land.

American reactions to the Arab-Israeli dispute generally followed Harry Truman's lead, and for good reasons. Presidents from Eisenhower to Carter continued to face the pressures the Missouri Democrat had encountered. Furthermore, Truman had seemingly demonstrated that he had chosen the path of least resistance. He may have failed to stop a war, but he did win the 1948 presidential election and kept the oil concessions for U.S. companies. Finally, Truman had left his successors a weakened United Nations. No U.S. president was able, or perhaps even wanted, to repair the damage caused by his fluctuations and his willingness to ignore the world organization.

Thus, both Republicans and Democrats acted largely unilaterally and advocated compromise in the Middle East while protecting Israel's continued existence. They urged the Arab governments to normalize their relations with the Jewish state and even tried to buy that cooperation with economic assistance to the Moslems, but they also chastised Jews for their treatment of Palestinian refugees and sought limits on Zionist expansion. Presidents Johnson, Nixon, Ford, and Carter endorsed Resolution 242.

Yet those presidents were reluctant to press their demands on either side. Instead, they continued to supply considerable economic and military assistance to the Jewish commonwealth and small quantities of aid to Arab countries, especially Jordan and Saudi Arabia. In the first twenty-five years after 1948 the U.S. provided $2.3 billion in loans and gifts to Israel. In addition, Washington sold the Zionists an impressive array of the latest military hardware. When war erupted in 1973, President Nixon asked Congress to supply Tel Aviv with $2.2 billion in emergency aid. Private American help was even more substantial. From 1950 to 1973, U.S. citizens purchased nearly $3 billion in State of Israel bonds.

Arab resentments toward the United States continued to grow through the 1950's, 1960's, and 1970's primarily because Washington was willing to grant the Israelis military assistance but was unwilling to force the Zionists to roll back their expansions and change their policies toward Palestinian refugees. After the 1973 war the Nixon administration faced the consequences of such U.S. failures, and the oil boycott finally forced some serious reconsideration. The United States cooperated with the Soviet Union in sponsoring a peace conference in Geneva, Switzerland. Secretary of State Henry Kissinger engaged in a highly publicized effort to win territorial concessions from the Israelis. In January, 1974, Israel signed the first Sinai agreement, giving up a small portion of the disputed peninsula. In the spring of that year the United States joined Japan and Great Britain in sweeping mines from the Suez Canal. Arab leaders finally became convinced that Washington was doing all it could to force compliance with Resolution 242, and in March they ended the oil boycott. One year later a second Sinai agreement resulted in additional Israeli concessions, including surrender of an oil field to Egypt.

By late 1977 there were signs that Egypt wanted to normalize relations with the Israelis. President Anwar Sadat even spoke to the Knesset in Jerusalem. And in the spring of 1979, Israel and Egypt signed a formal peace treaty with each other. Such progress toward peace did not, however, settle one gnawing problem—the resentment of the Palestinians. Within days after the signing of the Israeli-Egyptian accords, Palestinian raiders attacked Jewish settlements and the Israeli army retaliated against Arab refugee villages in southern Lebanon. Despite the new peace treaty, most Moslem countries continued to condemn the Zionist state and its U.S. backers.

Events of the twentieth century produced a tragic sequence. Zionism grew from the bigotry and jingoism of Christendom. Jewish leaders sought revenge for the Holocaust and found targets in hapless Arabs. Palestinian nationalism matured from the example of its Jewish counterpart. The Irgun and the Stern Gang sometimes employed the terrorism of their former Nazi oppressors, and the Palestinians then borrowed the tactics and vowed not to rest until they had reclaimed a homeland.

Sending one hundred thousand refugees to the Holy Land in 1945 did not necessitate creation of a Jewish state. The birth of Israel did not require displacement of one million Arabs or the policies of harassment of and discrimination against Palestinians. The continued existence of the Zionist state did not depend on expansion. Yet in light of the recent history of the Jewish people in Europe, such outcomes were understandable.

If world leaders hoped to prevent tragedy from begetting tragedy, they could not leave matters entirely in the hands of either embittered Jews or subsequently revengeful Arabs. The United Nations offered some prospects for finding a settlement based on justice, and through that organization Harry Truman had the opportunity to sponsor a collective solution to the Jewish refugee problem that might have minimized future conflict. Instead, he first denied responsibility for any political settlement in the Holy Land, then treated the United Nations as an instrument of U.S. foreign policy, freely ignoring or following its decisions as he saw fit. Neither Truman nor the American people were generally able to understand how to keep one solution from becoming the source of future conflict.

ARCHIVAL MATERIALS

Cambridge, Mass. Harvard University Library. Joseph C. Grew Papers.
————. William Yale Papers.
Charlottesville, Va. University of Virginia Library. Edward R. Stettinius Papers.
————. J. Rives Childs Papers.
Clemson, S.C. Clemson University Library. James F. Byrnes Papers.
Independence, Mo. Harry S Truman Presidential Library. Clark M. Clifford Papers.
————. George Elsey Papers.
————. Harry S Truman Papers.
————. Henry Grady Papers.
————. J. Howard McGrath Papers.
————. John Snyder Papers.
————. Myron C. Taylor Papers.
————. Philleo Nash Papers.
————. Samuel I. Rosenman Papers.
New Haven, Conn. Yale University, Sterling Memorial Library. Henry L. Stimson Papers.
————. Palestine Statehood Papers.
New York, N.Y. Columbia University Library. Herbert Lehman Collection, James G. McDonald Papers.
————. Oral History Collection. Reminiscences of Goldthwaite Dorr.
Princeton, N.J. Princeton University Library. Bernard M. Baruch Papers.
————. David E. Lilienthal Papers.
————. George F. Kennan Papers.
————. James V. Forrestal Papers.
Waltham, Mass. Brandeis University Library. Stephen Wise Papers.
Washington, D.C. Georgetown University Library. Robert F. Wagner Papers.
Washington, D.C. Library of Congress, Manuscript Division. Emanuel Celler Papers.
————. Felix Frankfurter Papers.

———. Francis Bowes Sayre Papers.
———. James M. Landis Papers.
———. Joseph W. and Stewart Alsop Papers.
———. Robert Patterson Papers.
———. Robert Taft Papers.
———. Tom Connally Papers.
———. William D. Leahy Papers.
———. William S. Culbertson Papers.
Washington, D.C. National Archives. Record Group 46, Records of the United States Senate, Foreign Relations Committee, 79th Congress.
———. Record Group 59, Records of the Department of State.
———. Record Group 80, Records of the Department of the Navy.
———. Record Group 107, Records of the Secretary of the Army.
———. Record Group 218, Records of the Joint Chiefs of Staff.

INTERVIEWS

Dorr, Goldthwaite. Interview with the author, July 11, 1974. New York, N.Y.
Henderson, Loy. Interview with the author, June 12, 1974. Washington, D.C.

UNPUBLISHED WORKS

Golding, David. "United States Foreign Policy in Palestine and Israel, 1945–1949." Ph.D. dissertation, New York University, 1961.
Grady, Henry. "Adventures in Diplomacy." Manuscript at Harry S Truman Presidential Library, Independence, Mo.
Ilan, A. "The Origin and Development of American Intervention in British Palestine Policy, 1938–1947." Ph.D. dissertation, Oxford University, 1974.
Nasir, Sari Jamil. "The Image of the Arab in American Popular Culture." Ph.D. dissertation, University of Illinois, 1962.
Oder, Irwin. "The United States and the Palestine Mandate, 1920–1948: A Study of the Impact of Interest Groups on Foreign Policy." Ph.D. dissertation, Columbia University, 1956.
Rigdon, William M. "Log of the President's Trip to the Berlin Conference (July 6, 1945, to August 7, 1945)." Manuscript at Harry S Truman Presidential Library, Independence, Mo.
Sachar, David B. "David K. Niles and United States Policy Toward Palestine." Undergraduate Honors Thesis, Harvard University, 1959.
Snetsinger, John G. "Truman and the Creation of Israel." Ph.D. dissertation, Stanford University, 1969.
Travis, Paul D. "Charlatans, Sharpers, and Climatology: The Symbolism

and Mythology of Late Nineteenth Century Expansionism in Kansas."
Ph.D. dissertation, University of Oklahoma, 1975.

GOVERNMENT DOCUMENTS

*Public Papers of the President of the United States: Harry S. Truman,
1945–1948.* Washington, D.C.: Government Printing Office, 1961–
1963.
U.S. Congress. *Congressional Record,* 67th, 77th–80th Congs., 1922,
1941–1948, 62, 87–94.
———, House of Representatives. *Report No. 179.* 78th Cong., 2d sess.,
1944.
———. Senate. *Hearings on the Palestine Refugee Problem before the
Senate Subcommittee on the Near East and Africa of the Committee
on Foreign Relations,* 82d Cong., 2d sess., 1953.
———, ———, Special Committee Investigating Petroleum Reserves.
American Petroleum Interests in Foreign Countries, Hearings, 79th
Cong., 1st sess., 1945.
U.S. Department of State. *Department of State Bulletin* 4–16 (1941–
1947).
———. *Foreign Relations of the United States, 1941–1947.* Washington,
D.C.: Government Printing Office, 1958–1972.
———. *Foreign Relations of the United States: The Conference of Ber-
lin (The Potsdam Conference), 1945.* 2 Vols. Washington, D.C.: Gov-
ernment Printing Office, 1960.

BOOKS AND ARTICLES

Abu-Lughod, Ibrahim, ed. *The Transformation of Palestine: Essays on
the Origin and Development of the Arab-Israeli Conflict.* Evanston,
Ill.: Northwestern University Press, 1971.
Acheson, Dean. *Present at the Creation: My Years in the State Depart-
ment.* New York: The New American Library, 1970.
Adler, Frank J. *Roots in a Moving Stream: The Centennial History of
Congregation B'nai Jehudah of Kansas City, 1870–1970.* Kansas City:
The Temple, Congregation B'nai, 1972.
Adler, Selig. "Franklin D. Roosevelt and Zionism—The Wartime Record,"
Judaism 21 (Summer, 1972): 265–276.
———. "The Palestine Question in the Wilson Era," *Jewish Social Stud-
ies* 10 (October, 1948): 314–320.
Ahlstrom, Sydney E. *A Religious History of the American People.* New
Haven: Yale University Press, 1972.
Albright, W. F. "Palestine Transformed," *The Nation* 158 (June 3, 1944):
656.

Annual of the Southern Baptist Convention, 1948, Ninety-first Session.
Nashville, Tenn.: Broadman Press, 1948.

Antonius, George. *The Arab Awakening: The Story of the Arab National Movement.* New York: G. P. Putnam's Sons, 1946.

Atkinson, Henry A. "Betrayal from the Left," *Churchman* 45 (November 1, 1945): 78.

"Atlantic Report on the World Today: Palestine," *Atlantic Monthly* 173 (September, 1946): 17–22.

"Aydelotte, Frank," *Current Biography* 2 (October, 1941): 4–6.

Bain, Kenneth R. "American Foreign Policy and the Palestine Resolution: 1944," *Paisano: The Historian of the University of Texas* 9–10 (1970–1972): 63–76.

Baly, Denis. *Palestine and the Bible.* New York: Association Press, 1961.

Barbour, Nevil. *Palestine: Star or Crescent.* New York: The Odyssey Press, 1947.

Bell, J. Bowyer. *The Long War: Israel and the Arabs since 1946.* Englewood Cliffs, N.J.: Prentice-Hall, 1969.

Ben-Horin, Eliahu. "The Cockpit of the Middle East," *Harper's* 193 (July, 1946): 69–75.

———. "The Future of the Middle East," *Harper's* 190 (December, 1944): 82–90.

Bentwich, Norman. "The History of the Balfour Declaration, 1917–1948," *Contemporary Review* 211 (August, 1967): 74–81.

Berkman, Ted. "This is the Arab," *American Mercury* 65 (November, 1947): 528–538.

Berle, A. A. "Three Roads to War," *American* 142 (August, 1946): 21, 98–101.

Bickerton, Ian J. "President Truman's Recognition of Israel," *American Jewish Historical Quarterly* 58 (December, 1968): 173–239.

Bierbrier, Doreen, "American Zionist Emergency Council: An Analysis of a Pressure Group," *American Jewish Historical Quarterly* 60 (September, 1970): 82–105.

Bingay, Malcolm W. "What I Saw in Europe: What We Must Do About It," *Vital Speeches* 11 (August 1, 1945): 623–624.

Bradbury, John W. *The Sure Word of Prophecy.* New York: Fleming H. Revell Company, 1943.

Brody, David. "American Jewry, the Refugees, and Immigration Restriction (1932–1942)," *Publications of the American Jewish Historical Society* 45 (September, 1955–June, 1956): 219–247.

Brown, Charles E. *The Hope of His Coming.* Anderson, Ind.: Gospel Trumpet Company, 1927.

Burnham, James. "The Goal of Soviet Policy," *American Mercury* 64 (April, 1947): 389–406.

"Buxton, Frank," *Who's Who in America* 24 (1946–1947): 346.

Byrnes, James F. *Speaking Frankly.* New York: Harper and Brothers, 1947.

Cahman, Werner J. "Review: Palestine, Land of Promise," *American Journal of Sociology* 50 (September, 1944): 155–156.

Cameron, Robert. *Scriptural Truth About the Lord's Return.* New York: Fleming H. Revell Company, 1922.

Cantril, Hadley, and Mildred Strunk, eds. *Public Opinion, 1935–1946.* Princeton: Princeton University Press, 1951.

Carey, Gary. "The Long, Long Road to Brenda Patimkin," *National Jewish Monthly*, October, 1971. Reprinted in *The Black Man on Film: Racial Stereotyping*, ed. Richard A. Maynard. Rochelle Park, N.J.: Hayden, 1974.

Case, Shirley Jackson. *The Millennial Hope: A Phase of War-Time Thinking.* Chicago: University of Chicago Press, 1918.

Choveaux, Andree. "The New Palestine," *Geographical Review* 17 (January, 1927): 75–88.

Clifford, Clark M. "Recognizing Israel," *American Heritage* 28 (April, 1977): 4–11.

Cochran, Bert. *Harry Truman and the Crisis Presidency.* New York: Funk and Wagnalls, 1973.

Cohen, M. J. "Direction of Policy in Palestine, 1936–1945," *Middle East Studies* 11 (October, 1975): 237–267.

"The Contribution of Palestine," *New Republic* 109 (August 30, 1943): 314–315.

Crossman, Richard H. A. *Palestine Mission: A Personal Record.* New York: Harper and Brothers, 1947.

"Crum, Bartley," *Current Biography* 8 (May, 1947): 18–20.

Crum, Bartley C. *Behind the Silken Curtain.* New York: Simon and Schuster, 1947.

"Dachau: Experimental Murder," *Collier's* 115 (June 23, 1945): 16, 28, 30.

Daniel, Robert L. *American Philanthropy in the Near East, 1920–1960.* Athens, Ohio: Ohio University Press, 1970.

Daniels, Jonathan. *The Man of Independence.* Philadelphia: Lippincott, 1950.

Davis, George T. B. *Rebuilding Palestine According to Prophecy.* Philadelphia: The Million Testaments Campaign, 1935.

DeHaan, M. R. *The Second Coming of Jesus.* Grand Rapids, Mich.: Zondervan Publishing House, 1944.

Divine, Robert. *American Immigration Policy, 1924–1952.* New York: Da Capo Press, 1972.

———. *Foreign Policy and U.S. Presidential Elections, 1940–1948.* New York: New Viewpoints, 1974.

Dulles, John Foster. *War or Peace.* New York: Macmillan, 1950.

Encyclopedia Judaica. 10 vols. New York: Macmillan, 1971.

Epstein, Eliahu. "Middle Eastern Munich," *The Nation* 162 (March 9, 1946): 287–288.

Erskine, H. "Polls: Western Partisanship in the Middle East," *Public Opinion Quarterly* 33 (Winter, 1969–1970): 627–640.

"An Exclusive Interview with Clark Clifford," *American Heritage* 28 (April, 1977): 8–9.

Fairbairn, C. *The Interpretation of Prophecy*. London: The Banner of Truth Trust, 1964.

Feingold, Henry L. *The Politics of Rescue: The Roosevelt Administration and the Holocaust, 1938–1945*. New Brunswick, N.J.: Rutgers University Press, 1970.

————. "Roosevelt and the Holocaust: Reflections on New Deal Humanitarianism," *Judaism* 18 (Summer, 1969): 259–276.

Feis, Herbert. *The Birth of Israel: The Tousled Diplomatic Bed*. New York: Norton, 1969.

Ferrell, Robert. "American Policy in the Middle East," *Review of Politics* 37 (January, 1975): 3–19.

————. *George C. Marshall*. New York: Cooper Square Publishers, 1966.

Fink, Reuben, ed. *America and Palestine: The Attitude of Official America and of the American People Toward the Rebuilding of Palestine as a Free and Democratic Jewish Commonwealth*. New York: Herald Square Press, 1945.

Forrestal, James. *The Forrestal Diaries*, ed. Walter Millis. New York: Viking Press, 1951.

Frank, Gerold. "Fact and Legend about Palestine," *American Mercury* 61 (December, 1945): 685–692.

————. "The Tragedy of the DP's," *New Republic* 114 (April 1, 1946): 436–438.

Frankfurter, Felix N. *Felix Frankfurter Reminisces*. New York: Reynal, 1960.

Friedman, Saul S. *No Haven for the Oppressed: U.S. Policy Toward Jewish Refugees, 1938–1945*. Detroit: Wayne State University Press, 1973.

The Gallup Poll: Public Opinion, 1935–1971, Vol. I. New York: Random House, 1972.

Geissler, Eugene S. "Jewish Farming in Palestine," *America* 14 (January 19, 1946): 428.

Gervasi, Frank. "Terror in Palestine," *Collier's* 116 (August 11, 1945): 24, 64–65.

Grabill, Joseph L. *Protestant Diplomacy and the Near East: Missionary Influence on American Policy, 1810–1927*. Minneapolis: University of Minnesota Press, 1971.

Gruber, Ruth. *Destination Palestine*. New York: Current Books, 1948.

Haldeman, I. M. *The Signs of the Times*. New York: Charles C. Cook, 1914.

Halliwell, Leslie. *The Filmgoer's Companion*. London: Hart-Davis, MacGibbon, 1974.

Halperin, Samuel. *The Political World of American Zionism*. Detroit: Wayne State University Press, 1961.

————, and Irvin Oder. "The United States in Search of a Policy: Franklin D. Roosevelt and Palestine," *Review of Politics* 24 (July, 1962): 320–341.

Halpern, Ben. *The Idea of the Jewish State.* Cambridge, Mass.: Harvard University Press, 1969.

Hamby, Alonzo. *Beyond the New Deal: Harry S. Truman and American Liberalism.* New York: Columbia University Press: 1973.

Hamilton, Charles W. *Americans and Oil in the Middle East.* Houston: Gulf Publishing Company, 1962.

Handlin, Oscar. "American Views of the Jews at the Opening of the Twentieth Century," *Publications of the American Jewish Historical Society* 40 (June, 1951): 323–344.

Hanna, Paul L. *British Policy in Palestine.* Washington, D.C.: American Council of Public Affairs, 1942.

Hanser, Richard. "German Anti-Semitism Today," *American Mercury* 66 (April, 1948): 433–438.

Harrison, Earl G. "The Last Hundred Thousand," *Survey Graphic* 34 (December, 1945): 73–77.

Herring, George C. *Aid to Russia, 1941–1946.* New York: Columbia University Press, 1973.

Hillman, William, ed. *Mr. President: The First Publication From the Personal Diaries, Private Letters, Papers, and Revealing Interviews of Harry S. Truman, Thirty-Second President of the United States of America.* New York: Farrar, Straus and Young, 1952.

Hourani, Albert. *Arabic Thought in the Liberal Age, 1798–1939.* London: Oxford University Press.

Howard, Harry N. *The King Crane Commission.* Beirut: Khayat, 1963.

Huff, E. D. "The Study of a Successful Interest Group: The American Zionist Movement," *Western Political Quarterly* 25 (March, 1972): 109–124.

Hull, Cordell. *The Memoirs of Cordell Hull.* 2 vols. New York: Macmillan, 1948.

Hurewitz, Jacob C. *The Struggle for Palestine.* New York: W. W. Norton, 1950.

———. "United States Policies on Palestine," *Publication of the American Jewish Historical Society* 40 (December, 1950): 107–118.

"Hutcheson, Joseph C.," *Who's Who in the South and Southwest*, vol. X. Chicago: Marquis, 1967.

"Interim Policy for Palestine," *New Republic* 113 (November 26, 1945): 692–693.

Ismael, Jacqueline S., and Tareq Y. Ismael. "The Arab-Americans and the Middle East," *Middle East Journal* 30 (Summer, 1976): 390–405.

"The Jews of Europe: How to Help Them," *New Republic* 109 (August 30, 1943): 295–316.

Kelsey, W. K. "Problem: Palestine," *Forum* 104 (December, 1945): 352–354.

Kennan, George F. *Memoirs, 1925–1950.* Boston: Little, Brown, 1967.

Khouri, Fred J. *The Arab-Israeli Dilemma*. Syracuse, N.Y.: Syracuse University Press, 1968.

Kimche, Jon, and David Kimche. *A Clash of Destinies: The Arab-Jewish War and the Founding of the State of Israel*. New York: Praeger, 1960.

Kirchwey, Freda. "Palestine and Bevin," *The Nation* 162 (June 22, 1946): 737–739.

———. "The Palestine Inquiry," *The Nation* 162 (January 12, 1946): 33.

Krammer, Arnold, "Soviet Motives in the Partition of Palestine, 1947–1948," *Journal of Palestine Studies* 2 (Winter, 1973): 102–119.

Krock, Arthur. *Memoirs: Sixty Years on the Firing Line*. New York: Funk and Wagnalls, 1968.

Kurzman, Dan. *Genesis 1948: The First Arab-Israeli War*. New York: World Publishing Company, 1970.

Lamb, Harold. "The Middle East Explodes," *Saturday Evening Post*, August 18, 1945, pp. 18–19, 85–86.

Laqueur, Walter. *A History of Zionism*. New York: Rinehart and Winston, 1972.

———, ed. *The Israel-Arab Reader*. New York: Bantam Books, 1969.

Leahy, William D. *I Was There: The Personal Story of the Chief of Staff to Presidents Roosevelt and Truman, Based on His Notes and Diaries Made at the Time*. New York: McGraw-Hill, 1950.

Lehman, Herbert H. "Freeing Hitler's 15,000,000 Slaves," *American* 139 (May, 1945): 20–21, 104–108.

Lenczowski, George. *Oil and State in the Middle East*. Ithaca, N.Y.: Cornell University Press, 1960.

Lie, Trygve. *In the Cause of Peace*. New York: Macmillan, 1954.

Light On Prophecy, A Coordinated Constructive Teaching: The Proceedings and Addresses at the Philadelphia Prophetic Conference, May 28–30, 1918. New York: The Christian Herald Bible House, 1918.

Lilienthal, Alfred M. *The Other Side of the Coin*. New York: The Devin-Adair Company, 1965.

Lindberg, Milton B. *Palestine and Jews Today in the Light of Prophecy*. Chicago: Chicago Hebrew Mission, 1930.

Lowdermilk, Walter C. "The Land and the People," *The Nation* 165 (October 4, 1947): 360–361.

———. *Palestine, Land of Promise*. New York: Harper and Brothers, 1944.

McCown, Chester Charlton. *The Promise of His Coming*. New York: Macmillan, 1921.

McDonald, James G. *My Mission in Israel, 1948–1951*. New York: Simon and Schuster, 1951.

"McDonald, James G.," *Current Biography* 10 (April, 1949): 37–39.

McDonald, John. "What Road to Zion," *Fortune* 36 (September, 1947): 116–119, 146, 150, 153–157.

Manuel, Frank Edward. *The Realities of American-Palestine Relations.* New York: Public Affairs Press, 1949.

Massing, Paul W., and Maxwell Miller. "Should Jews Return to Germany?" *Atlantic Monthly* 176 (July, 1945): 87–90.

Meigs, Peveril. "Review: *Palestine: Land of Promise,*" *Geographical Review* 35 (January, 1945): 168–170.

Mikesell, Raymond F., and Hollis B. Chenery. *Arabian Oil: America's Stake in the Middle East.* Chapel Hill, N.C.: University of North Carolina Press, 1949.

Mowrer, Edgar Ansel. "Call the Mufti!" *Forum* 104 (March, 1946): 611–612.

Muller, Edwin. "The Arabs Are on the Move," *Reader's Digest* 49 (September, 1946): 49–53.

Munden, Kenneth W., ed. *The American Film Institute Catalog of Motion Pictures Produced in the United States: Feature Films, 1921–1930.* New York: R. R. Bowker, 1971.

Murphy, Robert D. *Diplomat Among Warriors.* Garden City: Doubleday, 1964.

Nadich, Judah. *Eisenhower and the Jews.* New York: Twayne Publisher, 1953.

Norris, George W. "TVA on the Jordan," *The Nation* 158 (May 20, 1944): 589.

"Nowhere to Lay Their Heads," *New Republic* 113 (October 29, 1945): 556–557.

Oder, Irwin. "American Zionism and the Congressional Resolution of 1922 on Palestine," *Publication of the American Jewish Historical Society* 45 (September, 1955–June, 1956): 35–47.

O'Shaughnessy, Thomas. "Soviet Shadows in the Arab East," *America* 14 (January 26, 1946): 456–458.

"Palestine . . . Much Promised Land," *Scholastic* 47 (December 3, 1945): 6–7.

"The Palestine Problem and Proposals for Its Solution," *The Nation* 164 (May 17, 1947): 585–613.

Pankhurst, Christabel. *Seeing the Future.* New York: Harper and Brothers, 1929.

Parzan, Herbert. "President Truman and the Palestine Quandary: His Initial Experience, April–December, 1945," *Jewish Social Studies* 35 (January, 1973): 42–72.

———. "The Roosevelt Palestine Policy, 1943–1945," *American Jewish Archives* 26 (April, 1974): 31–65.

Patai, Raphael. *Encyclopedia of Zionism and Israel,* 2 vols. New York: Herzl Press, 1971.

Patch, George H. *Prophecy Explained, Past, Present, and Future.* New York: The Christian Herald Bible House, 1921.

Philby, J. St. John B. *Arabian Jubilee.* London: Hale, 1952.

Phillips, William. *Ventures in Diplomacy*. Boston: privately published, 1952.

Plesur, Milton. "The Relations Between the United States and Palestine," *Judaism* 3 (Fall, 1954): 469–479.

Polk, William R., David M. Stamler, and Edmund Asfour. *Backdrop to Tragedy: The Struggle for Palestine*. Boston: Beacon Press, 1957.

Postal, Bernard, and Henry W. Levy. *And the Hills Shouted for Joy: The Day Israel Was Born*. New York: David McKay Company, 1973.

"A Program for Palestine," *New Republic* 115 (July 15, 1946): 31–32.

Proskauer, Joseph. *A Segment of My Times*. New York: Farrar, Strauss, 1950.

Renner, George T. "America's Outpost for Peace," *American* 139 (May, 1945): 116.

Rimmer, Harry, *The Shadow of Coming Events*. Grand Rapids, Mich.: William B. Eerdmans Publishing Company, 1946.

Rodinson, Maxime. *Israel and the Arabs*. New York: Pantheon, 1968.

Roosevelt, Eleanor. *This I Remember*. New York: Harper, 1949.

Roosevelt, Franklin, *Franklin Roosevelt and Frankfurter: Their Correspondence, 1928–1945*, annotated by Max Freedman. Boston: Little, Brown, 1968.

Roosevelt, Kermit. "The Arabs Live There Too," *Harper's* 193 (October, 1946): 289–294.

———. "The Partition of Palestine: A Lesson in Pressure Politics," *Middle East Journal* 2 (January, 1948): 1–16.

Rosenwald, Lessing J. "The Fallacies of Palestine," *Collier's* 121 (March 13, 1948): 30–32.

Sachar, Howard M. *A History of Israel: From the Rise of Zionism to Our Time*. New York: Knopf, 1976.

Sakran, Frank Charles. *Palestine Dilemma: Arab Rights versus Zionist Aspirations*. Washington, D.C.: Public Affairs Press, 1948.

Sandeen, Ernest R. *The Roots of Fundamentalism: British and American Millenarianism, 1800–1930*. Chicago: University of Chicago Press, 1970.

Schechtman, Joseph B. "Roosevelt and the Jews—I," *Jewish World* 1 (February, 1955): 7–10.

———. *The United States and the Jewish State Movement: The Crucial Decade, 1939–1949*. New York: Thomas Yoseloff, 1966.

Selim, George Dimitri. *American Doctoral Dissertations on the Arab World, 1883–1968*. Washington, D.C.: Government Printing Office, 1970.

Selznick, Gertrude J., and Stephen Steinberg. *The Tenacity of Prejudice: Anti-Semitism in Contemporary America*. New York: Harper and Row, 1969.

"Send Them to Palestine," *New Republic* 114 (January 7, 1946): 7–8.

"The Shape of Things," *The Nation* 165 (October 11, 1947): 367–369.

Sherwood, Robert E. *Roosevelt and Hopkins*. New York: Harper, 1948.

Shwadran, Benjamin. *The Middle East, Oil and the Great Powers.* New York: Praeger, 1955.

Silver, Abba Hillel. "Why the Jews Should Have Palestine," *American Magazine* 144 (December, 1947): 34–35, 126–130.

Simpson, A. B. *The Coming One.* New York: Christian Alliance Publishing Company, 1912.

Snetsinger, John. *Truman, the Jewish Vote, and the Creation of Israel.* Stanford, Calif.: Stanford University Press, 1974.

Spear, Sheldon. "The United States and the Persecution of the Jews in Germany, 1933–1939," *Jewish Social Studies* 30 (October, 1968): 215–242.

Stace, W. T. "The Zionist Illusion," *Atlantic Monthly* 179 (February, 1947): 82–86.

Stein, Leonard. *The Balfour Declaration.* London: Vallentine-Mitchell, 1961.

Steinberg, Milton. "The Creed of an American Zionist," *Atlantic Monthly* 175 (February, 1945): 101–106.

Stettinius, Edward R. *Roosevelt and the Russians.* Garden City, N.Y.: Doubleday, 1949.

Stevens, Richard P. *American Zionism and U.S. Foreign Policy, 1942–1947.* New York: Pageant Press, 1962.

Stocking, George W. *Middle East Oil: A Study in Political and Economic Controversy.* Kingsport, Tenn.: Vanderbilt University Press, 1970.

Stone, I. F. "The Case of the Mufti," *The Nation* 162 (May 4, 1946): 526–527.

———. "Jewry in a Blind Alley," *The Nation* 161 (November 24, 1945): 543–544.

———. "The Palestine Report," *The Nation* 162 (May 11, 1946): 562–564.

Stringer, William H. "A Peace for Palestine," *New Republic* 113 (November 12, 1945): 633–635.

Sulzberger, Cyrus Leo. *A Long Row of Candles: Memoirs and Diaries, 1934–1954.* New York: Macmillan, 1969.

Sykes, Christopher. *Crossroads to Israel, 1917–1948.* Bloomington: Indiana University Press, 1973.

Talmon, Yonina. "Millenarism," in *International Encyclopedia of the Social Sciences,* ed. David L. Sills, vol. X. New York: Macmillan, 1968.

Thomas, Norman. "Blood and Oil in Palestine," *Progressive* 12 (April, 1948): 22–24.

Truman, Harry. *Memoirs: Year of Decisions.* Garden City, N.Y.: Doubleday, 1955.

———. *Memoirs: Years of Trial and Hope, 1946–1952.* Garden City, N.Y.: Doubleday, 1956.

———. *Mr. Citizen.* New York: Stratford Press, 1953.

Truman, Margaret. *Harry S. Truman.* New York: Morrow, 1973.

Trumbull, Charles G. *Prophecy's Light on Today.* New York: Fleming H. Revell Company, 1937.

Vernant, Jacques. *The Refugee in the Post-War World.* New Haven: Yale University Press, 1973.

Wagner, Robert F. "Palestine—A World Responsibility," *The Nation* 161 (September 15, 1945): 247–249.

Wallace, Henry. "The Problem of Palestine," *New Republic* 116 (April 21, 1947): 12–13.

Weinberg, Albert K. *Manifest Destiny: A Study of Nationalist Expansionism in American History.* Gloucester, Mass.: P. Smith, 1958.

Weizmann, Chaim. *Trial and Error: The Autobiography of Chaim Weizmann.* New York: Harper, 1949.

Wells, Sumner. *We Need Not Fail.* Boston: Houghton Mifflin, 1948.

Wilkinson, John. *God's Plan for the Jews.* London: The Paternoster Press, 1944.

Wilson, Evan. "The Palestine Papers, 1943–1947," *Journal of Palestine Studies* 2 (Summer, 1973): 33–54.

Wood, Ross. *The Present in the Light of Prophecy.* Cincinnati: privately published, 1933.

Zeine, Zeine N. *Arab-Turkish Relations and the Emergence of Arab Nationalism.* Beirut: Khayat, 1958.

NEWSPAPERS AND PERIODICALS

Alabama Baptist
America
American Magazine
American Mercury
Atlantic Monthly
Baptist and Reflector
Booklist
Catholic World
Christian Social Relations
Churchman
Collier's
Florida Baptist Witness
Foreign Affairs
Forth
Fortune
Forum
Harper's
Illinois Baptist
Life
Living Church
The Nation
New Republic

Newsweek
New York Times
Opinion News
Pentecostal Evangel
The Progressive
Reader's Digest
Scholastic
Survey Graphic
Time
Washington Post
Word and Way

MOTION PICTURES

The Desert Song
Lest We Forget
The Lost Patrol
March of Time
Nazi Concentration Camps
Night Train
One Stolen Night
Paramount News
The Sheik
She's a Sheik
A Son of the Desert
A Son of the Sahara
The Son of the Sheik
The Thief of Bagdad
United News

DATE DUE